THE SILVER SPOON PASTA

THE

SILVER

SPOON

PASTA

AUTHENTIC ITALIAN RECIPES

DRIED PASTA

FRESH PASTA

132

VIVA LA PASTA

Pasta is the most popular of Italy's many culinary delights. Its almost infinite variety means that it can take pride of place on the most sophisticated tables and also satisfy the need for fast yet tasty food. One thing is certain: this "absurd Italian culinary religion," as writer and founder of the Futurist movement Filippo Marinetti referred to it in the 1930s, remains the most Italian of all foods. It is synonymous with Italy, playing a huge part in its worldwide fame, and a symbol of the ingenuity of the Italian people.

A BALANCED DIET

There is no more natural and simple food than pasta, which can be made from only two ingredients—flour and water. No artificial additives are required. Simply drying the product makes it last for much longer, while its natural appearance is already full of the sun's brightness, absorbed by the wheat grains as they grow in the fields. Furthermore, pasta is one of the most balanced foods in terms of nutrition. Starch, which makes up the highest percentage of the carbohydrates in pasta, is an excellent source of energy and easy to digest. Nutritionists recommend that the greatest part of an adult's daily supply of calories should come from carbohydrates, the rest from lipids and proteins. The composition of durum wheat pasta is 74 percent carbohydrates, 1.2 percent fats, and 11.5 percent proteins. Other nutritional needs are then met by the traditional ways of serving pasta. Sprinkling pasta with cheese, for example, supplies the essential amino acid that balances the proteins already in pasta, and tossing it with tomatoes and vegetables provides vitamins. It has only to be combined with richer sauces to make it into a one-course meal.

THE HISTORY OF PASTA

Who invented pasta? Countless stories and legends surround this famous food. The truth is as simple as its ingredients and is linked to the discovery and use of cereals. Some 7,000 years ago, people began to abandon their nomadic existence and to farm the land. With each harvest, they learned to improve the process, grinding wheat, mixing it with water, rolling it out into thin sheets on hot stones, and, eventually, boiling it in sea water. The oldest evidence dates back to 3,000 BC, while the ancient Greeks and Etruscans produced and ate the first types of pasta many years before the birth of Christ. After varying fortunes, the foundations for pasta's shining future were laid in the eleventh century in Sicily, which became the first focal point for the production of dried pasta and was responsible for its great popularity. From Sicily, pasta spread across the Mediterranean Sea, arriving in Amalfi in the south of Italy and Genoa in the northwest. The oldest documentary evidence for the use of dried pasta dates back to 1316 and was found in Genoa, naming the first pasta maker in history, Maria Borgogno, owner of a house in which *faciebat lasagnas*—"lasagna was made." In 1363, in the inventory of a house in Recco, near Genoa, the colander is first mentioned. When the power of Genoa declined, its famous pasta faded in comparison with that of other areas, notably Naples. For centuries, pasta was a luxury foodstuff, and it was only in the seventeenth century that noble *maccherone*, the generic name for all types of pasta, became a common dish among the general population. Its consumption was boosted by the introduction into Europe of tomatoes, used sporadically in the sixteenth century. The unusual appearance of this food, the pasta makers' stalls, and, above all, their entertaining customers, were a source of great curiosity. Despite its fragile structure, spaghetti soon became legendary, and synonymous with Italy and the Italians.

CHANGES IN TASTE

For Italians, the only way pasta can be cooked is *al dente* or *vierde vierde*, as they say in Naples, and overcooked pasta is considered inedible. *Al dente* literally means "to the tooth," while *vierde vierde* means "very green," or "unripened," both describing pasta that is tender but still firm to the bite. Nowadays, historical recipes for pasta provoke mixed feelings of disapproval and amusement, even those of recognized "masters," such as Martino, cook to a distinguished prelate, who in 1450 recommended very long cooking times—up to two hours—and sauces with salt, cheese, and sweet spices. The same is true for the authors of magnificent sixteenth-century recipe books, such as Cristoforo di Messisbugo or Bartolomeo Scappi, the former specifying one hour's cooking time for dried vermicelli and the latter 30 minutes for maccaraoni alla romanesca, a type of fresh pasta. The famous cookbook writer Pellegrino Artusi, at the end of the nineteenth century, advised draining spaghetti while it still had some bite. The first ingredients for pasta sauces were still sweet—honey, spices, and cinnamon sugar— although they do not really constitute sauces because they were added raw and after cooking. The only savory ingredient that has always been used is cheese: pecorino, provolone, and Parmesan. It was only in the eighteenth century that savory sauces became known. The first real recipe in which tomatoes are used with pasta dates from 1839 and was created by Ippolito Cavalcanti, Duke of Buonvicino, in southern Italy.

LEGENDS

Vegetarian

Vegan

Dairy-free

Nut-free

Thirty minutes or less

Five ingredients or fewer

DRIED PASTA

HOW DRIED PASTA IS PRODUCED

From the time of Roman writer and architect Vitruvius (first century BC) until almost the end of the eighteenth century, flour mills remained virtually unchanged: two wheel-shaped grindstones turned to produce semolina flour from durum wheat. This flour was then added to the tank of a kneading machine, the most important part of the pasta factory, and kneaded with warm water, first by hand and later with a grinding stone. Increased demand led to the invention of the first hydraulic presses in about 1870. Mechanization was gradual, producing hydraulic or steam-powered machines toward the end of the nineteenth century. The first machine able to carry out all phases of the production process was patented in 1933. It was only when artificial drying was introduced that pasta could become a truly industrialized product that could be manufactured throughout Italy. Until then, newly extruded spaghetti was collected, hung on long wooden rods, and exposed to the sun and air to dry, giving pasta factories located in areas with a warm, dry climate an advantage. This problem vanished with the advent of the drying units of the modern pasta factory, where the semolina flour is hydrated with 30 to 35 percent water to make the dough. Mixing and kneading are carried out in a vacuum to produce a more compact and translucent dough, which is then driven toward metal cutters to make long strands of pasta. These strands are then hung over rods. Finally, each strand is cut cleanly to the required size, and the resulting pasta is immediately collected on other rods, moving toward the enormous drying unit where the pasta remains for about eight hours until the total moisture content is reduced to below 12.5 percent.

COOKING INSTRUCTIONS

QUANTITY	As a general rule, allow 3 ounces (70 g) per serving for a first course and 3½ ounces (100 g) per serving for a main course.
POT	Use a large pot, preferably made from aluminum or steel, which should be taller than it is wide.
SALT	Allow 4 cups (1 litre) water and 2½ teaspoons salt for 3½ ounces (100 g) pasta.
TIMING	Follow the package directions but check the pasta at least twice to avoid overcooking.
WATER	Only add the pasta when the salted water has reached a rolling boil. If using spaghetti, fan out a handful in the pan, then stir immediately. Cover the pan, and as soon as the water comes back to a boil, remove the lid and leave uncovered.
COOKING AND PREPARATION TIME	The times indicated for both pasta and sauces in the recipes have been calculated as an average. Times vary depending on the type of heat, the quality of the ingredients, and the skill of the cook.
SAUCE AND CHEESE	If you require cheese, always use fresh and grate it just before sprinkling it on the pasta. Do not overdo the quantity. Those who want to can add more at the table from the cheese dish.

LONG PASTA

BAVETTE

Bavette (meaning "little threads" in Italian), along with its smaller relation bavettine, is a type of dried pasta from Genoa, northwest Italy. Bavette closely resembles slightly convex, flattened spaghetti. It is about 10 inches (25 cm) long, 1/16 inch (1 mm) thick, and 1/4 inch (5 mm) wide and is traditionally accompanied by sauces without meat—especially pesto. Any other long, flat pasta can be substituted.

SPRING BAVETTE

BAVETTE PRIMAVERILI

Preparation time: 30 *min*
Cooking time: 30 *min*
Serves 4

— 4 tablespoons (50 g) butter
— 2 tablespoons olive oil
— 2 scallions (spring onions), chopped
— 2¾ cups (400 g) shelled peas
— 14 ounces (400 g) asparagus, trimmed and cut into short lengths
— ⅔ cup (150 ml) hot water
— 12 ounces (350 g) bavette
— ⅔ cup (50 g) grated Parmesan cheese
— salt and pepper

Melt half the butter with the oil in a shallow saucepan over medium heat. Add the scallions (spring onions) and cook for 3–5 minutes, until soft and translucent. Add the peas and asparagus, season with salt and pepper, stir in the hot water, and simmer for 25 minutes. Meanwhile, cook the bavette in plenty of salted boiling water until al dente. Drain, tip into the pan with the vegetables, and mix. Stir in the remaining butter and the Parmesan and serve immediately.

BAVETTE WITH CLAMS AND ZUCCHINI

BAVETTE ALLE VONGOLE E ZUCCHINE

Preparation time: 30 *min*
Cooking time: 45 *min*
Serves 4

— 1¾ pounds (800 g) clams, scrubbed
— 3 tablespoons olive oil
— 1 shallot, chopped
— 1 garlic clove
— ½ fresh chile, seeded and chopped
— 11 ounces (300 g) zucchini (courgettes), cut into strips
— 1 tablespoon chopped fresh flat-leaf parsley
— scant ½ cup (100 ml) dry white wine
— 3 tomatoes, blanched, peeled, and diced
— 12 ounces (350 g) bavette
— salt

Discard any clams with broken shells or that do not shut immediately when sharply tapped. Put the clams in a dry skillet or frying pan and cook over high heat for about 5 minutes, until they open. Discard any that remain closed. Remove the clams from their shells and set aside. Heat the oil in a saucepan, add the shallot, garlic clove, and chile, and cook over low heat, stirring occasionally, for 5 minutes, until soft. Remove and discard the garlic clove, add the clams, zucchini (courgettes), and flat-leaf parsley, and cook for 5 minutes. Pour in the wine and cook until the alcohol has evaporated. Add the tomatoes, season with salt, and cook for 20–30 minutes, until thickened. Cook the bavette in a large pan of salted, boiling water until al dente. Drain, add to the clam-and-zucchini mixture, and toss well. Serve immediately.

BUCATINI

A type of dried pasta from the Lazio region in central Italy, approximately ⅛ inch (3 mm) in diameter and made from durum wheat semolina flour. Bucatini looks like thick spaghetti and is so called because it is hollow (*buco* means "hole" in Italian). The hole allows air to circulate inside the pasta, which facilitates the slow drying process. It also means that the pasta can absorb a large quantity of sauce. Bucatini is, therefore, best combined with smooth and aromatic sauces, such as Amatriciana (see page 20), the traditional tomato-based recipe from Amatrice, near Rome. In central and southern Italy, where bucatini goes by the name *perciatelli*, it is common to combine it with more robust and full-bodied sauces, such as ragù (meat sauce), whereas in Sicily it is usually combined with a traditional sardine and wild fennel sauce. Bucatini can be substituted with any other type of long, thick pasta.

BUCATINI WITH MOZZARELLA AND EGGPLANT

BUCATINI ALLA MOZZARELLA E MELANZANE

Preparation time: *35 min*
Cooking time: *35 min*
Serves *4*

— 1 eggplant (aubergine), cut into julienne strips
— 5 tablespoons olive oil
— 2 ounces (50 g) diced pancetta or bacon
— 4 tomatoes, blanched, peeled, seeded, and chopped
— ½–1 fresh chile, seeded and chopped
— 3½ ounces (100 g) mozzarella cheese, diced
— 12 ounces (350 g) bucatini
— 1 egg, hard-boiled and finely chopped
— salt

Layer the eggplant (aubergine) strips in a colander, sprinkling each with salt, and let drain for 30 minutes, then rinse and pat dry. Heat the oil in a skillet or frying pan. Add the eggplant strips and cook over medium heat, stirring occasionally, for 5–8 minutes, until lightly browned. Remove them from the pan with a slotted spoon and drain on paper towels. Meanwhile, cook the pancetta or bacon in another skillet or frying pan over medium–low heat, without adding any oil, for 5 minutes, stirring occasionally. Add the tomatoes and chopped chile to taste and season with salt. Lower the heat and simmer, stirring occasionally, for 15 minutes. Add the eggplant strips and simmer for another few minutes. Remove the pan from the heat and stir in the mozzarella. Cook the bucatini in plenty of salted water until al dente. Drain and tip into a warmed serving dish, then pour the sauce over the pasta. Sprinkle with the chopped egg and serve immediately.

BUCATINI WITH GREEN TOMATOES

BUCATINI AI POMODORI VERDI

Preparation time: *15 min*
Cooking time: *45 min*
Serves 4

— 2 tablespoons olive oil
— 3½ ounces (100 g) diced
   pancetta or bacon
— ½ garlic clove, crushed
— 1 sprig fresh flat-leaf
   parsley, chopped
— 4 green tomatoes, seeded
   and chopped
— 3 ounces (80 g) canned tuna
   in oil, drained and flaked
— 12 ounces (350 g) bucatini
— salt

Heat the oil in a saucepan, add the pancetta or bacon, garlic, and parsley, and cook over medium heat for 5 minutes, until lightly browned. Add the tomatoes and tuna, season with salt if necessary, and cook over low heat for 40 minutes. Cook the bucatini in a large saucepan of salted, boiling water until al dente, then drain and tip into the pan of sauce. Mix well and serve.

BUCATINI WITH SHRIMP, WHITE WINE, AND GARLIC

BUCATINI CON LE CANOCCHIE, VINO BIANCO, E AGLIO

Preparation time: *30 min*
Cooking time: *40 min*
Serves 4

— 1 pound 2 ounces (500 g)
   tomatoes, blanched, peeled,
   seeded, and diced
— 8–12 raw mantis shrimp or
   Mediterranean shrimp (prawns)
— 2 tablespoons olive oil
— 1 garlic clove
— pinch of chili powder
— scant 1 cup (200 ml) dry
   white wine
— 12 ounces (350 g) bucatini
— 1 tablespoon finely chopped
   fresh flat-leaf parsley
— salt

Put the tomatoes into a dish, sprinkle with salt, tilt the dish, and let drain. Pull the heads off the shrimp (prawns) if this has not already been done and cut a slit along the back of each down to the tail. Drain the tomatoes fully and pat dry with paper towels.

Heat the oil in a large saucepan. Add the garlic clove and chili powder and cook over low heat, stirring frequently, for a few minutes until the garlic is golden brown. Remove the garlic clove with a slotted spoon and discard. Add the tomatoes to the pan, increase the heat to medium–high, and cook, gently stirring occasionally, until softened but not mushy. Add the shrimp and cook for 5 minutes. Pour in the wine, cover, and cook for another 5 minutes.

Meanwhile, cook the pasta in plenty of salted boiling water until al dente. Remove the shrimp from the pan and keep warm. Drain the pasta, tip into the pan with the sauce, and stir. Transfer to a warmed serving dish, put the shrimp on top, sprinkle with the parsley, and serve immediately.

BUCATINI AMATRICIANA

Preparation time: *20 min*
Cooking time: *30 min*
Serves 4

— 2 tablespoons olive oil
— ½ onion, chopped
— 1 fresh chile, seeded
  and chopped
— 3 ounces (80 g) guanciale
  or pancetta, diced
— 4 tomatoes, blanched,
  peeled, seeded, and sliced
— 12 ounces (350 g) bucatini
— ½ cup (40 g) grated
  pecorino cheese
— salt

Heat the oil in a shallow saucepan. Add the onion and cook over low heat, stirring occasionally, for 5 minutes. Add the chile and pork, increase the heat to medium, and cook, stirring frequently, for 5–8 minutes, until the meat has browned. Remove the meat from the pan with a slotted spoon and keep warm. Add the tomatoes to the pan and cook, stirring occasionally, for 5 minutes. Cook the bucatini in plenty of salted boiling water until al dente. Drain and tip into a warmed serving dish. Add the meat and the tomato sauce, sprinkle with the pecorino, and toss well. Serve immediately.

Tip: The bucatini can be replaced by other types of pasta— spaghetti, macaroni, vermicelli, or rigatoni.

A local and ancient specialty in Lazio in central Italy, this popular dish is still causing controversy. There is wide and fierce debate over whether the sauce is named "Matriciana" or "Amatriciana." Either way, most sources agree that it is named after Amatrice, a small town in the province of Rieti. However, since Amatrice once belonged to the neighboring region of L'Aquila, it is argued that this dish belongs to the cuisine of Abruzzo rather than Lazio.

BUCATINI WITH FENNEL

Preparation time: *15 min*
Cooking time: *20 min*
Serves 4

— ⅓ cup (50 g) raisins
— 3½ ounces (100 g)
  fennel, trimmed
— 2 tablespoons olive oil
— 1 onion, very thinly sliced
— ¼ cup (25 g) pine nuts
— pinch of saffron threads
— 12 ounces (350 g) bucatini
— salt

Put the raisins into a heatproof bowl, pour in warm water to cover, and let soak. Blanch the fennel in boiling water for 3–4 seconds, then drain and chop. Heat the oil in a saucepan. Add the onion and cook over low heat, stirring occasionally, for 5 minutes. Add the fennel and cook, stirring occasionally, for another 10 minutes. Drain the raisins and squeeze out the excess liquid, then add to the pan with the pine nuts and saffron. Cook the bucatini in plenty of salted boiling water until al dente. Drain, tip into a warmed serving dish, and pour the sauce on top. Serve immediately.

SPICY BUCATINI

Preparation time: 20 *min*
Cooking time: 25 *min*
Serves 6

— ½ cup (120 ml) olive oil
— 3 garlic cloves
— 6 fresh red chiles
— 1 pound (450 g) bucatini
— salt

Heat 2 teaspoons of the oil in a skillet or frying pan. Add 2 of the garlic cloves and cook over low heat, stirring frequently, until lightly browned. Add the whole chiles and cook, stirring frequently, until they are puffed up and shiny. Remove the chiles and garlic from the pan with a slotted spoon, transfer to a mortar, and pound to a paste with a pestle. Cook the pasta in plenty of salted boiling water until al dente, then drain. Heat the remaining oil in a saucepan with the remaining garlic clove until it is lightly browned. Remove and discard the garlic, add the chile and pasta to the pan and quickly tosstogether. Transfer to a warmed serving dish and serve immediately.

This is a recipe from the sun-drenched region of Basilicata in southern Italy, an area fragrant with the aromatic herbs that grow wild on the hills and the bright strings of red chiles drying on the doors and walls of houses. Wheat is farmed intensively, leading to a rich tradition of pasta-making with many original shapes created by skillful, local hands. The inclusion of the forte *("strength"), the ubiquitous chile, is virtually compulsory in every dish.*

BUCATINI WITH OLIVES

Preparation time: 15 *min*
Cooking time: 30 *min*
Serves 4

— 2 tablespoons olive oil
— 1½ tablespoons butter
— 1 garlic clove
— 4 anchovy fillets
— 6 tablespoons capers, drained and chopped
— 1 cup (250 g) canned, diced tomatoes
— 1 cup (100 g) green olives, pitted and cut into circles
— 12 ounces (350 g) bucatini
— 1 tablespoon black olive paste (tapenade)
— salt
— chopped fresh flat-leaf parsley, to serve

Heat the oil and butter with a pinch of salt in a large skillet or frying pan. Add the garlic and cook over low heat, stirring frequently, until golden brown, then remove and discard. Add the anchovies, capers, and tomatoes to the pan and cook over low heat, stirring occasionally, for 15 minutes. Add the olives and season lightly with salt if necessary. Mix well and simmer for another 15 minutes. Meanwhile, cook the bucatini in plenty of salted boiling water until al dente. Drain, tip into the pan with the sauce, and stir in the olive paste (tapenade). Transfer to a warmed serving dish, sprinkle with the parsley, and serve immediately.

BUCATINI WITH PANCETTA

BUCATINI CON PANCETTA

Preparation time: *15 min*
Cooking time: 20 *min*
Serves 4

— 1 tablespoon olive oil
— 2 tablespoons (25 g) butter
— 3½ ounces (100 g) pancetta
  or bacon, diced
— 3 eggs, lightly beaten
— 1 cup (80 g) grated
  pecorino cheese
— 1 tablespoon heavy
  (double) cream
— 10 ounces (275 g) bucatini
— salt and pepper

Heat the oil with the butter in a large skillet or frying pan. Add the pancetta or bacon and cook over medium heat, stirring occasionally, for a few minutes until lightly browned. Beat together the eggs, pecorino, and cream in a bowl and lightly season with salt. Cook the bucatini in plenty of salted boiling water until al dente. Drain, tip into the pan with the pancetta or bacon, toss well, and remove from the heat. Pour the egg mixture over the pasta and toss well. Season with plenty of pepper and serve immediately.

BUCATINI WITH BELL PEPPER SAUCE

BUCATINI CON SALSA AI PEPERONI

Preparation time: 20 *min*
Cooking time: 30 *min*
Serves 4

— 2 tablespoons olive oil
— 1 pearl onion, chopped
— ½ garlic clove, chopped
— 3 red or yellow bell peppers,
  halved, seeded, and sliced
— scant ½ cup (100 ml)
  heavy (double) cream
— 12 ounces (350 g) bucatini
— 2 teaspoons chopped fresh
  marjoram
— salt and pepper

Heat the oil in a saucepan, add the onion and garlic, and cook over low heat, stirring occasionally, for 10 minutes, until lightly browned. Add the bell peppers, mix well, and cook for another 10 minutes, until tender. Transfer to a food processor and process to a puree. Return to the pan, stir in the cream, and season with salt and pepper to taste. Keep warm over very low heat. Cook the bucatini in a large saucepan of salted, boiling water until al dente, then drain, and tip into the sauce. Cook for 1 minute, stir in the marjoram, and serve.

BUCATINI WITH MUSHROOM SAUCE

Preparation time: *30 min*
plus 20 min soaking
Cooking time: *45 min*
Serves *4*

— 1 ounce (25 g) dried
  mushrooms
— 7 ounces (200 g) fresh
  porcini mushrooms
— 4 tablespoons olive oil
— ½ garlic clove, crushed,
  and 1 whole garlic clove
— ⅔ cup (150 ml) water
— ¼ cup (50 g) ricotta cheese
— 1 tablespoon concentrated
  tomato paste (puree)
— 12 ounces (350 g) bucatini
— salt and pepper

Place the dried mushrooms in a bowl, add warm water to cover, and let soak for 20 minutes, then drain and squeeze dry. Chop half the fresh porcini. Thinly slice the rest and reserve for later. Heat 3 tablespoons of the oil with 1 whole garlic clove in a saucepan, add the drained dried mushrooms and chopped porcini, and cook for about 10 minutes, until the mushrooms have released their liquid. Remove and discard the garlic. Add the water and cook for 20 minutes. Transfer the mixture to a food processor and process to a puree, then stir in the ricotta. Put the reserved porcini into a saucepan with the remaining oil, the remaining garlic, and the tomato paste (puree). Mix well, add 2 tablespoons water, and cook for 15 minutes. Season with salt and pepper. Meanwhile, cook the pasta in a large pan of salted, boiling water until al dente. Drain, place in a warmed serving dish, and spoon the ricotta mixture and mushrooms on top.

BUCATINI WITH MUSSELS

Preparation time: *30 min*
Cooking time: *35 min*
Serves *4*

— 2¼ pounds (1 kg) mussels
— 4 tablespoons olive oil
— 4 tablespoons (50 g) butter
— 1 tablespoon anchovy paste
— 1 cup (100 g) black olives,
  pitted and sliced
— 9 ounces (250 g) tomatoes,
  blanched, peeled, and chopped
— 1 garlic clove, finely chopped
— 1 tablespoon finely chopped
  fresh flat-leaf parsley
— 12 ounces (350 g) bucatini
— salt and pepper

Scrub the mussels under cold running water and remove the "beards." Discard any with damaged shells or that do not shut immediately when sharply tapped. Put them into a saucepan, add 2 tablespoons of the oil, cover, and cook over high heat, shaking the pan occasionally, for 4–5 minutes, until they open. Remove the pan from the heat and lift out the mussels with a slotted spoon. Discard any that remain shut. Set aside a few mussels in their shells for the garnish and remove the remainder from their shells. Pour the cooking liquid through a strainer lined with cheesecloth (muslin) into a bowl. Melt the butter with the remaining oil in another saucepan. Mix the anchovy paste with 1 tablespoon water in a small bowl and stir into the pan. Add the olives, tomatoes, and 3–4 tablespoons of the reserved cooking liquid and simmer for 20 minutes. Stir in the garlic and parsley and simmer for another few minutes, then remove from the heat. Cook the bucatini in plenty of salted boiling water until al dente. Drain and return to the pan, pour the sauce over the pasta, add the shelled mussels, and stir. Season with pepper and divide the mixture among warmed plates. Garnish with the reserved mussels in their shells and serve immediately.

CAPELLINI

Capellini (whose name means "fine hair" in Italian) is a type of dried pasta similar to the more commonly known capelli d'angelo, or "angel hair". Capellini is very long and looks like thin spaghetti, with a diameter less than ¹⁄₁₆ inch (1 mm) thick. Because of the fineness of its texture, it is often served in a broth (stock), or combined with light sauces. Capellini is most suitable for oven-baked recipes, including soufflés.

Preparation time: *40 min*
Cooking time: *25 min*
Serves 4

— 11 ounces (300 g) capellini
— 6 tablespoons (80 g) butter, plus extra for greasing
— 3 tablespoons all-purpose (plain) flour
— 2 eggs, separated
— salt and pepper

For the tomato sauce:
— 1 cup (250 g) canned, diced tomatoes or fresh tomatoes, blanched, peeled and chopped
— pinch of sugar
— 2 garlic cloves
— 2 tablespoons olive oil
— 10 torn fresh basil leaves
— salt

BAKED CAPELLINI

SFORMATO DI CAPELLINI

Cook the capellini in plenty of salted boiling water until al dente. Drain, reserving the cooking water, and set aside. Melt 1½ tablespoons of the butter in a small saucepan. Stir in the flour and cook, stirring constantly, for 2–3 minutes, until lightly browned. Gradually stir in scant 1 cup (200 ml) of the reserved cooking water, a little at a time. Bring to a boil, stirring constantly, and lower the heat. Simmer gently, stirring constantly, for 20 minutes until thickened and smooth. Remove from the heat and season with salt. Pour the sauce over the capellini, add the remaining butter, and season with pepper. Toss to combine and let cool.

To make the tomato sauce, put the tomatoes, with their juice if using canned tomatoes, into a saucepan, and add the sugar, garlic, and a pinch of salt. Cover and cook over very low heat for about 30 minutes without stirring. Mash the tomatoes with a wooden spoon and, if using canned tomatoes, cook for another 15 minutes. Remove the garlic with a slotted spoon and discard. Remove the pan from the heat and let cool. Stir in the olive oil and basil.

Preheat the oven to 350°F (180°C/Gas Mark 4) and generously grease a cake pan with butter. Stiffly whisk the egg whites in a grease-free bowl until stiff peaks form. Stir the egg yolks into the cooled pasta mixture, then fold in the egg whites. Pour the mixture into the prepared pan and bake for 10–15 minutes, or until light golden brown. Remove the pan from the oven, turn out onto a warmed serving dish, and serve with the hot tomato sauce on the side.

CAPELLINI IN CREAM AND CHEESE SAUCE

CAPELLINI IN BIANCO

Preparation time: *10 min*
Cooking time: *10 min*
Serves 4

— 3 tablespoons (40 g) butter
— scant ½ cup (100 ml) heavy (double) cream
— 14 ounces (400 g) capellini
— 3 ounces (80 g) Gruyère cheese, diced
— salt and freshly ground white pepper

Put the butter into a heatproof bowl set over a saucepan of simmering water and melt. Stir occasionally while the butter melts. Stir in the cream and heat through for a few minutes. Cook the capellini in plenty of salted boiling water until al dente. Drain, tip into a warmed serving dish, pour the cream mixture over the pasta, add the Gruyère, and stir. Season with pepper and serve immediately.

SOUFFLÉ OF CAPELLINI

SOUFFLÉ DI CAPELLINI

Preparation time: *40 min*
Cooking time: *45 min*
Serves 4

— 3 tablespoons (40 g) butter, plus extra for greasing
— ⅓ cup (40 g) all-purpose (plain) flour
— 2 cups (500 ml) lukewarm milk
— 9 ounces (250 g) capellini
— 3 eggs, separated
— ¾ cup (80 g) grated Gruyère cheese
— salt

Preheat the oven to 325°F (160°C/Gas Mark 3) and grease a soufflé dish with butter. Melt the butter in a saucepan. Stir in the flour and cook over medium heat, stirring constantly, for 2–3 minutes, until golden brown. Gradually stir in the milk, a little at a time. Bring to a boil, stirring constantly. Lower the heat and simmer gently, stirring constantly, for 20 minutes, until thickened and smooth. Meanwhile, cook the pasta in plenty of salted boiling water until al dente, then drain. Remove the pan of béchamel sauce from the heat. Beat in the egg yolks, one at a time, then stir in the Gruyère and the pasta, mixing with 2 forks. Stiffly whisk the egg whites in a grease-free bowl until stiff peaks form, then fold into the mixture. Gently spoon or pour the pasta mixture into the prepared dish, filling it three-quarters full to allow room for it to rise. Bake for about 20 minutes, until well risen and golden. Remove from the oven and serve immediately straight from the dish.

LINGUINE

Linguine, whose name means "little tongues" in Italian, is a type of dried pasta produced industrially or by hand from durum wheat semolina flour and water. It is flat and thick in the middle, about 10½ inches (26 cm) long and ⅛ inch (3 mm) wide. It originates from the Liguria region in the northwest of Italy, where the very similar bavette and trenette are also found. Linguine is ideal combined with sauces based on oil and aromatic herbs, but is rarely served with meat. The most traditional dishes are Linguine al Pesto Genovese (Linguine with Genoese Pesto, see page 29) and Linguine ai Frutti di Mare (Seafood Linguine, see page 33) from the Calabria region in the south.

Preparation time: *30 min*
Cooking time: *30 min*
Serves 4

— 20 fresh anchovies
— 3 tablespoons extra virgin olive oil
— 1 teaspoon anchovy paste
— 2 garlic cloves, crushed
— 4 tomatoes, blanched, peeled, seeded, and chopped
— 2 tablespoons chopped fresh flat-leaf parsley
— 12 ounces (350 g) linguine
— salt and pepper

LINGUINE WITH ANCHOVIES

LINGUINE ALLE ACCIUGHE

Pinch the head of an anchovy between your thumb and index finger and pull it off—the innards should come away with it. Pinch along the top edge of the anchovy and pull out the backbone. Repeat with the remaining fish, then rinse them and pat dry. Heat the oil in a skillet or frying pan. Add the anchovies and cook over medium heat, turning occasionally, for 4–5 minutes. Remove with a slotted spoon and drain on paper towels. Stir the anchovy paste into the pan, add the garlic and tomatoes, and cook, stirring occasionally, for 10 minutes. Season to taste with salt and pepper and sprinkle with the parsley. Cook the pasta in plenty of salted boiling water until al dente. Drain, tip into the pan, add the anchovies, and toss gently. Serve immediately.

Preparation time: *10 min*
Cooking time: *20 min*
Serves 4

— 4 tablespoons (50 g) butter
— 4 ounces (120 g) canned crab meat, drained
— 4 tomatoes, blanched, peeled, and diced
— 3 ounces (80 g) smoked salmon, cut into strips
— dash of vodka
— 10 ounces (275 g) linguine
— salt

LINGUINE WITH CRAB AND SALMON

LINGUINE AL GRANCHIO E SALMONE

Melt the butter in a small saucepan. Add the crab meat and cook over low heat for a few minutes, then add the tomatoes and cook, stirring occasionally, for another 10 minutes. Add the strips of salmon, sprinkle with vodka, and cook until the alcohol has evaporated. Stir and remove the pan from the heat. Cook the linguine in plenty of salted boiling water until al dente. Drain, toss with the sauce, and serve immediately.

Preparation time: *10 min*
Cooking time: *10 min*
Serves 4

— 12 ounces (350 g) linguine
— 2 potatoes, cut into
    thin batons
— ½ cup (50 g) green (French)
    beans

For the pesto:
— 25 fresh basil leaves
— 2 garlic cloves, crushed
— 5 tablespoons olive oil
— ⅓ cup (25 g) grated
    pecorino cheese
— ⅓ cup (25 g) grated
    Parmesan cheese
— salt

LINGUINE WITH GENOESE PESTO

LINGUINE AL PESTO GENOVESE

To make the pesto, put the basil, garlic, a pinch of salt, and the oil into a food processor and process briefly at medium speed. Add both cheeses and process again until blended. Alternatively, pound the ingredients in a mortar with a pestle until a smooth paste is obtained. Cook the linguine, potatoes, and green (French) beans together in a large saucepan of salted boiling water until al dente, then drain. Toss with the pesto and serve.

Tip: Instead of linguine, you can also make this recipe with reginette, another traditional type of pasta from the Liguria region in northwest Italy.

Preparation time: *1 hour*
Cooking time: *40 min*
Serves 4

— 1 lobster, about
    1½ pounds (700 g)
— 2 tablespoons olive oil
— 1 garlic clove
— 1 onion, finely chopped
— ½ cup (150 g) peeled, seeded,
    and chopped tomatoes
— pinch of dried oregano
— 12 ounces (350 g) linguine
— salt

LINGUINE WITH LOBSTER

LINGUINE ALL'ARAGOSTA

Plunge the lobster into a large pot of boiling salted water, cover, bring back to a boil, and boil for 10 minutes. Remove from the pot and let cool. Put the lobster, belly side down, on a cutting (chopping) board and cut it in half. Open it out and remove the tail meat from both halves of the shell. Remove the dark intestinal tract with the point of the knife and discard. Snap off the claws and break them into pieces at the joints, then crack the shells with a heavy knife. Remove the meat. Cut all the lobster meat into small pieces. Heat the oil in a shallow saucepan. Add the garlic clove and cook over low heat, stirring frequently, until lightly browned. Remove with a slotted spoon and discard. Add the onion, tomatoes, and oregano to the pan, season with salt, and simmer, stirring occasionally, for 10–15 minutes, until thickened. Cook the linguine in plenty of salted boiling water until al dente. Drain, tip into the sauce, and toss. Add the diced lobster, toss again, and serve immediately.

LINGUINE WITH BROCCOLI AND PANCETTA

LINGUINE BROCCOLETTI E PANCETTA

Preparation time: *30 min*
Cooking time: *30 min*
Serves 4

— 2 tablespoons olive oil
— 4½ ounces (120 g) diced pancetta or bacon
— 1 garlic clove, finely chopped
— 1 pound 5 ounces (600 g) broccoli, cut into florets
— 1 tablespoon concentrated tomato paste (puree)
— ⅔ cup (150 ml) vegetable broth (stock)
— 12 ounces (350 g) linguine
— ½ cup (40 g) grated Parmesan cheese
— salt

Heat the oil in a saucepan. Add the pancetta or bacon and cook over medium–low heat, stirring occasionally, for 4–5 minutes. Stir in the garlic and half the broccoli and cook, stirring occasionally, for 5 minutes. Stir in the tomato paste (puree) and broth (stock), lower the heat, and simmer for 10 minutes, until the broccoli is tender but still firm. Cook the pasta with the remaining broccoli in plenty of salted boiling water until al dente. Drain, tip into the pan with the sauce, and toss over the heat for a few minutes. Transfer to a warmed serving dish, sprinkle with the Parmesan, and serve immediately.

LINGUINE WITH ARTICHOKES AND HAM

LINGUINE AI CARCIOFI E PROSCIUTTO

Preparation time: *20 min*
Cooking time: *30 min*
Serves 4

— 4 tablespoons olive oil
— ½ onion, finely chopped
— 4 baby globe artichokes, trimmed and sliced
— 5 ounces (150 g) ham, cut into strips
— 12 ounces (350 g) linguine
— ⅔ cup (50 g) grated Parmesan cheese
— salt

Heat the oil in a shallow saucepan. Add the onion and cook over low heat, stirring occasionally, for 5 minutes. Add the artichokes, cover, and cook, stirring occasionally, for 25 minutes, until tender. Stir in the ham, increase the heat to medium, and cook for another 2 minutes. Remove the pan from the heat. Cook the linguine in plenty of salted boiling water until al dente. Drain, tip into a warmed serving dish, and toss with the artichokes and ham. Sprinkle with the Parmesan and serve immediately.

LINGUINE WITH BROCCOLI AND PANCETTA

LINGUINE WITH SMOKED SALMON AND TOMATO SAUCE

LINGUINE AL SALMONE E SALSA DI POMODORO

Preparation time: 25 *min*
Cooking time: 30 *min*
Serves 4

— 3 tablespoons (40 g) butter
— ½ onion, chopped
— ½ cup (120 ml) brandy
— 1 pound 2 ounces (500 g) fresh
  tomatoes, blanched, peeled,
  and diced, or 2 cups (500 g)
  canned diced tomatoes
— 4 ounces (120 g) smoked
  salmon, cut into strips
— scant ½ cup (100 ml) heavy
  (double) cream
— 12 ounces (350 g) linguine
— salt and pepper

Melt the butter in a saucepan. Add the onion and cook over low heat, stirring occasionally, for 5 minutes. Pour in the brandy and cook until the alcohol has evaporated. Add the tomatoes and simmer, stirring occasionally, for about 10 minutes, until thickened. Add the salmon, season with pepper, stir in the cream and heat gently. Meanwhile, cook the linguine in plenty of salted boiling water until al dente. Drain, tip into the pan with the sauce, and toss for a few seconds. Transfer to a warmed serving dish and serve immediately.

SEAFOOD LINGUINE

LINGUINE AI FRUTTI DI MARE

Preparation time: 20 *min*
Cooking time: 30 *min*
Serves 4

— 11 ounces (300 g) mussels
— 14 ounces (400 g) clams
— 5 tablespoons olive oil
— 3 garlic cloves, crushed
— pinch of dried oregano
— 12 ounces (350 g) linguine
— 14 ounces (400 g) canned
  chopped tomatoes
— 1 tablespoon chopped
  fresh basil
— salt and pepper

Scrub the mussels and clams under cold running water. Remove the "beards" from the mussels. Discard any with broken shells or that do not shut immediately when sharply tapped. Preheat the oven to 425°F (220°C/Gas Mark 7). Heat 1 tablespoon of the oil in a skillet or frying pan. Add 1 of the crushed garlic cloves and the oregano. When hot, add the clams and cook over high heat, shaking the pan occasionally, for 3–5 minutes, until they open. Remove the pan from the heat and lift out the clams with a slotted spoon. Reserve the cooking juices. Heat 1 tablespoon of the remaining oil in another skillet or frying pan. Add the mussels and cook over high heat, shaking the pan occasionally, for 5 minutes, until they open. Remove from the heat and lift out the mussels with a slotted spoon. Reserve the cooking juices. Discard any shellfish that remain shut and remove the rest from their shells. If desired, leave some in their shells to serve. Cook the pasta in plenty of salted boiling water until al dente, then drain. Heat the remaining oil in a large saucepan. Add the remaining garlic and cook over low heat, stirring frequently, for 1 minute, then add the tomatoes, pasta, shellfish, basil, and 1 tablespoon of the reserved cooking juices. Season with salt and pepper. Tip the mixture into the middle of a large sheet of aluminum foil. Bring up the sides of the foil and fold over the edges securely to close. Put the package on a baking sheet. Bake for 5 minutes and serve immediately.

LINGUINE WITH CAVIAR

LINGUINE AL CAVIALE

Preparation time: *15 min*
Cooking time: *25 min*
Serves 4

— 4 tablespoons (50 g) butter
— 1 small onion, thinly sliced
— scant ½ cup (100 ml) vodka
— 12 ounces (350 g) linguine
— 2 tablespoons caviar or
   lumpfish roe
— salt and pepper
— finely chopped fresh flat-leaf
   parsley, to garnish

Melt the butter in a shallow saucepan. Add the onion and cook over low heat, stirring occasionally, for 5 minutes. Drizzle with the vodka and cook gently until the alcohol has evaporated, then season with salt and pepper. Cook the linguine in plenty of salted boiling water until al dente. Drain, tip into the pan with the sauce, and stir well. Transfer to individual warmed plates, form a "nest" in the middle of each, and add a heaping teaspoon of caviar or lumpfish roe. Alternatively, you can mix the caviar or lumpfish roe into the pasta. Sprinkle with the finely chopped parsley and serve immediately.

Tip: Fresh caviar should never have a fishy smell or piquant taste. The eggs should be whole and individual, not sticky or dry.

LINGUINE WITH CUTTLEFISH

LINGUINE CON LE SEPPIE

Preparation time: *1 hour*
Cooking time: *50 min*
Serves 4

— 12 ounces (350 g) small
   cuttlefish, about 4–4½ inches
   (10–12 cm) long
— 2 tablespoons olive oil
— 1 onion, chopped
— scant 1 cup (200 ml) dry
   white wine
— 3 tablespoons peeled and
   diced tomato
— 1 tablespoon chopped
   fresh flat-leaf parsley
— 12 ounces (350 g) linguine
— salt and pepper

To clean the cuttlefish, cut off the tentacles just in front of the eyes, squeeze out the beak from the middle, and discard. Separate and skin the tentacles and pull off the skin from the body. Cut along the back and remove and discard the cuttlebone. Open out the body sac, carefully remove the ink sac, and reserve. Remove and discard the innards and head. Cut the body sacs and tentacles into strips. Heat the oil in a saucepan. Add the cuttlefish and onion and cook over low heat, stirring occasionally, for 5 minutes. Pour in the wine and cook until the alcohol has evaporated. Add the tomato, season with salt and pepper, cover, and simmer for about 20 minutes. Squeeze the ink into the pan, discarding the ink sacs, and cook for 5 minutes. Stir in the parsley and cook for another 20 minutes, until the sauce has thickened. Cook the linguine in plenty of salted boiling water until al dente. Drain, tip into a warmed serving dish, add the cuttlefish sauce, and serve.

The coastal region of Liguria in northwest Italy has mild temperatures throughout the year. The Gulf Stream brings cooling breezes in summer and the surrounding mountains protect the area from low temperatures during the winter. Therefore, the tomato season begins here in May, rather than running from June to September, as in other regions.

REGINETTE

Reginette is a type of dried pasta originating from Naples in the south of Italy. It is long, flat, and ½ inch (1 cm) wide, similar to tagliatelle, but with at least one side curled. The name, meaning "little queens," refers to Princess Mafalda of Savoy (1125–1158), for whom the shape was created. In the Liguria region, in the northwest, the term reginette can also be used for taglierini and linguine. Reginette is thought to complement any sauce, but its shape suits thicker and full-bodied sauces particularly well.

Preparation time: 20 *min*
Cooking time: 20 *min*
Serves 4

— 1 cup (100 g) baby peas (petit pois)
— 3 tablespoons olive oil
— 1 small shallot, very finely chopped
— 16 small langoustines, shelled and deveined (see Spaghetti with Langoustines, page 56)
— 12 ounces (350 g) reginette
— 2 tomatoes, blanched, peeled, and diced
— salt and freshly ground white pepper

REGINETTE WITH LANGOUSTINES

REGINETTE CON GLI SCAMPI

Cook the peas in lightly salted boiling water for about 5 minutes until tender, then drain. Meanwhile, heat the oil in a saucepan. Add the shallot and cook over medium heat, stirring occasionally, for 3 minutes. Add the langoustines, season with salt and white pepper, lower the heat, and cook for 6–7 minutes. Cook the reginette in plenty of salted boiling water until al dente. Drain, tip into the pan with the langoustines, add the peas, and stir. Add the tomatoes and cook for 2 minutes, shaking the pan. Transfer to a warmed serving dish and serve immediately.

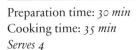

Preparation time: 30 *min*
Cooking time: 35 *min*
Serves 4

— 2 tablespoons lemon juice
— 4 young globe artichokes
— 2 tablespoons olive oil
— 1¼ cup (200 g) chopped onions
— scant 1 cup (200 ml) dry white wine
— 12 ounces (350 g) reginette
— 1 stick (120 g) butter
— salt and pepper
— grated Parmesan cheese, to serve

REGINETTE WITH ONIONS AND ARTICHOKES

REGINETTE ALLE CIPOLLE E CARCIOFI

Fill a bowl halfway with water and stir in the lemon juice. Trim the artichokes, slice, and put into the bowl to prevent discoloration. Heat the oil in a large saucepan. Add the onions, season with salt, and cook over low heat for 5 minutes. Drain the artichokes, add to the pan, and cook for 5–8 minutes, until softened. Pour in the wine and cook until the alcohol has evaporated. Pour in ½ cup (120 ml) hot water, cover, and simmer for about 25 minutes, until the artichokes are tender and the sauce is thicker. Meanwhile, cook the pasta in plenty of salted boiling water until al dente. Drain, tip into the pan with the sauce, add the butter, and season with pepper. Toss over the heat for a few minutes, then transfer to a warmed serving dish. Serve immediately with the Parmesan.

REGINETTE WITH LANGOUSTINES

SPAGHETTI

Spaghetti (meaning "small strings" in Italian) is the classic dried pasta shape. It is also Italy's most popular dish, with Italians eating an average of 62 pounds (28 kg) each per year. According to Italian law, only durum wheat semolina flour is to be used for making spaghetti. However, European laws now permit the use of soft wheat flour, so check the label carefully. The thickness of spaghetti varies, but it is usually about ½ inch (1.5 mm) thick with a length of 10 inches (25 cm). Thinner versions include spaghettini, which is 1⁄16 inch (1 mm) thick and is often called vermicelli in southern Italy. Good-quality spaghetti can be recognized by its appearance and texture before tasting it. It should be amber yellow, with a shiny surface and a firm consistency. Many Italian cooks believe spaghetti should not be drained in a colander, but simply lifted out of the water to keep it moist before the sauce is added. Spaghetti goes well with tomato-based sauces, and fish and shellfish sauces, but surprisingly not Bolognese sauce, which is traditionally served with tagliatelle. Perhaps the best-known and most widely cooked spaghetti recipe is Spaghetti alla Carbonara (Spaghetti Carbonara, see page 45), from the central Italian region of Lazio.

Preparation time: *20 min*
Cooking time: *25 min*
Serves 4

— 2 tablespoons olive oil
— 2 ripe tomatoes, blanched, peeled, and chopped
— 1 red bell pepper, seeded and cut into julienne strips
— 1 cup (100 g) green olives, pitted
— 12 ounces (350 g) spaghetti
— ½ cup (40 g) grated Parmesan cheese
— salt and pepper

SPAGHETTI FROM CIOCIARA

SPAGHETTI ALLA CIOCIARA

Heat the oil in a saucepan. Add the tomatoes, red bell pepper, and olives and season with salt and pepper. Cook over low heat, stirring occasionally and adding a little hot water, if necessary, for 15 minutes. Cook the spaghetti in plenty of salted boiling water until al dente. Drain, tip into the pan with the sauce, and toss well over the heat for 1 minute. Sprinkle with the Parmesan and serve immediately.

It was not until the end of the eighteenth century that growing tomatoes as a food crop became common in Europe, mainly in France and southern Italy. However, in France tomatoes were eaten only at the royal court, whereas in Naples they quickly became popular among ordinary people, who had long suffered from food shortages.

SPAGHETTI WITH FRESH HERBS AND ZUCCHINI

SPAGHETTI ALLE ERBE FRESCHE E ZUCCHINE

Preparation time: *25 min*
Cooking time: *25 min*
Serves 4

— 2 tablespoons olive oil
— 3 cups (400 g) sliced zucchini (courgettes)
— 4–5 sprigs fresh flat-leaf parsley
— 4 fresh basil leaves, torn
— pinch of dried oregano
— 12 ounces (350 g) spaghetti
— ½ cup (40 g) grated Parmesan cheese
— salt and pepper

Heat the oil with 1 tablespoon water in a skillet or frying pan. Add the zucchini (courgettes) and cook over medium–low heat, stirring occasionally, for 15 minutes. Add a sprig of parsley, the basil leaves, and oregano and season with salt and pepper. Cook the spaghetti in plenty of salted boiling water until al dente. Drain, tip into a warmed serving dish, add the zucchini and Parmesan, and toss well. Garnish with the remaining parsley sprigs and serve immediately.

SPAGHETTI WITH HAM AND MASCARPONE

SPAGHETTI AL PROSCIUTTO E MASCARPONE

Preparation time: *10 min*
Cooking time: *7 min*
Serves 4

— 12 ounces (350 g) spaghetti
— 2 egg yolks
— ⅓ cup (80 g) mascarpone cheese
— ⅔ cup (50 g) grated Parmesan cheese
— generous ½ cup (100 g) diced ham
— salt and pepper

Cook the spaghetti in plenty of salted boiling water until al dente. Meanwhile, beat together the egg yolks, mascarpone, Parmesan, and ham in a bowl and season with salt and pepper. If necessary, stir in a little of the pasta cooking water to give a creamy consistency. Drain the pasta, tip it into a serving dish, pour the sauce over the pasta, and toss well. Serve immediately.

SPAGHETTI WITH CAULIFLOWER

SPAGHETTI CON CAVOLFIORE

Preparation time: *10 min*
Cooking time: *15 min*
Serves 4

— 1¾ pounds (800 g) cauliflower, cut into florets
— 3 tablespoons olive oil
— 1 garlic clove
— 10 ounces (275 g) spaghetti
— salt and pepper
— grated Parmesan cheese, to serve

Cook the cauliflower florets in plenty of lightly salted boiling water for 5–10 minutes until tender, then remove with a slotted spoon. Reserve the cooking water. Heat the oil in a skillet or frying pan. Add the garlic clove and cook over low heat, stirring frequently, for a few minutes until browned. Remove with a slotted spoon and discard. Add the cauliflower florets to the pan. Bring the reserved cooking water back to a boil, add the spaghetti, and cook until al dente. Drain, tip into the pan, season with salt and pepper, and toss well. Serve immediately, handing the Parmesan separately.

SPAGHETTI FROM NORCIA

SPAGHETTI ALLA NURSINA

Preparation time: *15 min*
Cooking time: *15 min*
Serves 4

— scant ½ cup (100 ml) olive oil
— 4 anchovy fillets
— 3½ ounces (100 g) black truffles, sliced
— 12 ounces (350 g) spaghetti
— 1 sprig chopped fresh flat-leaf parsley
— salt

Heat the oil in a shallow pan. Add the anchovies and cook over medium heat for a couple of minutes until tender but not crisp. Remove from the heat and add the truffles to the pan. Return the pan to the heat and cook gently for a few minutes, making sure that the mixture does not boil. Cook the spaghetti in plenty of salted boiling water until al dente. Drain, tip into a warmed serving dish, add the sauce, and toss. Sprinkle with the chopped parsley and serve.

Tip: Truffles must not be kept for long as the aroma quickly disappears or, at least, fades. Store for a maximum of 2 days in an airtight glass jar, after carefully brushing but not washing them. Add a handful of uncooked rice to the jar. This will absorb some of their aroma and if used later for risotto, will produce a very fragrant dish.

This is possibly the simplest dish in Umbrian cuisine, yet it is one that requires careful preparation. Pan-frying rather than gently sautéing the anchovies, or using poor quality olive oil, can result in a mediocre dish. The choice of truffles is crucial. The most famous are black truffles from Norcia—which give this dish its name—and Spoleto, for sale from Christmas Eve to March. During the rest of the year truffles are less strong.

SPAGHETTI WITH ZUCCHINI

SPAGHETTI CON LE ZUCCHINE

Preparation time: *20 min*
Cooking time: *30 min*
Serves 4

— 3 tablespoons olive oil
— 1 garlic clove
— 1 small onion
— 2 fresh sage leaves
— 1 celery stalk
— 3 tomatoes, blanched, peeled, seeded, and chopped
— 2⅔ cups (350 g) thinly sliced zucchini (courgettes)
— 12 ounces (350 g) spaghetti
— 5 ounces (150 g) mozzarella cheese, diced
— ⅓ cup (25 g) grated Parmesan cheese
— salt and pepper

Heat the oil in a pan, add the garlic clove, whole onion, sage leaves, and celery stalk and cook over low heat for 5 minutes. Add the tomatoes and bring to a boil over medium heat, then add the zucchini (courgettes). Season with salt and pepper, cover, and cook for 15 minutes, then remove the onion, garlic, celery, and sage. Meanwhile, cook the spaghetti in a large pan of salted water until al dente, then drain, and return to the pan. Toss with the sauce, mozzarella, and Parmesan and serve.

SPAGHETTI WITH TOMATO AND BASIL

Preparation time: *20 min*
Cooking time: *1 hour 15 min*
Serves 4

— 2¼ pounds (1 kg)
  tomatoes, diced
— 1 garlic clove, crushed
— 1 onion, chopped
— 1 carrot, chopped
— 1 celery stalk, chopped
— 2 tablespoons butter
— 2 tablespoons olive oil
— 14 ounces (400 g) spaghetti
— salt and pepper
— fresh basil leaves, to garnish
— grated Parmesan cheese,
  to serve

Put the tomatoes, garlic, onion, carrot, and celery into a pan and add a pinch of salt. Bring to a boil, stirring frequently, then lower the heat, and simmer, stirring occasionally, for 1 hour. Remove the pan from the heat and spoon the mixture into a food processor or blender. Process to a puree and season to taste with salt and pepper. Melt the butter with the oil in a skillet or frying pan. Add the vegetable puree and cook over low heat, stirring constantly, for a few minutes. Cook the spaghetti in plenty of salted boiling water until al dente. Drain, tip into a warmed serving dish, and spoon the sauce over it. Garnish with a few small basil leaves and serve immediately with the Parmesan.

Tip: Alternatively, return the spaghetti to the pan in which it was cooked after draining, pour the sauce over it and mix well. The residual heat of the pan will add to the creaminess.

SPAGHETTI WITH TUNA AND BORLOTTI BEANS

Preparation time: *15 min*
Cooking time: *10 min*
Serves 4

— 1 tablespoon olive oil
— 2 tablespoons hot mustard
— 2 tablespoons chopped fresh
  flat-leaf parsley
— 3½ ounces (100 g) canned
  tuna, drained and flaked
— 1 small red onion,
  finely chopped
— 3¼ cup (100 g) cooked or
  canned borlotti beans, drained
— 1 garlic clove, minced
— 12 ounces (350 g) spaghetti
— 1 bell pepper, seeded and cut
  into strips
— salt and pepper

Whisk together the oil, mustard, and parsley in a bowl and season with salt and pepper. Put the tuna, onion, beans, and garlic into a serving dish. Cook the spaghetti in plenty of salted boiling water until al dente. Drain, tip into the dish, and toss well. Pour the oil dressing over the pasta, garnish with the bell pepper strips, and serve immediately.

SPAGHETTI MARINARA

SPAGHETTI ALLA MARINARA

Preparation time: *25 min*
Cooking time: *30 min*
Serves 4

— 1 scorpion fish, ocean perch, or rockfish, cleaned and boned
— 7 ounces (200 g) clams
— 3 tablespoons olive oil
— 2 garlic cloves
— 6 tomatoes, blanched, peeled, and diced
— 7 ounces (200 g) uncooked shrimp (prawns), peeled and chopped
— 12 ounces spaghetti
— salt
— fresh flat-leaf parsley, chopped, to garnish

Remove and discard the skin from the fish and cut the flesh into pieces, then put them into a food processor, and process to a puree. Scrub the clams under cold running water and discard any with broken shells or that do not shut immediately when sharply tapped. Heat the oil in a pan. Add the garlic cloves and cook over low heat, stirring frequently, for a few minutes until browned. Remove with a slotted spoon and discard. Add the tomatoes to the pan, season with salt and pepper, and cook, stirring occasionally, for 15 minutes. Stir the pureed fish into the pan, followed by the clams and shrimp (prawns). Cook for another 10 minutes and discard any clams that remain shut. Cook the spaghetti in plenty of salted boiling water until al dente. Drain, toss with the sauce, and serve immediately, sprinkled with parsley.

SPAGHETTI BAKED IN ALUMINUM FOIL

SPAGHETTI AL CARTOCCIO

Preparation time: *15 min*
Cooking time: *35 min*
Serves 4

— 11 ounces (300 g) tomatoes, blanched, peeled, and diced
— 2 tablespoons olive oil
— 2 tablespoons lemon juice
— 1 tablespoon capers, drained
— 1 garlic clove, crushed
— 1 sprig fresh basil, finely chopped
— 12 (350 g) ounces spaghetti
— salt and pepper

Preheat the oven to 350°F (180°C/Gas Mark 4). Put the tomatoes, oil, lemon juice, and capers into a skillet or frying pan, season with salt and pepper, and cook over low heat, stirring occasionally, for 15 minutes until thickened. Stir in the garlic and basil. Cook the spaghetti in plenty of salted boiling water until al dente. Drain, return to the pan, pour in the sauce, and toss. Tip the mixture on to the middle of a large sheet of aluminum foil, bring up the sides, and fold over securely to seal. Put the parcel on a baking sheet and bake for 15 minutes. Serve immediately straight from the parcel.

SPAGHETTI CARBONARA

SPAGHETTI ALLA CARBONARA

Preparation time: *30 min*
Cooking time: *20 min*
Serves 4

— 2 tablespoons butter
— generous ½ cup (100 g) diced pancetta
— 1 garlic clove
— 12 ounces (350 g) spaghetti
— 2 eggs, beaten
— ½ cup (40 g) grated Parmesan cheese
— ½ cup (40 g) grated pecorino cheese
— salt and pepper

Melt the butter in a pan, add the pancetta and garlic, and cook until the garlic turns brown. Remove and discard the garlic. Meanwhile, cook the spaghetti in a large pan of salted boiling water until al dente, then drain, and add to the pancetta. Remove the pan from the heat, pour in the eggs, add half the Parmesan and half the pecorino, and season with pepper. Mix well so that the egg coats the spaghetti. Add the remaining cheese, mix again, and serve.

Along with Bucatini Amatriciana (see page 20), this is among the best-known dishes of Lazio in central Italy. It is named Carbonara because it was a staple meal of the workers who collected wood in the Appenine Mountains to make charcoal or carbone.

SPAGHETTI WITH ANCHOVY AND BLACK TRUFFLE SAUCE

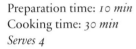

SPAGHETTI ALLA SALSA D'ACCIUGHE E TARTUFO NERO

Preparation time: *10 min*
Cooking time: *30 min*
Serves 4

— 3 tablespoons olive oil
— 1 garlic clove
— 1 tablespoon anchovy paste
— 14 ounces (400 g) tomatoes, peeled, deseeded and chopped
— 12 ounces (350 g) spaghetti
— 1 tablespoon chopped fresh flat-leaf parsley
— 1 ounce (25 g) black truffle, thinly sliced
— salt and pepper

Heat the oil in a pan. Add the garlic clove and cook over low heat, stirring frequently, for a few minutes until lightly browned, then remove the garlic with a slotted spoon and discard. Stir the anchovy paste into the oil, then add the tomatoes and season with salt and pepper. Stir well and simmer for about 15 minutes until thickened. Cook the spaghetti in plenty of salted boiling water until al dente. Drain, return to the pan, pour the anchovy sauce over and sprinkle with the parsley. Transfer to a warmed serving dish, sprinkle with the truffle slices and serve immediately.

SPAGHETTI PARCEL WITH CLAMS

Preparation time: *30 min*
Cooking time: *40 min*
Serves *4*

— 2¼ pounds (1 kg) clams
— 2 garlic cloves
— 1 sprig fresh flat-leaf parsley
— scant 1 cup (200 ml) dry white wine
— scant ½ cup (100 ml) olive oil
— 12 ounces (350 g) spaghetti
— 1 ounce (25 g) bottarga (salted pressed grey [striped] mullet or tuna roe), grated
— 1 teaspoon chopped fresh flat-leaf parsley
— salt and pepper

Preheat the oven to 425°F (220°C/Gas Mark 7). Scrub the clams under cold running water. Discard any with damaged shells or that do not shut immediately when sharply tapped. Put them into a large pan with the garlic cloves and parsley sprig. Pour in the wine, cover, and cook over high heat, shaking the pan occasionally, for 3–5 minutes until the clams open. Drain, reserving the cooking liquid, and discard any clams that remain shut. Set aside a few whole clams for the garnish and remove the remainder from their shells. Pour the reserved cooking liquid through a strainer lined with cheesecloth (muslin) into a clean pan. Add the olive oil, season lightly with salt and pepper, and bring to a boil over medium heat. Continue to boil until reduced and thickened. Cook the spaghetti in plenty of salted boiling water until al dente. Drain, tip into the reduced cooking liquid, and toss. Turn off the heat and stir in the bottarga, parsley, and shelled clams. Spoon the mixture into the middle of a large sheet of wax (greaseproof) paper, garnish with the whole clams, bring up the sides of the paper, and fold over the edges securely to seal. Put the parcel onto a baking sheet and bake for 5 minutes. Transfer the parcel to a warmed serving dish, open slightly at the top, and serve immediately.

Tip: Chopped parsley should be added after the sauce is cooked, otherwise it loses some of its color and flavor.

SPAGHETTI WITH ANCHOVIES

Preparation time: *30 min*
Cooking time: *30 min*
Serves *4*

— 5 ounces (150 g) salted anchovies
— 1 sprig fresh flat-leaf parsley
— ½ garlic clove
— 2 tablespoons olive oil
— 12 ounces (350 g) spaghetti
— salt and pepper

Pinch the heads of the anchovies between your thumb and forefinger and pull them off. Pinch along the top edge of each anchovy and pull out the backbones. Put them into a dish, add water to cover and let soak for 10 minutes to remove some of the salt. Chop the filleted anchovies very finely with the parsley and garlic, then put the mixture in a salad bowl and stir in the olive oil. Cook the spaghetti in a large pan of salted boiling water until al dente, then drain and tip into the salad bowl. Toss well and season with pepper.

SPAGHETTI WITH BLACK OLIVES AND LEMON

SPAGHETTI CON OLIVE NERE E LIMONE

Preparation time: *10 min*
Cooking time: *5 min*
Serves 4

— 10 ounces (275 g) spaghetti
— 30 black olives, pitted
   and chopped
— 10 fresh basil leaves, torn
— juice of 1 large lemon, strained
— 6–8 tablespoons extra virgin
   olive oil
— salt

Cook the spaghetti in plenty of salted boiling water until al dente. Drain, return to the pan, and immediately add the olives, basil, lemon juice, and enough oil to coat. Toss well and serve immediately or let cool, then chill in the refrigerator. This makes an excellent summery first course.

SPAGHETTI AND SHELLFISH PARCEL

SPAGHETTI AI FRUTTI DI MARE NEL CARTOCCIO

Preparation time: *40 min*
Cooking time: *35 min*
Serves 4

— 10 clams
— 2 tablespoons olive oil
— 2 garlic cloves
— 1 fresh chile
— 4 ripe tomatoes, blanched,
   peeled, and chopped
— 4 baby octopuses, cleaned
   and sliced
— 10 baby squid, cleaned
   and sliced
— 8 large raw shrimp (prawns),
   peeled and deveined
   (see Spaghetti with
   Langoustines, page 56)
— 12 ounces (350 g) spaghetti
— 1 sprig fresh basil, torn
— 1 sprig fresh flat-leaf
   parsley, chopped
— salt and pepper

Scrub the clams under cold running water. Discard any with damaged shells or that do not shut immediately when sharply tapped. Heat the oil in a pan with the garlic cloves. When the garlic turns golden brown remove with a slotted spoon and discard. Add the whole chile and clams to the pan, cover, and cook over high heat, shaking the pan occasionally, for 4–5 minutes until the shells open. Lift out the shellfish with a slotted spoon and when cool enough to handle remove the clams from the shells. Discard any that remain shut. Remove the chile from the pan and discard. Add the tomatoes, octopuses, and squid to the pan, season with salt and pepper, and cook, stirring occasionally, for a few minutes. Stir in the clams and the shrimp. Preheat the oven to 350°F (180°C/Gas Mark 4). Meanwhile, cook the spaghetti in plenty of salted boiling water until al dente. Drain, tip into the pan of seafood, sprinkle with the basil and parsley, and toss, then remove the pan from the heat. Tip the mixture onto the middle of a large sheet of wax (greaseproof) paper. Bring up the sides and fold over the edges to seal. Transfer the parcel to a baking sheet and bake for 5 minutes. Transfer the parcel to a warmed serving dish, open the top slightly, and serve immediately.

SPAGHETTI WITH CAPERS

SPAGHETTI AI CAPPERI

Preparation time: *15 min*
Cooking time: *20 min*
Serves 4

— 1 salted anchovy
— 4 tablespoons olive oil
— 2 garlic cloves
— 2 tablespoons capers,
    rinsed and drained
— 12 ounces (350 g) spaghetti
— salt

Pinch the head of the anchovy between your thumb and forefinger and pull it off. Pinch along the top edge of the anchovy and pull out the backbone. Put it into a dish, add water to cover and let soak for 10 minutes to remove some of the salt. Heat the oil in a pan, add the anchovy and garlic and cook over low heat, stirring frequently, until the anchovy has disintegrated and the garlic has turned golden brown. Remove the pan from the heat, discard the garlic, and add the capers. Meanwhile, cook the spaghetti in a large pan of salted, boiling water until al dente, then drain, toss with the sauce, and serve.

In the Aeolian Islands of southern Italy caper bushes grow wild everywhere and are also intensively cultivated. The island of Salina produces the biggest quantity of capers, and the buds from Pollara (an area situated on the slopes of a dormant volcano) are particularly prized for their firm consistency and fragrance. The most common type of caper plant throughout the islands is the tondino, *which produces the firmest caper buds. Traditionally preserved in dried sea salt the capers are ready for consumption after a couple of months.*

SPAGHETTI WITH ROSEMARY

SPAGHETTI AL ROSMARINO

Preparation time: *10 min*
Cooking time: *40 min*
Serves 4

— 2 tablespoons olive oil
— 2 tablespoons fresh rosemary
    needles, finely chopped
— 1 garlic clove, finely chopped
— ½ fresh chile, seeded and
    finely chopped
— 9 ounces (250 g) canned
    chopped tomatoes
— 1 tablespoon all-purpose
    (plain) flour
— 1 tablespoon milk
— 12 ounces (350 g) spaghetti
— ½ cup (40 g) grated
    Parmesan cheese
— salt

Heat the oil in a pan, add the rosemary, garlic, and chile and cook for about 2 minutes. Stir in the tomatoes with their juice and bring to a boil, then lower the heat, cover, and simmer for 30 minutes. Stir the flour with 1–2 tablespoons warm water. Season the rosemary sauce with salt, stir in the flour mixture and milk, and cook for another 5 minutes. Cook the spaghetti in a large pan of salted, boiling water until al dente, then drain, and transfer to a warmed serving dish. Sprinkle with the Parmesan and pour on the sauce.

SPAGHETTI WITH EGGPLANT AND PARSLEY

SPAGHETTI ALLE MELANZANE E PREZZEMOLO

Preparation time: *45 min*
Cooking time: *25 min*
Serves 4

— 2 eggplants (aubergines), diced
— 2 tablespoons olive oil
— 1 tablespoon finely chopped
   fresh flat-leaf parsley
— 2 egg yolks
— 1 egg white
— scant 1 cup (200 g)
   ricotta cheese
— 12 ounces (350 g) spaghetti
— salt and pepper

Put the eggplants (aubergines) into a colander, sprinkle with salt, and let drain for 30 minutes, then rinse, and pat dry with paper towels. Heat the oil in a skillet or frying pan. Add the eggplants and parsley and cook over medium heat, stirring frequently, for 15 minutes. Remove from the pan with a slotted spoon and drain well. Beat together the egg yolks and egg white in a serving dish, then beat in the ricotta until smooth. Season lightly with salt and pepper. Cook the spaghetti in plenty of salted boiling water until al dente. Drain, tip into the dish, and mix well. Add the eggplants and serve immediately.

SPAGHETTI WITH GARLIC AND CHILE OIL

SPAGHETTI AGLIO, OLIO E PEPERONCINO

Preparation time: *5 min*
Cooking time: *15 min*
Serves 4

— 5 tablespoons olive oil
— 2 garlic cloves, thinly sliced
— ½ fresh chile, seeded and
   chopped
— 1 sprig fresh flat-leaf parsley,
   chopped
— 12 ounces (350 g) spaghetti
— salt

Heat the oil in a small pan, add the garlic and chile, and cook over low heat for a few minutes until the garlic is golden brown. Season lightly with salt, remove the pan from the heat, and add the parsley. Cook the spaghetti in a large pan of salted boiling water until al dente, then drain, toss with the garlic and chile oil, and serve.

SPAGHETTI WITH GORGONZOLA AND PANCETTA

SPAGHETTI AL GORGONZOLA E PANCETTA

Preparation time: *15 min*
Cooking time: *20 min*
Serves 4

— 2 tablespoons olive oil
— ⅔ cup (120 g) diced
   pancetta or bacon
— ¼–½ fresh chile, seeded
   and chopped
— 4 ounces (120 g) mild
   Gorgonzola cheese
— scant 1 cup (200 ml) heavy
   (double) cream
— 12 ounces (350 g) spaghetti
— grated Parmesan cheese,
   to serve
— salt

Heat the oil in a shallow pan. Add the pancetta or bacon and chile to taste, and cook over low heat, stirring occasionally, for 5 minutes. Gradually crumble the Gorgonzola into the pan, stirring constantly, then pour in the cream. Cook the spaghetti in plenty of salted boiling water until al dente. Drain, tip into a warmed serving dish, and pour the sauce over the pasta. Serve immediately, offering the Parmesan separately.

SPAGHETTI WITH CHICKEN

SPAGHETTI AL POLLO

Preparation time: 20 *min*
Cooking time: 55 *min*
Serves 4

— 1 skinless boneless
  chicken breast
— 4 tablespoons (50 g) butter
— 2 cups (150 g) sliced cremini
  (chestnut) mushrooms
— 1 cup (250 ml) heavy
  (double) cream
— 12 ounces (350 g) spaghetti
— ½ cup (40 g) grated
  Parmesan cheese
— salt and pepper

Put the chicken into a pan and add water to cover. Bring just to a boil, then lower the heat so that it barely bubbles. Cover and poach for 25–30 minutes until cooked through and tender. Drain and let cool, then dice. Melt the butter in a skillet or frying pan. Add the diced chicken and cook over medium heat, stirring frequently, for 5 minutes until lightly browned all over. Lower the heat, add the mushrooms, season with salt and pepper and cook, stirring occasionally, for 15 minutes. Stir in the cream and heat through gently. Meanwhile, cook the spaghetti in plenty of salted boiling water until al dente. Drain, tip into a serving dish, spoon the sauce on top, and sprinkle with the Parmesan. Serve immediately.

SPAGHETTI WITH ZUCCHINI FLOWERS

SPAGHETTI AI FIORI GIALLI

Preparation time: 25 *min*
Cooking time: 35 *min*
Serves 4

— 2 tablespoons olive oil
— 1 garlic clove
— 4 tomatoes, blanched,
  peeled, seeded, and chopped
— 16 zucchini (courgette)
  flowers, cut into strips
— 12 ounces (350 g) spaghetti
— 8 fresh basil leaves, torn
— salt and pepper

Heat the oil in a pan. Add the garlic clove and cook over low heat, stirring frequently, for a few minutes until golden brown, then remove the garlic with a slotted spoon and discard. Add the tomatoes and cook, stirring occasionally, for 15 minutes. Add the zucchini (courgette) flowers and cook for 5 minutes more. Season with salt and pepper. Cook the spaghetti in plenty of salted boiling water until al dente. Drain, tip into a warmed serving dish, pour the sauce over the pasta, garnish with the basil, and serve immediately.

SPAGHETTI WITH CHEESE AND PEPPER

SPAGHETTI CACIO E PEPE

Preparation time: 5 *min*
Cooking time: 7 *min*
Serves 4

— 12 ounces (350 g) spaghetti
— generous 1 cup (100 g) grated
  pecorino cheese
— salt and pepper

Cook the spaghetti in plenty of salted boiling water until al dente. Drain, reserving a few tablespoons of the cooking liquid, and tip into a warmed serving dish. Sprinkle with the pecorino and season well with pepper. Add the reserved pasta cooking water, toss, and serve immediately.

Preparation time: *10 min*
Cooking time: *7 min*
Serves 4

— 2 egg yolks
— ⅔ cup (50 g) grated
   Parmesan cheese
— 3 tablespoons butter, diced
— 2 tablespoons heavy
   (double) cream
— 12 ounces (350 g) spaghetti
— 10 green peppercorns
— salt

SPAGHETTI WITH GREEN PEPPERCORNS

SPAGHETTI AL PEPE VERDE

Combine the egg yolks, ½ cup (40 g) of the Parmesan, the butter, and cream in a serving dish. Cook the pasta in plenty of salted boiling water until al dente. Drain, tip it into the dish, and stir gently. Add the green peppercorns and the remaining cheese and serve immediately.

Tip: Green peppercorns are unripe and milder than black or white pepper. They are preserved by freeze-drying, dehydrating, or bottling in brine or vinegar. If the peppercorns are preserved in brine, drain and rinse first. Avoid those preserved in vinegar.

Preparation time: *25 min*
Cooking time: *20 min*
Serves 6

— scant ½ cup (100 ml) olive oil
— 2 garlic cloves
— 9 ounces (250 g) oily fish
   fillets, such as anchovies,
   mackerel, or tuna, cut
   into cubes
— scant 1 cup (200 ml) dry
   white wine
— 5 ounces (150 g) mild green
   chiles, seeded and chopped
— 4 tablespoons chopped
   fresh oregano
— 15 ounces (425 g) spaghetti
— salt

SPAGHETTI WITH FISH, GREEN CHILES, AND OREGANO

SPAGHETTI CON PESCE AZZURRO, PEPERONI VERDI, E OREGANO

Heat the oil in a pan. Add the garlic cloves and cook over low heat, stirring occasionally, for a few minutes until lightly browned. Remove with a slotted spoon and discard. Add the fish to the pan and cook for 3 minutes. Pour in the wine and cook until the alcohol has evaporated. Stir in the chiles and oregano and cook for a few minutes more. Cook the spaghetti in plenty of salted boiling water until al dente. Drain, tip into the pan with the sauce, and toss over the heat for a few minutes. Transfer to a warmed serving dish and serve immediately.

Preparation time: *10 min*
Cooking time: *7 min*
Serves 4

— 1⅓ cups (330 g) ricotta cheese
— 6 fresh sage leaves
— 6 fresh basil leaves
— 1 tablespoon rosemary
— 1 tablespoon fresh marjoram
— 12 ounces (350 g) spaghetti
— salt and freshly ground
   white pepper

SPAGHETTI WITH RICOTTA AND HERBS

SPAGHETTI ALLA RICOTTA CON LE ERBE

Process the ricotta and herbs in a food processor or blender. Cook the spaghetti in plenty of salted boiling water until al dente. Drain, reserving 2 tablespoons of the cooking water, and tip into a warmed serving dish. Dilute the sauce with the reserved cooking water and pour it over the spaghetti. Season with a little white pepper, toss well, and serve immediately.

Preparation time: *40 min*
Cooking time: *45 min*
Serves 4

— 2¼ pounds (1 kg) grouper,
   cleaned and boned
— 4 tablespoons olive oil
— ½ onion, thinly sliced
— 1 leek, thinly sliced
— 1 carrot, coarsely chopped
— 1 celery heart, coarsely
   chopped
— 3 small tomatoes, blanched,
   peeled, and chopped
— 1 sprig fresh flat-leaf parsley,
   chopped
— scant ½ cup (100 ml) dry
   white wine
— 12 ounces (350 g) spaghetti
— salt and pepper

SPAGHETTI WITH GROUPER

SPAGHETTI ALLA CERNIA

Cut the fish into chunks. Heat the oil in a shallow pan. Add the onion and leek and cook over low heat, stirring occasionally, for 5 minutes. Increase the heat to medium, add the carrot and celery, and cook, stirring occasionally, for 5–7 minutes more, until lightly browned. Add the tomatoes and parsley, season with salt and pepper, and simmer, stirring occasionally, for 15 minutes. Add the fish, lower the heat, and cook, occasionally stirring gently, for a few minutes until the fish is lightly browned. Drizzle with the wine and cook until the alcohol has evaporated. Cover and simmer for 15 minutes. Cook the spaghetti in plenty of salted boiling water until al dente. Drain, tip into a warmed serving dish, pour the sauce over the pasta, toss well, and serve immediately.

Preparation time: *40 min*
Cooking time: *30 min*
Serves 4

— 1 cup (250 ml) dry white wine
— 1 bay leaf
— strip of thinly pared
   lemon zest
— 24 langoustines or lobsterettes
— 3 tablespoons olive oil
— 1 shallot, chopped
— 1 tablespoon pine nuts
— 2 sprigs fresh basil, chopped
— 12 ounces (350 g) spaghetti
— salt and pepper

SPAGHETTI WITH LANGOUSTINES

SPAGHETTI CON GLI SCAMPI

Pour 8¾ cups (2 litres) of water into a pan and add half the wine, the bay leaf, lemon zest, and a pinch of salt. Add the langoustines, bring to a boil, and cook for 7 minutes. Drain and leave until cool enough to handle, then peel them and remove the black intestinal vein. Heat the oil in a pan. Add the shallot and cook over low heat, stirring occasionally, for 5 minutes. Pour in ½ cup (120 ml) water, add the langoustines and pine nuts, drizzle with the remaining wine, and season with salt and pepper. Simmer for 5 minutes, then stir in the basil. Cook the spaghetti in plenty of salted boiling water until al dente. Drain, tip into a warmed serving dish, and top with the langoustine sauce.

SPAGHETTI WITH MASCARPONE

SPAGHETTI AL MASCARPONE

Preparation time: *10 min*
Cooking time: *10 min*
Serves 4

— 4 tablespoons (50 g) butter
— 1 cup (250 ml) heavy
   (double) cream
— ⅔ cup (150 g)
   mascarpone cheese
— 12 ounces (350 g) spaghetti
— ½ cup (40 g) grated
   Parmesan cheese
— salt

Melt the butter with the cream in a flameproof dish over low heat. Add the mascarpone and stir until smooth and thoroughly incorporated. Cook the spaghetti in plenty of salted boiling water until al dente. Drain, tip into the dish and toss with the sauce. Increase the heat, sprinkle with the Parmesan, and serve.

SPAGHETTI WITH MUSHROOM SAUCE

SPAGHETTI ALLA BOSCAIOLA

Preparation time: *25 min*
Cooking time: *45 min*
Serves 4

— 2 tablespoons olive oil
— 2 garlic cloves
— 3⅔ cups (250 g) sliced
   porcini mushrooms
— 1 pound 5 ounces (600 g)
   tomatoes, blanched, peeled,
   and diced
— 12 ounces (350 g) spaghetti
— 2 tablespoons butter
— 1 tablespoon finely chopped
   fresh flat-leaf parsley
— salt and pepper

Heat the oil in a shallow pan with the garlic cloves. When the garlic has turned golden brown, remove with a slotted spoon and discard. Add the mushrooms, increase the heat to medium–high, and cook until they have released their liquid. Lower the heat, add the tomatoes, season with salt and pepper, and simmer for 20 minutes. Cook the spaghetti in plenty of salted boiling water until al dente. Drain, tip into a warmed serving dish, and pour over the mushroom sauce. Add the butter, sprinkle with the parsley, and serve immediately.

Tip: If fresh porcini mushrooms (or "ceps") are not available, you can replace them with ⅓ cup (20 g) dried mushrooms, soaked in lukewarm water for 30 minutes, rinsed, and drained.

SPAGHETTI WITH OLIVES

SPAGHETTI ALLE OLIVE

Preparation time: *15 min*
Cooking time: *30 min*
Serves 4

— 2 tablespoons extra-virgin olive
   oil, plus extra for drizzling
— 2 leeks, sliced
— scant 1 cup (100 g) black
   olives, pitted
— 14 ounces (400 g) spaghetti
— 2 tablespoons chopped fresh
   flat-leaf parsley
— ⅔ cup (50 g) grated
   pecorino cheese
— salt

Heat the oil in a pan. Add the leeks, cover, and cook over low heat, stirring occasionally, for 15 minutes. Stir in the olives and cook for another 5 minutes. Meanwhile, cook the pasta in plenty of salted boiling water until al dente. Drain, tip into the pan with the leeks, and toss. Sprinkle with the parsley and pecorino, drizzle with olive oil, and serve immediately.

Preparation time: *15 min*
Cooking time: *35 min*
Serves *4*

— 1 pound 2 ounces (500 g)
  broccoli, cut into florets
— 3 tablespoons olive oil
— 2 tablespoons butter
— 1 onion, chopped
— 4 tablespoons heavy
  (double) cream
— 12 ounces (350 g) spaghetti
— ⅓ cup (25 g) grated
  Parmesan cheese
— salt and pepper

Preparation time: *50 min*
Cooking time: *35 min*
Serves *4*

— 2¼ pounds (1 kg) small
  octopuses, cleaned
— 4 tablespoons olive oil
— 2 garlic cloves
— 7 ounces (200 g) tomatoes,
  blanched, peeled, and chopped
— 12 ounces (350 g) spaghetti
— 1 sprig fresh flat-leaf parsley,
  chopped
— salt and pepper

Preparation time: *30 min*
Cooking time: *5 min*
Serves *4*

— 1 pound 2 ounces (500 g)
  ripe vine tomatoes, blanched,
  peeled, seeded, and chopped
— 4 tablespoons olive oil
— 10 fresh basil leaves, torn
— 2 garlic cloves
— 12 ounces (350 g) spaghetti
— salt and pepper

SPAGHETTI WITH BROCCOLI

SPAGHETTI AI BROCCOLETTI

Boil the broccoli in salted water for 8 minutes. Heat the oil and butter in a skillet or frying pan, add the onion, and cook over low heat, stirring occasionally, for 5 minutes until softened. Drain the broccoli, add to the pan, and mix well. Stir in the cream and simmer gently for 10 minutes. Transfer the mixture to a food processor and process to a puree. Season with salt and pepper to taste. Meanwhile, cook the spaghetti in a large pan of salted boiling water until al dente, then drain, toss with the broccoli and cream mixture, sprinkle with the Parmesan, and serve.

SPAGHETTI WITH OCTOPUS

SPAGHETTI AL POLPO

Rinse the octopuses and, without draining all the water, put them into a flameproof earthenware dish or heavy pan and set over medium heat until the water has dried out. Add the oil and garlic cloves and cook, stirring frequently, for a few minutes until the garlic is lightly browned. Remove the garlic with a slotted spoon and discard. Add the tomatoes to the dish or pan, season with salt and pepper, lower the heat, and simmer for 20 minutes. Cook the spaghetti in plenty of salted boiling water until al dente. Drain, tip into a warmed serving dish, and pour the sauce over the pasta. Sprinkle with the parsley and serve immediately.

SPAGHETTI WITH RAW TOMATO

SPAGHETTI AL POMODORO CRUDO

Put the tomatoes into a salad bowl, add the oil, basil, and garlic, and season with salt and pepper. Mix well, cover, and set aside in a cool place for 30 minutes, then remove and discard the garlic. Cook the spaghetti in a large pan of salted boiling water until al dente, then drain, toss with the raw tomato sauce, and serve.

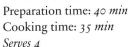

SPAGHETTI WITH SHRIMP AND GLOBE ARTICHOKES

SPAGHETTI CON GAMBERI E CARCIOFI

Preparation time: *40 min*
Cooking time: *35 min*
Serves 4

— 2 tablespoons lemon juice
— 4–5 young globe artichokes, trimmed
— 2 tablespoons olive oil
— 1 shallot, finely chopped
— 1 celery stalk, finely chopped
— ½ carrot, finely chopped
— 1 tablespoon white wine
— 4 tablespoons warm water
— 1 pound 2 ounces (500 g) uncooked shrimp (prawns)
— 12 ounces (350 g) spaghetti
— salt and pepper

To garnish:
— chopped fresh flat-leaf parsley
— grated bottarga (salted pressed grey [striped] mullet or tuna roe)

Half fill a bowl with water and stir in the lemon juice. Trim the artichokes, cut into thin wedges, and put them into the acidulated water. Heat the oil in a large pan. Add the shallot, celery, and carrot and cook over low heat, stirring occasionally, for 5–8 minutes until softened. Sprinkle with the wine and cook for a few minutes until the alcohol has evaporated. Add the warm water and cook for 5 minutes. Add the artichokes stalk ends up, season with salt and pepper, and cook, adding a few tablespoons of warm water if necessary, for 20 minutes, until tender but firm. Meanwhile, rinse the shrimp, set 4 of them aside, and peel and devein the remainder. When the artichokes are almost cooked add the 4 whole shrimp, cook for another 2 minutes, and add the peeled shrimp. Cook, stirring constantly, for 5 minutes, then remove the whole shrimp, and keep warm. Cook the pasta in plenty of salted boiling water until al dente. Drain, tip into the pan with the artichokes, and toss over low heat. Transfer to a warmed serving dish, garnish with the whole shrimp, parsley, and bottarga, and serve immediately.

Tip: Even when cooked in a sauce (for example, in a broth of oil and water with a garlic clove), artichokes should be cooked with the stalk ends up so that only the leaves are cooked in the liquid, while the more tender parts are steamed.

SPAGHETTI WITH ARUGULA AND WALNUTS

SPAGHETTI CON RUCOLA E NOCI

Preparation time: *10 min*
Cooking time: *10 min*
Serves 4

— ¾ cup (80 g) walnuts
— 1 garlic clove
— 1 bunch of arugula (rocket), shredded
— 4 tablespoons olive oil
— 12 ounces (350 g) spaghetti
— grated Parmesan cheese, to serve
— salt and pepper

Blanch the walnuts in boiling water for a few minutes, then drain, and rub off the skins. Chop the garlic with half the walnuts and put the mixture into a bowl. Add the arugula (rocket) and oil, season with salt and pepper, and mix well. Chop the remaining walnuts. Cook the spaghetti in plenty of salted boiling water until al dente. Drain, tip into a serving dish, add the arugula mixture, and toss. Sprinkle with the remaining walnuts and Parmesan and serve immediately.

SPAGHETTI WITH SARDINES

SPAGHETTI ALLE SARDE

Preparation time: *30 min*
Cooking time: *30 min*
Serves 4

— 11 ounces (300 g)
  fresh sardines
— all-purpose (plain) flour,
  for dusting
— 3 tablespoons olive oil
— 2 garlic cloves
— 1 sprig fresh flat-leaf parsley,
  chopped, plus extra to garnish
— 12 ounces (350 g) spaghetti
— salt and pepper

Rub off the fish scales with your fingers or the back of a knife and rinse under cold running water. Cut off the head of each fish. Gently squeeze the belly until the guts are visible then pull them out with a knife. Rinse well, then slit open the belly of each fish, and place, skin side up, on a cutting (chopping) board. Press firmly along the backbone with your fingers until the fish is flat. Turn it over and gently pull out the bones, snipping the backbone at the tail end with kitchen scissors. Rinse well, pat dry with paper towels and dust with flour. Heat the oil in a shallow pan. Add the garlic cloves and cook over low heat, stirring frequently, for a few minutes until lightly browned, then remove with a slotted spoon and discard. Add the fish to the pan and brown on both sides, then mash with a fork. Cook over low heat for 15 minutes and, if necessary, drizzle with a little hot water. Season with salt and pepper and sprinkle with the parsley. Cook the spaghetti in plenty of salted boiling water until al dente. Drain, tip into the pan with the fish, and toss over the heat for a few minutes. Transfer to a warmed serving dish, garnish with parsley sprigs, and serve immediately.

— 6 tablespoons olive oil
— 2 garlic cloves
— 12 ounces (350 g) sardines,
  scaled, cleaned, and boned
  (as above)
— 2 large tomatoes, blanched,
  peeled, and chopped
— 1 tablespoon hot water
— 1 tablespoon chopped fresh
  flat-leaf parsley
— 1 cup (50 g) fresh
  bread crumbs
— 12 ounces (350 g) spaghetti
— salt and pepper

Variation: Heat 4 tablespoons of the oil in a pan. Add the garlic cloves and cook over low heat, stirring frequently, for a few minutes until lightly browned, then remove with a slotted spoon and discard. Add the sardines, tomatoes, and hot water to the pan, and cook for 5 minutes. Season with salt and pepper, add the parsley, and cook for another 5 minutes. Meanwhile, heat the remaining olive oil in a small skillet or frying pan. Add the bread crumbs and cook, stirring constantly, for a few minutes until golden, then add to the sardines. Cook the spaghetti in plenty of salted boiling water until al dente. Drain, tip into a warm serving dish, pour the sardine sauce over it, and serve.

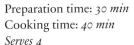

SPAGHETTI WITH VEGETABLES AND HERBS

SPAGHETTI CON SUGO BRILLANTE

Preparation time: 30 *min*
Cooking time: 40 *min*
Serves 4

— 14 ounces (400 g)
  tomatoes, chopped
— 1 green bell pepper,
  seeded and diced
— 1 onion, chopped
— 1 celery stalk, chopped
— 1 zucchini (courgette), diced
— 1 garlic clove, finely chopped
— 1 tablespoon chopped mixed
  fresh herbs, such as marjoram,
  savory, and oregano
— 3 tablespoons olive oil
— 12 ounces (350 g) spaghetti
— torn fresh basil leaves,
  to garnish
— 1 tablespoon grated ricotta
  salata cheese
— salt and pepper

Put the tomatoes, green bell pepper, onion, celery, zucchini (courgette), garlic and herbs into a pan, season with salt, cover, and cook over low heat, stirring occasionally, for 25–30 minutes until the tomatoes have broken up and the vegetables are soft. Uncover the pan, increase the heat to medium, and cook, stirring frequently, until the liquid has reduced. Remove the pan from the heat and press the mixture through a strainer into a bowl with the back of a spoon. If necessary, return it to the pan and reduce the remaining liquid, stirring constantly. Heat the oil in a shallow pan. Add the tomato and vegetable sauce and mix well. Season to taste with salt and pepper and cook until the oil separates from the tomato mixture, creating a shiny effect. Cook the pasta in plenty of salted boiling water until al dente. Drain, tip into a warmed serving dish and pour the sauce over. Garnish with basil and serve immediately, handing the ricotta separately.

SPAGHETTI WITH WALNUT SAUCE

SPAGHETTI ALLA SALSA DI NOCI

Preparation time: 30 *min*
Cooking time: 15 *min*
Serves 4

— ¾ cup (80 g) walnuts
— pinch of sugar
— pinch of freshly grated nutmeg
— scant ½ cup (100 ml) olive oil
— 12 ounces (350 g) spaghetti
— 1½ tablespoons butter, plus
  extra for serving
— ¾ cup (40 g) fresh
  bread crumbs
— grated Parmesan cheese,
  to serve
— salt

Blanch the walnuts in boiling water for a few minutes, then drain, and rub off the skins. Chop finely and mix with the sugar and nutmeg in a bowl. Gradually stir in the oil and season with salt. Cook the spaghetti in plenty of salted boiling water until al dente. Meanwhile, melt the butter in a skillet or frying pan. Add the bread crumbs and cook, stirring constantly, for a few minutes until golden brown. Drain the spaghetti, tip it into the pan with the bread crumbs, and toss over the heat for 2 minutes. Pour the walnut sauce into the pan and stir. Transfer to a warmed serving dish, sprinkle with Parmesan, and serve immediately. To ensure the ingredients are thoroughly mixed, put a few pats of butter on the pasta before adding the sauce and Parmesan.

Walnut sauce, usually served with pansotti (see Genoese Pansotti page 246), is also good with spaghetti. This sauce is a traditional recipe from Liguria, a narrow coastal region between the sea and mountains in northwest Italy, where a limited amount of fresh produce grows in the wild. As a result, Ligurians must make the most of the crops that thrive, such as garlic, borage, olives, basil, walnuts, pine nuts, and onions.

SPAGHETTINI WITH CHEESE AND ARTICHOKES

SPAGHETTINI FORMAGGIO E CARCIOFI

Preparation time: 25 *min*
Cooking time: 50 *min*
Serves 4

— 2 tablespoons lemon juice
— 4 young globe artichokes, trimmed
— 2 tablespoons butter
— 4 tablespoons olive oil
— 1 onion, chopped
— 1 garlic clove, chopped
— scant 1 cup (200 ml) dry white wine
— scant ½ cup (100 ml) lukewarm water (optional)
— 1 sprig fresh marjoram, finely chopped
— 12 ounces (350 g) spaghettini
— 2 ounces (50 g) diced mild provolone cheese
— 3½ ounces (100 g) diced white scamorza cheese
— ½ cup (40 g) grated Parmesan cheese
— salt and pepper

Half fill a bowl with water and stir in the lemon juice. Cut the artichokes into wedges and put them into the acidulated water to prevent discoloration. Melt the butter with half the oil in a shallow pan. Add the onion and garlic and cook over low heat, stirring occasionally, for 5 minutes. Drain the artichokes, add to the pan, and cook, stirring occasionally, for 10 minutes. Pour in the wine and cook until the alcohol has evaporated. Add a little lukewarm water if necessary. Stir in the marjoram, cover, and simmer gently for 20 minutes. Cook the spaghettini in plenty of salted boiling water until al dente. Drain, tip into a warmed serving dish, drizzle with the remaining oil, pour in the artichoke sauce, and add all the cheeses. Mix together thoroughly, season with pepper, and serve immediately.

SPAGHETTINI WITH MOZZARELLA AND ANCHOVIES

SPAGHETTINI CON MOZZARELLA E ACCIUGHE

Preparation time: 15 *min*
Cooking time: 7 *min*
Serves 4

— 2 ounces (50 g) salted anchovies
— 5 ounces (150 g) mozzarella cheese, diced
— 2 egg yolks
— 12 ounces (350 g) spaghettini
— salt

Pinch the heads of the anchovies between your thumb and index finger and pull them off, taking the innards with them. Pinch along the top edge of each anchovy and pull out the backbones. Put the fish into a bowl, pour in water to cover, and let soak for 10 minutes to remove some of the salt, then drain and chop. Put them into a serving dish and add the mozzarella. Beat the egg yolks with a pinch of salt in a bowl and add to the dish. Cook the spaghettini in plenty of salted boiling water until al dente. Drain, transfer to the dish, mix with the sauce, and serve immediately.

SPAGHETTINI WITH TUNA AND OLIVES

SPAGHETTINI CON OLIVE E TONNO

Preparation time: *15 min*
Cooking time: *20 min*
Serves 4

— 6 anchovy fillets in oil, drained
— 3½ ounces (100 g) canned
   tuna in oil, drained and flaked
— 1¼ cups (150 g) green
   olives, pitted
— 1 tablespoon capers, rinsed
   and drained
— 6 tablespoons olive oil
— 2 garlic cloves
— 12 ounces (350 g) spaghettini
— salt and pepper

Put the anchovies, tuna, olives, and capers into a bowl, season with salt and pepper, and mix well. Heat the oil in a pan. Add the garlic cloves and cook over low heat, stirring frequently, for a few minutes. Remove with a slotted spoon and discard. Add the tuna mixture and cook over medium heat, stirring occasionally, for 5 minutes. Cook the spaghettini in plenty of salted boiling water until al dente. Drain and tip into a serving dish. Add the sauce, toss, and serve immediately.

Tip: Capers are available preserved in salt or vinegar. The first option keeps the original flavor better.

SPAGHETTINI WITH CAPERS AND HERBS

SPAGHETTINI AI CAPPERI E ERBE

Preparation time: *10 min*
Cooking time: *7 min*
Serves 4

— 1 ounce (25 g) canned anchovy
   fillets, drained and chopped
— 2 ounces (50 g) capers, drained
— 3 tablespoons fresh flat-leaf
   parsley, chopped
— 1 teaspoon dried oregano
— 2 tablespoons olive oil
— 2 tablespoons butter, diced
— 2 egg yolks
— 12 ounces (350 g) spaghettini
— ½ cup (40 g) grated
   Parmesan cheese
— salt and pepper

Put the anchovy fillets, capers, parsley, oregano, oil, and butter into a serving dish. Beat the egg yolks with a pinch of salt in a bowl. Cook the spaghettini in plenty of salted boiling water until al dente. Drain, tip into the dish, add the egg yolks, and stir. Season with pepper, sprinkle with the Parmesan, and serve immediately.

VERMICELLI

Vermicelli is a type of dried pasta made from durum wheat semolina flour, like a thinner version of spaghetti. It is believed to be of Neapolitan origin, and in the south of Italy the two terms spaghetti and vermicelli are used interchangeably. The name means "little worms," and the first evidence of the existence of vermicelli dates back to 1154. The twelfth-century Arab geographer al-Idrisi writes that at Trabia in Sicily, *itriya* ("vermicelli") was produced and exported throughout the island and into Muslim territories. This claim is confirmed by the survival of the Sicilian dialect word *tria*, which means both modern spaghetti and the metal cutter that is used to produce it. Vermicelli is often served with fish-based sauces, but also works well in oven-baked dishes.

Preparation time: *30 min*
Cooking time: *35 min*
Serves 4

— 2 tablespoons olive oil
— 1 garlic clove, crushed
— ½ dried chile, crumbled
— 11 ounces (300 g) tomatoes, blanched, peeled, and chopped
— 1 teaspoon sugar (optional)
— 3½ ounces (100 g) clams
— 7 ounces (200 g) baby octopus, cleaned and cut into pieces
— scant 1 cup (200 ml) dry white wine
— 12 ounces (350 g) vermicelli
— 1 tablespoon chopped fresh flat-leaf parsley
— salt

FISHERMAN'S VERMICELLI

VERMICELLI DEL MARINAIO

Heat the oil in a shallow pan. Add the garlic and chile and cook over low heat, stirring frequently, for 2–3 minutes. Add the tomatoes, season with salt, and simmer for 15 minutes. You can add 1 teaspoon sugar to remove any acidity. Meanwhile, scrub the clams under cold running water. Discard any with damaged shells or that do not shut immediately when sharply tapped. Put the clams into another pan, cover, and cook over high heat, shaking the pan occasionally, for 3–5 minutes until the shells open. Discard any that remain shut and remove the remainder from their shells. If desired, leave some in their shells to serve. Add the octopus to the tomato sauce, pour in the wine, stir well, and simmer for 10 minutes. Add the clams and stir. Cook the vermicelli in plenty of salted boiling water until al dente. Drain, tip into a warmed serving dish, pour the sauce over the pasta, and sprinkle with the chopped parsley. Serve immediately.

Preparation time: *30 min*
Cooking time: *30 min*
Serves 4

— 2¼ pounds (1 kg) clams,
  scrubbed
— ⅔ cup (150 ml) olive oil
— 2 garlic cloves
— 12 ounces (350 g) vermicelli
— 1 tablespoon chopped fresh
  flat-leaf parsley
— salt and pepper

VERMICELLI WITH CLAMS

VERMICELLI CON LE VONGOLE

Scrub the clams under cold running water. Discard any
with broken shells or that do not shut immediately when
sharply tapped. Heat the oil in a pan, add the garlic and
clams, and cook for about 5 minutes until the shells open.
Remove the pan from the heat and lift out the clams with
a slotted spoon. Discard any that remain closed. Discard the
garlic. Remove the clams from their shells. Strain the
cooking liquid into a skillet or frying pan and add the clams.
Meanwhile, cook the vermicelli in plenty of salted boiling
water until al dente, then drain and tip into the skillet
or frying pan. Cook for 2 minutes, tossing frequently, then
season with salt and pepper to taste, and sprinkle with the
parsley. Tip onto a warmed serving dish.

Tip: To create a perfect dish of pasta with clams, drain the pasta
when half cooked, then add it to the pan with the clams to
finish the cooking process. This way the pasta will absorb the
liquid from the clams and enhance the flavor. For a variation
to this dish, add some chopped tomatoes (blanched, peeled,
and seeded), or canned tomatoes. This recipe also works with
the slightly thicker spaghettini.

Preparation time: *10 min*
Cooking time: *15 min*
Serves 4

— 2 eggs
— ⅔ cup (50 g) grated
  Parmesan cheese
— 12 ounces (350 g) vermicelli
— 4 tablespoons (50 g) butter
— salt and pepper

VERMICELLI WITH PARMESAN

VERMICELLI AL PARMIGIANO

Break the eggs into a bowl, mix with half the Parmesan, and
season with salt and pepper. Cook the vermicelli in plenty of
salted boiling water until al dente. Meanwhile, put the butter
into a heatproof bowl, set it over a pan of simmering water,
and melt. Drain the pasta, tip into the bowl with the eggs and
cheese, and mix. Add the melted butter and the remaining
Parmesan, mix together carefully, and serve immediately.

ZITE

Zite, or ziti, is a type of dried pasta originally from the city of Naples, and is now widespread throughout southern Italy. Similar to spaghetti but thicker, tubular, and hollow, zite is made of durum wheat semolina flour and can be smooth or ridged. As zite strands are made very long, they are usually broken up before cooking. In Naples, zite is traditionally served as part of a wedding feast, and the name comes from the word *zita* in the Neapolitan dialect, which means "wife." Further south, in Puglia, it is typically served as Zite alla Sangiovanniello (Zite Sangiovanniello, see below) with a tomato, anchovy, and caper sauce. Zite is also particularly suited to baked pasta dishes, such as the Sicilian Pasta con le Sarde (Pasta with Sardines, see page 68).

Ⓧ Ⓧ

Preparation time: *10 min*
Cooking time: *30 min*
Serves 4

— 2 fresh anchovies
— 2 tablespoons olive oil
— 1 garlic clove
— 14 ounces (400 g) fresh tomatoes, blanched, peeled, and chopped, or canned chopped tomatoes
— 1 hot red chile, seeded and chopped
— 1 tablespoon capers, drained
— 1 sprig fresh flat-leaf parsley, chopped
— 12 ounces (350 g) zite
— salt

ZITE SANGIOVANNIELLO

ZITE ALLA SANGIOVANNIELLO

Pinch the heads of the anchovies between your thumb and forefinger and pull them off, taking the innards with them. Pinch along the top edge of each anchovy and pull out the backbones. Heat the oil in a shallow pan. Add the garlic clove and cook over low heat, stirring frequently, for a few minutes until lightly browned. Remove the garlic with a slotted spoon and discard. Add the anchovies and cook, stirring constantly, until they have almost disintegrated. Add the tomatoes and chile and simmer for about 20 minutes until thickened. Stir in the capers and parsley. Cook the zite in plenty of salted boiling water until al dente. Drain, tip into a warmed serving dish, pour the sauce over the pasta, and serve immediately.

In Puglia there is a strong tradition of homemade pasta and many Puglian women are rightfully proud of their skill in making orecchiette and zite, both of which are staples. This ancient art is still very much alive, and these varieties of pasta continue the legacy of the women who first made them, and whose lives were dedicated, with unfailing love and a spirit of sacrifice, to the family.

PASTA WITH SARDINES

Preparation time: *30 min*
Cooking time: *1 hour*
Serves 4

— 3 tablespoons golden
  raisins (sultanas)
— 4 salted anchovy fillets
— 7 ounces (200 g) wild fennel
— 2 tablespoons olive oil,
  plus extra for brushing
— 1 onion, chopped
— ¼ cup (25 g) pine nuts
— pinch of saffron threads
— 12 ounces (350 g) fresh
  sardines, scaled and cleaned
— all-purpose (plain) flour,
  for dusting
— vegetable oil, for deep-frying
— 11 ounces (300 g) zite
— salt

Put the golden raisins (sultanas) in a bowl, add hot water to cover, and let soak. In another bowl, cover the anchovies with water and soak for 10 minutes. Cook the fennel in lightly salted boiling water for 15–20 minutes, then drain, reserving the cooking liquid, and chop. Heat the oil in a pan, add the onion, and cook over low heat, stirring occasionally, for 5 minutes. Drain the anchovies, add to the pan and mash with a wooden spoon. Drain the raisins, squeezing out the excess liquid, and add to the pan along with the fennel and pine nuts. Sprinkle with the saffron, cover, and cook over low heat for 15 minutes.

Open the sardines out like the pages of a book, leaving them attached along their backs. Rinse well, pat dry, and dust with flour, shaking off any excess. Heat the vegetable oil in a deep-fryer or large pan to 350–375°F (180–190°C/Gas Mark 4–5) or until a cube of day-old bread browns in 30 seconds. Add the sardines and deep-fry until golden brown, then remove, and drain on paper towels. Season with a little salt. Preheat the oven to 400°F (200°C/Gas Mark 6) and brush an ovenproof dish with oil.

Cook the zite in the reserved cooking water, topped up with more boiling water if necessary, until al dente, then drain, return to the pan, and stir in half the sauce. Spoon a layer of pasta onto the base of the prepared dish and place a layer of sardines on top. Add a layer of the sauce and continue making layers of pasta, sardines, and sauce until all the ingredients are used, ending with a layer of sauce. Bake for 10 minutes.

Tip: Wild fennel grows all over the coastal areas of the eastern Mediterranean, where it is widely used as a vegetable, eaten raw or cooked, and a herb. The leaves are feathery and dill-like and the bulbs have a more pronounced anise taste than ordinary fennel. If not available, you can use regular fennel.

SHORT PASTA

CONCHIGLIE

A popular type of dried short pasta, conchiglie can be smooth or ridged and are so called because they resemble mollusk shells—*conchiglie* in Italian. The classic seashell shape has always been a feature of the decorative arts in Italy, and has been adopted by pasta makers too. The cavity of the conchiglie is good for catching and holding sauces, making it ideal for light sauces of tomato, ricotta, or pesto. Depending on the size, the larger version is called conchiglioni, the smaller, conchigli-ette. Conchiglie can also be colored with natural ingredients such as tomato or squid ink.

CONCHIGLIE WITH GORGONZOLA AND PISTACHIOS

CONCHIGLIE CON GORGONZOLA E PISTACCHI

Preparation time: *15 min*
Cooking time: *10 min*
Serves 4

— ½ cup (50 g) pistachio nuts
— 3½ ounces (100 g) strong Gorgonzola cheese, diced
— 2 tablespoons heavy (double) cream
— 11 ounces (300 g) conchiglie
— ½ cup (40 g) grated Parmesan cheese
— salt

Put the pistachios into a heatproof bowl, pour over boiling water to cover, and let stand for 3 minutes. Drain well and when cool enough to handle, rub off the skins with your fingers. Chop the kernels and set aside. Put the Gorgonzola and cream into a pan and melt over low heat, stirring constantly until smooth, then remove from the heat. Cook the pasta in plenty of salted boiling water until al dente. Drain, tip into a warmed serving dish, and toss with the melted Gorgonzola mixture, chopped pistachios, and Parmesan. Serve immediately.

CONCHIGLIE WITH SPINACH

CONCHIGLIE CON GLI SPINACI

Preparation time: *20 min*
Cooking time: *20 min*
Serves 4

— 4 tablespoons (50 g) butter
— 1 shallot, chopped
— 4⅔ cups (400 g) frozen chopped spinach
— 1 egg
— scant ½ cup (100 g) ricotta cheese
— 12 ounces (350 g) conchiglie
— salt and pepper

Melt the butter in a pan. Add the shallot and cook over low heat, stirring occasionally, for 5 minutes. Add the spinach and stir well, then season with salt, cover, and cook for a few minutes until heated through. Be careful to remove the pan from the heat before the mixture dries out. Put the egg and ricotta into a serving dish, season lightly with pepper, and beat until smooth and combined. Alternatively, you can replace the egg with 4 tablespoons light (single) cream. Cook the pasta in plenty of salted boiling water until al dente. Drain and stir into the ricotta mixture. Add the spinach mixture, toss lightly, and serve immediately.

CONCHIGLIE WITH GORGONZOLA AND PISTACHIOS

CONCHIGLIE WITH MOZZARELLA

CONCHIGLIE WITH HERBS

CONCHIGLIE ALLE ERBE

Preparation time: *20 min,*
plus marinating
Cooking time: *25 min*
Serves 4

— generous ½ cup (130 ml)
 olive oil
— juice of ½ lemon, strained
— 1 bunch of chopped fresh
 mixed herbs, such as thyme,
 sage, rue, and mint
— ½ onion, finely chopped
— 5–6 tomatoes, blanched,
 peeled, and diced
— 12 ounces (350 g) conchiglie
— salt

Combine scant ½ cup (100 ml) of the oil and the lemon juice in a bowl with a fork. Add the herbs and let marinate for 2 hours. Heat the remaining oil in a small shallow pan. Add the onion and cook over low heat, stirring occasionally, for 5 minutes. Add the herbs and their marinade and cook, stirring occasionally, for another 5 minutes. Add the tomatoes and simmer, stirring occasionally, for about 15 minutes, until thickened. Season to taste with salt. Meanwhile, cook the pasta in plenty of salted boiling water until al dente. Drain, tip into a warmed serving dish and pour the sauce over the pasta. Serve immediately.

CONCHIGLIE WITH MOZZARELLA

CONCHIGLIE ALLA MOZZARELLA

Preparation time: *15 min*
Cooking time: *8 min*
Serves 4

— 11 ounces (300 g) tomatoes,
 blanched, peeled, and diced
— 7 ounces (200 g) diced
 mozzarella cheese
— 10 torn fresh basil leaves
— ⅔ cup (150 ml) olive oil
— 12 ounces (350 g) conchiglie
— 1 tablespoon capers in oil,
 drained
— salt

Put the tomatoes, mozzarella, basil, and olive oil into a serving dish. Cook the pasta in plenty of salted boiling water until al dente. Drain and immediately tip on top of the mixture in the dish so that the mozzarella melts slightly. Add the capers, toss well, and serve immediately.

Tip: You can use this sauce to make a cold pasta salad. Proceed as above but slightly undercook the pasta and cool it down under running water. For best results, chill the seasoned pasta in the refrigerator for at least an hour before serving.

Preparation time: *20 min*
Cooking time: *30 min*
Serves 4

— 4 Sardinian globe
    artichokes, trimmed
— 2 tablespoons olive oil
— 1 garlic clove, finely chopped
— 2 tablespoons chopped fresh
    flat-leaf parsley
— 12 ounces (350 g) conchiglie
— salt and pepper

CONCHIGLIE WITH SARDINIAN ARTICHOKES

CONCHIGLIE CON I CARCIOFI SARDI

Quarter the artichokes, remove and discard the chokes, and slice very thinly. Heat the oil in a shallow pan. Add the garlic and parsley and cook over low heat, stirring frequently, for 2 minutes. Stir in the artichokes, cover, and cook over low heat, stirring occasionally and adding a little hot water if necessary, for 20 minutes. Season to taste with salt. Meanwhile, cook the pasta in plenty of salted boiling water until al dente. Drain and toss with the artichoke sauce. Transfer to a warmed serving dish, season generously with pepper, and serve immediately.

Ⓐ

Preparation time: *40 min*
Cooking time: *1 hour 5 min*
Serves 4

— 4 tablespoons (50 g) butter,
    plus extra for greasing
— ½ onion, finely chopped
— 3 ounces (80 g) ground
    (minced) veal
— 3 ounces (80 g) ground
    (minced) chicken
— scant ½ cup (100 ml) dry
    white wine
— 1 black truffle, chopped
— ½ cup (80 g) diced ham
— 2 ounces (50 g) chicken livers,
    trimmed and cut into pieces
— scant ½ cup (100 ml) heavy
    (double) cream
— 9 ounces (250 g) conchiglioni
— ½ cup (50 g) grated
    Emmenthal cheese
— salt and pepper

TIMBALE OF FILLED CONCHIGLIONI

TIMBALLO DI CONCHIGLIONI FARCITI

Melt half the butter in a shallow pan. Add the onion, veal, and chicken and cook over medium heat, stirring frequently, for 8–10 minutes until the meat is lightly browned. Pour in the wine and cook until the alcohol has evaporated. Lower the heat and simmer for 10 minutes. Stir in the truffle, ham, and chicken livers and cook, stirring occasionally, for another 5 minutes. Stir in the cream and season with salt and pepper. Remove the pan from the heat. Preheat the oven to 350°F (180°c/Gas Mark 4) and grease an ovenproof dish with butter. Cook the pasta in plenty of salted boiling water until al dente. Drain and fill each shell with a teaspoon of the mixture. Put the filled conchiglioni into the prepared dish. Dot with the remaining butter and sprinkle with the Emmenthal. Bake for 40 minutes, then serve.

DITALINI WITH ZUCCHINI

DITALINI

Ditalini, meaning "small thimbles" in Italian, is a smooth or ridged cylindrical type of dried short pasta. In the regions of Lazio in central Italy, and Calabria in the south, ditalini is traditionally combined with broccoli and is also commonly used in soups, paired with beans and peas, and in timbales.

DITALINI WITH ZUCCHINI

DITALINI CON ZUCCHINE

Preparation time: *20 min*
Cooking time: *45 min*
Serves 4

— 4 tablespoons (50 g) butter
— 2 tablespoons olive oil
— ½ small onion, chopped
— 3 ounces (80 g) smoked bacon, cut into strips
— 1¾ cups (200 g) shelled peas
— 6 young zucchini (courgettes), sliced
— 11 ounces (300 g) ditalini or ditali
— grated Parmesan cheese, to serve
— salt

Melt the butter with the oil in a skillet or frying pan. Add the onion and cook over low heat, stirring occasionally, for 5 minutes. Add the bacon and cook for 4–6 minutes, then add the peas. Cover and cook gently for 20 minutes. Add the zucchini (courgettes) and stir, then re-cover the pan, and cook for another 15 minutes. Season to taste with salt and pepper. Meanwhile, cook the ditalini in plenty of salted boiling water until al dente. Drain, tip into the pan and toss. Serve immediately, with the Parmesan alongside.

EGGPLANT AND DITALINI TIMBALE

TIMBALLO DI MELANZANE E DITALINI

Preparation time: *1 hour*
Cooking time: *50 min*
Serves 6

— 3 tablespoons butter, plus extra for greasing
— 4 tablespoons very fine fresh bread crumbs
— 2 eggplants (aubergines), thinly sliced into long strips
— all-purpose (plain) flour, for dusting
— olive oil or vegetable oil, for deep-frying
— 12 ounces (350 g) ditalini
— 7 ounces (200 g) mozzarella cheese, diced
— 3½ ounces (100 g) provolone cheese, shaved
— ⅓ cup (25 g) grated Parmesan cheese
— 7 ounces (200 g) luganega or other Italian sausage, cut into pieces
— salt and pepper

Preheat the oven to 350°F (180°C/Gas Mark 4). Grease a 1½ inch (4-cm) deep, round ovenproof dish or cake pan with butter and sprinkle with the bread crumbs. Dust the eggplants (aubergines) with flour, shaking off any excess. Heat the oil in a deep-fryer to 350–375°F (180–190°C) or until a cube of day-old bread browns in 30 seconds. Add the eggplant slices, in batches if necessary, and deep-fry for 5–10 minutes until golden brown on both sides. Remove with a slotted spoon and drain on paper towels. Line the base and sides of the prepared dish with the eggplant slices, slightly overlapping the edges. Cook the ditalini in plenty of salted boiling water until al dente. Drain, return to the pan, and add the mozzarella, provolone, and Parmesan. Toss, season with salt and pepper, and stir in the sausage pieces. Spoon the mixture evenly into the prepared dish and fold the overlapping pieces of eggplant over the filling. Dot with the butter and bake for about 30 minutes. Serve immediately.

FARFALLE

A type of short, dried pasta made of durum wheat semolina flour, *farfalle* literally means "butterflies" in Italian, and is sometimes also referred to as bow-tie pasta in English. Farfalle are made from tightly scalloped 2-inch (5-cm) squares of pasta pinched in at the middle. The shape dates back to the sixteenth century, originating in the Lombardy and Emilia-Romagna regions of northern Italy. Known as *gassa* in the city of Genoa in the northwest, *strichetto* and *galani* in the cities of Bologna and Parma in Emilia-Romagna, other variations include the larger farfallone and the smaller farfalline. Farfalle are ideal for holding tomato sauce and other light sauces with butter, peas, and cream, and are also good in cold pasta salads.

Preparation time: *5 min*
Cooking time: *10 min*
Serves 4

— 3½ ounces (100 g)
   Gorgonzola cheese
— 3½ ounces (100 g) crescenza
   or other stracchino cheese
— 1 teaspoon butter
— 2–3 tablespoons milk
— pinch of grated nutmeg
— 12 ounces (350 g) farfalle
— scant 1 cup (70 g) grated
   Parmesan cheese
— salt

FARFALLE WITH CHEESE

FARFALLE AI FORMAGGI

Put the Gorgonzola, crescenza, and butter into a small pan, add the milk, and melt over low heat, stirring until smooth. Add the nutmeg and season to taste with salt. Cook the pasta in plenty of salted boiling water until al dente. Drain and tip into a warmed serving dish. Pour the sauce on top, toss well, and sprinkle with the Parmesan. Serve immediately.

Gorgonzola is one of the best-known Italian cheeses. The name comes from the village of Gorgonzola, near Milan, where it seems that the cheese was invented by chance when a herdsman inadvertently left some milk in a bucket for a few days. The milk coagulated and became a very tasty cheese marbled with green veins of the mold Penicillium glaucum: *the first Gorgonzola.*

FARFALLE WITH SHRIMP

FARFALLE CON I GAMBERI

Preparation time: 20 *min*
Cooking time: 30 *min*
Serves 4

— 2 tablespoons olive oil
— 1 shallot, chopped
— 1 cup (120 g) shelled peas
— 12 uncooked shrimp (prawns), peeled, and deveined (see Spaghetti with Langoustines, page 56)
— scant ½ cup (100 ml) dry white wine
— 12 ounces (350 g) farfalle
— 2 tablespoons chopped fresh flat-leaf parsley
— salt and pepper

Heat the oil in a pan. Add the shallot and cook over low heat, stirring occasionally, for 5 minutes. Add the peas and cook, stirring occasionally, for 10 minutes. Add the shrimp (prawns), pour in the wine, and cook until the alcohol has evaporated. Stir and cook for 3 minutes more. Meanwhile, cook the pasta in plenty of salted boiling water until al dente. Drain, tip into the pan with the sauce, and toss over the heat for 2 minutes. Season with pepper and transfer to a warmed serving dish. Sprinkle with the parsley and serve immediately.

FARFALLE WITH PROSCIUTTO AND PESTO

FARFALLE AL PROSCIUTTO E PESTO

Preparation time: 30 *min*
Cooking time: 20 *min*
Serves 6

— 3½ ounces (100 g) prosciutto, thinly sliced
— 4 tablespoons (50 g) butter
— ½ cup (50 g) pine nuts
— scant ½ cup (100 ml) white wine
— 1 tablespoon pesto (see Trenette with Pesto, page 206)
— 15 ounces (425 g) farfalle
— grated Parmesan cheese, to serve
— salt

Spread out the slices of prosciutto on a tray and put into the freezer for 30 minutes, then cut into julienne strips. Melt the butter in a shallow pan. Add the prosciutto and cook, stirring occasionally, for 3–5 minutes, then stir in the pine nuts. Pour in the wine and cook until the alcohol has evaporated, then simmer gently for another 10 minutes. Remove from the heat and stir in the pesto. Meanwhile, cook the pasta in plenty of salted boiling water until al dente. Drain, tip into a warmed serving dish, and pour the sauce over the pasta. Sprinkle with plenty of Parmesan and serve immediately.

The only way of sampling a true Genoese pesto sauce is to go to Liguria, a region in northwest Italy famous for a type of basil with small leaves and a delicate aroma. Common basil with large leaves has a stronger fragrance.

FARFALLE WITH RADICCHIO

FARFALLE WITH RADICCHIO

Preparation time: *20 min*
Cooking time: *30 min*
Serves *4*

— 1½ tablespoons butter
— 1 small white onion, chopped
— 1 head of Treviso radicchio, coarsely chopped
— 8-inch (20-cm) length of luganega or other Italian sausage, cut into pieces
— scant ½ cup (100 ml) heavy (double) cream
— 12 ounces (350 g) farfalle
— ½ cup (40 g) grated Parmesan cheese
— salt

Melt the butter in a shallow pan. Add the onion and cook over low heat, stirring occasionally, for 5 minutes. Add the radicchio and cook, stirring occasionally, for a few minutes until wilted. Add the sausage and cook, stirring occasionally, for about 10 minutes. Stir in the cream and cook, stirring frequently, until thickened. Season to taste with salt. Cook the pasta in plenty of salted boiling water until al dente. Drain, tip into a warmed serving dish and pour the sauce over the pasta. Sprinkle with the Parmesan and serve immediately.

Tip: For a healthier version of this dish, replace the cream with ¼ cup (50 g) ricotta cheese mixed with 1–2 tablespoons of the pasta cooking water.

FARFALLE WITH MASCARPONE

FARFALLE AL MASCARPONE

Preparation time: *20 min*
Cooking time: *25 min*
Serves *4*

— 9 ounces (250 g) tomatoes, blanched and peeled
— 2 tablespoons butter
— 2 tablespoons olive oil
— 1 small onion, chopped
— 10 fresh basil leaves, torn
— ⅓ cup (80 g) mascarpone cheese
— 11 ounces (300 g) farfalle
— grated Parmesan cheese, to serve
— salt

Put the tomatoes, butter, oil, onion, basil, and a pinch of salt into a pan and cook over low heat, stirring occasionally, for 20 minutes. Remove the pan from the heat and transfer the mixture to a food processor. Process to a puree and scrape into a bowl, then stir in the mascarpone. Cook the pasta in plenty of salted boiling water until al dente. Drain, transfer to a warmed serving dish, and toss with the sauce. Sprinkle with Parmesan and serve immediately.

Mascarpone is a delicate-tasting white cheese with a soft consistency suitable for use in both sweet and savory dishes. It is made from cream which has been skimmed off milk and treated with heat and acidity. Mascarpone originates from Lodi and Abbiategrasso in Lombardy, northern Italy, and the name comes from the word mascherpa, *which in certain areas of Lombardy means "cream."*

FARFALLE WITH SMOKED PANCETTA

FARFALLE ALLA PANCETTA AFFUMICATA

Preparation time: *20 min*
Cooking time: *40 min*
Serves 4

— 1 tablespoon olive oil
— generous ½ cup (100 g) diced smoked pancetta
— 1 fresh chile, seeded and chopped
— 9 ounces (250 g) tomatoes, blanched, peeled, and chopped
— scant 1 cup (200 ml) heavy (double) cream
— 12 ounces (350 g) farfalle
— ⅓ cup (25 g) grated Parmesan cheese
— salt

Heat the oil in a pan, add the pancetta and chile, and cook over medium heat for 5 minutes until lightly browned. Add the tomatoes, season with salt, and cook over low heat for 25 minutes. Stir in the cream and cook over very low heat for 5 minutes until thickened. Meanwhile, cook the pasta in plenty of salted boiling water until al dente. Drain, tip into the sauce, and cook, stirring constantly, for 30 seconds. Sprinkle with the Parmesan and serve.

SUMMER FARFALLE

FARFALLE GRAND'ESTATE

Preparation time: *30 min*
Cooking time: *20 min*
Serves 4

— 2 tablespoons olive oil
— 1 scallion (spring onion), finely chopped
— 1 garlic clove, finely chopped
— 6 fresh basil leaves, torn
— 1 tablespoon chopped fresh marjoram
— 2 young zucchini (courgettes), cut into julienne strips
— 1 yellow bell pepper, seeded and cut into julienne strips
— 1 eggplant (aubergine), cut into julienne strips
— scant 1 cup (200 ml) dry white wine
— 12 ounces (350 g) farfalle
— salt and pepper

Heat the oil in a large pan. Add the scallion (spring onion), garlic, basil, and marjoram and cook over low heat, stirring occasionally, for 5 minutes. Stir in the zucchini (courgette), yellow bell pepper, and eggplant (aubergine), pour in the wine, and cook until the alcohol has evaporated. Season with salt and pepper and simmer for 20–25 minutes until the vegetables are tender. Cook the pasta in plenty of salted boiling water until al dente. Drain, tip into the pan with the vegetables, and toss over the heat for a few minutes. Transfer to a warmed serving dish and serve immediately.

FARFALLE WITH CRAB

Preparation time: *30 min*
Cooking time: *35 min*
Serves 4

— 2 tablespoons butter
— 2 tablespoons olive oil
— 2 shallots, thinly sliced
— scant ½ cup (100 ml) lukewarm water
— 8 globe artichoke hearts, trimmed and cut into quarters
— 7 ounces (200 g) crab meat, drained if canned
— scant ½ cup (100 ml) heavy (double) cream
— 12 ounces (350 g) farfalle
— salt and pepper

Melt the butter with the oil in a shallow pan. Add the shallots and cook over low heat, stirring occasionally, for 5 minutes. Pour in the lukewarm water, add the quartered artichoke hearts and crab meat, stir, and cook for 15 minutes. Pour in the cream, season with salt and pepper, cover, and simmer for a few minutes more. Cook the pasta in plenty of salted boiling water until al dente. Drain and tip into the pan with the sauce. Increase the heat and toss well. Transfer to a warmed serving dish and serve immediately.

FARFALLE WITH RICOTTA

FARFALLE ALLA RICOTTA

Preparation time: *10 min*
Cooking time: *5 min*
Serves 4

— generous 1 cup (250 g) ricotta cheese
— 2 ounces (50 g) finely diced smoked scamorza or provolone cheese, finely diced
— 2 tablespoons grated Parmesan cheese
— 2 egg yolks
— 12 ounces (350 g) farfalle
— salt

Put the ricotta into a bowl and break it up with a fork. Add the diced and grated cheeses and stir in the egg yolks—the mixture should be fairly thick. Cook the pasta in plenty of salted boiling water until al dente. Drain, tip into the ricotta mixture, and toss well so that everything is a nice golden yellow. Serve immediately.

Ricotta is the whey produced during the first phase of cheese making, which is then re-cooked (ricotta in Italian) to evaporate the liquid.

FARFALLE WITH SAFFRON

FARFALLE AL ZAFFERANO

Preparation time: *25 min*
Cooking time: *18 min*
Serves 4

— 12 ounces (350 g) farfalle
— 4 tablespoons (50 g) butter
— pinch of saffron threads
— ⅔ cup (50 g) grated Parmesan cheese
— salt

Cook the pasta in plenty of salted boiling water until al dente. Meanwhile, melt the butter in a heatproof bowl set over a pan of simmering water. Remove the butter from the heat and stir in the saffron. Drain the pasta, transfer to a warmed serving dish, and pour the saffron butter over. Sprinkle with the Parmesan, toss, and serve immediately.

FARFALLE WITH SARDINES

FARFALLE ALLE SARDE

Preparation time: *30 min*
Cooking time: *40 min*
Serves 4

— 1¾ pounds (800 g)
  fresh sardines
— 2 tablespoons olive oil
— 1 small onion, chopped
— 1 celery stalk, chopped
— 1 garlic clove, chopped
— 1 bunch of fresh flat-leaf
  parsley, chopped
— scant 1 cup (200 ml)
  white wine
— 12 ounces (350 g) farfalle
— 1 potato, diced
— salt and pepper

Rub off the scales of the fish with your fingers or the back of a knife and rinse under cold running water. Cut off the head of each fish. Gently squeeze the belly until the guts protrude, trap them with the knife, and pull them out. Rinse well, then slit open the belly of each fish, and place, skin side up, on a cutting (chopping) board. Press firmly along the backbone with your fingers until the fish is flat. Turn it over and gently pull out the bones, snipping the backbone at the tail end with kitchen scissors. Heat the oil in a pan. Add the onion, celery, and garlic, and cook over low heat, stirring occasionally, for 5 minutes. Stir in the parsley, add the sardines, and season lightly with salt and pepper. Increase the heat, pour in the wine, and cook until the alcohol has evaporated. Lower the heat and simmer, adding a little hot water if necessary, for 15 minutes. Cook the pasta and potato in plenty of salted boiling water until al dente. Drain, tip into a serving dish, and pour the sardine sauce over. Serve immediately.

This is a simplified version of the well-known Sicilian dish Pasta con le Sarde (Pasta with Sardines, see page 68), which includes wild fennel, pine nuts, and golden raisins (sultanas).

FARFALLE WITH SAUSAGE

FARFALLE ALLA SALSICCIA

Preparation time: *15 min*
Cooking time: *35 min*
Serves 4

— 2 tablespoons butter
— 4 tablespoons olive oil
— 1 onion, chopped
— 1 celery stalk, chopped
— 1 carrot, chopped
— 1 garlic clove
— 1 pound 2 ounces (500 g)
  tomatoes, blanched,
  peeled and diced
— 10 fresh basil leaves, torn
— 2 small sausages, skinned
  and diced
— scant 1 cup (200 ml) dry
  white wine
— 12 ounces (350 g) farfalle
— salt and pepper

Melt the butter with the oil in a pan. Add the onion, celery, and carrot and cook over low heat, stirring occasionally, for 5 minutes. Add the garlic clove and cook, stirring frequently, for a few minutes until golden brown. Remove the garlic with a slotted spoon and discard. Add the tomatoes, basil, and sausages, pour in the wine, increase the heat, and cook until the alcohol has evaporated. Lower the heat, stir, and season to taste with salt and pepper, then simmer for 20–25 minutes until thickened. Meanwhile, cook the pasta in plenty of salted boiling water until al dente. Drain, tip into the pan with the sauce, and toss well. Serve immediately.

FUSILLI IN CUTTLEFISH INK

FUSILLI

Fusilli, meaning "little spindles" in Italian, is a corkscrew-shaped dried pasta made of durum wheat semolina flour, water, and salt. It is made using a special, thin utensil like a knitting needle with a rounded end, so that the pieces slide off easily. Fusilli can be long or short, hollow or solid. This flexible pasta shape, springy and with bite, originated in the regions of Molise and Basilicata in southern Italy, but has since spread throughout the country. Best suited to strong-tasting sauces, fusilli is perfect with vegetable sauces that stick to its coils, or with shellfish.

Preparation time: *20 min*
Cooking time: *1 hour 15 min*
Serves 4

— 1½ pounds (675 g) baby cuttlefish, ink sacs reserved
— 2 tablespoons olive oil
— 1 onion, very thinly sliced
— scant 1 cup (200 ml) dry white wine
— 2 tablespoons tomato paste (puree)
— 12 ounces (350 g) fusilli
— 1 tablespoon chopped fresh flat-leaf parsley
— salt and pepper

FUSILLI IN CUTTLEFISH INK

FUSILLI AL NERO DI SEPPIA

To clean the cuttlefish, cut off the tentacles just in front of the eyes, squeeze out the beak from the middle, and discard. Separate and skin the tentacles and pull off the skin from the body. Cut along the back and remove and discard the cuttlebone. Remove and discard the innards and head. Cut the cuttlefish into strips. Heat the oil in a pan, add the onion, and cook over low heat, stirring occasionally, until softened. Add the cuttlefish and cook over medium heat, stirring occasionally, until lightly browned. Add the wine and cook until the alcohol has evaporated. Stir in the tomato paste (puree), season with salt and pepper, lower the heat, cover, and cook for 1 hour, checking occasionally to make sure the pan isn't getting too dry. Cook the fusilli in plenty of salted boiling water until al dente. Pour the cuttlefish ink into the sauce and stir in the parsley. Drain the pasta, tip it into the sauce, mix well, and transfer to a warmed serving dish.

FUSILLI PIZZA

FUSILLI PIZZA

Preparation time: 20 *min*
Cooking time: 30 *min*
Serves 4

— butter, for greasing
— 14 ounces (400 g) tomatoes,
  blanched, peeled, and chopped
— 1 tablespoon olive oil, plus
  extra for drizzling
— pinch of dried oregano
— 1 tablespoon chopped
  fresh basil
— 12 ounces (350 g) fusilli
  or other short pasta
— ½ cup (40 g) grated
  Parmesan cheese
— 3½ ounces (100 g) mozzarella
  cheese, diced
— salt

Preheat the oven to 350°F (180°C/Gas Mark 4) and grease an ovenproof dish with butter. Puree the tomatoes in a food processor or blender. Heat the oil in a pan. Add the pureed tomatoes and cook over low heat, stirring occasionally, for 10–15 minutes until thickened. Stir in the oregano and basil and remove from the heat. Cook the pasta in plenty of salted boiling water until al dente. Drain, return to the pan, and pour the sauce over the pasta. Sprinkle with the Parmesan and toss well to mix. Spoon the mixture into the prepared dish, top with the diced mozzarella, and drizzle with oil. Bake for about 10 minutes until the mozzarella starts to melt. Serve immediately straight from the dish.

FUSILLI WITH ARTICHOKES

FUSILLI AI CARCIOFI

Preparation time: 25 *min*
Cooking time: 30 *min*
Serves 4

— ⅓ cup (20 g) dried mushrooms
— 2 tablespoons olive oil
— ½ onion, chopped
— 1 garlic clove
— 1 tablespoon chopped fresh
  flat-leaf parsley
— 3 young globe artichokes,
  trimmed and thinly sliced
— 1 teaspoon concentrated
  tomato paste (puree)
— scant ½ cup (100 ml) dry
  white wine
— 1½ teaspoons butter
— 12 ounces (350 g) fusilli
— salt and pepper

Put the mushrooms into a heatproof bowl, pour in lukewarm water to cover, and let soak for 30 minutes. Drain, squeeze out the excess liquid, and chop. Heat the oil in a pan. Add the onion, garlic, parsley, and mushrooms and cook over low heat, stirring occasionally, for 8–10 minutes until lightly browned. Meanwhile, cut the artichokes into strips. Add the artichokes to the pan, season with salt and pepper, and cook, stirring occasionally, for 10 minutes. Mix the tomato paste (puree) with 1 tablespoon water in a small bowl and add to the pan. Pour in the wine and cook until the alcohol has evaporated. Stir in the butter and simmer for 10 minutes, then remove the pan from the heat. Cook the pasta in plenty of salted boiling water until al dente. Drain, return to the pan, and pour the artichoke sauce over it. Transfer to a warmed serving dish and serve immediately.

FUSILLI IN PUMPKIN CREAM

Preparation time: *30 min*
Cooking time: *1 hour*
Serves 4

— 1 pumpkin, weighing about
  1½ pounds (700 g)
— 1 pound 2 ounces (500 g)
  turnip greens (tops)
— 3 tablespoons olive oil
— 1 onion, chopped
— 1 garlic clove, finely chopped
— 12 ounces (350 g) fusilli
— ⅔ cup (150 ml) heavy
  (double) cream
— ½ cup (40 g) grated
  Parmesan cheese
— salt and pepper

Preheat the oven to 350°F (180°C/Gas Mark 4). Cut off the top of the pumpkin and scoop out the flesh, reserving the "shell." Discard the seeds and membranes and slice the flesh. Put the slices into an ovenproof dish in a single layer and bake, turning once, for 40 minutes. Meanwhile, cook the turnip greens (tops) in just enough boiling water to cover for 5–10 minutes until tender. Drain and let cool. Remove the pumpkin from the oven and mash with a potato masher. Heat the oil in a large pan. Add the onion and garlic and cook over low heat, stirring occasionally, for 5 minutes. Meanwhile, cook the fusilli in plenty of salted boiling water until al dente. Drain, tip into the pan, and add the turnip greens, mashed pumpkin, cream, and Parmesan. Season to taste with salt and pepper, mix gently, and heat through for a few minutes. Spoon the mixture into the reserved pumpkin shell and serve immediately.

FUSILLI WITH ZUCCHINI

Preparation time: *20 min*
Cooking time: *30 min*
Serves 4

— 2 tablespoons butter
— 2 tablespoons olive oil
— 1 onion, chopped
— 6 young zucchini
  (courgettes), sliced
— 12 ounces (350 g) fusilli
— 1 egg yolk
— ½ cup (40 g) grated
  pecorino cheese
— salt and pepper

Melt the butter with the oil in a pan. Add the onion and cook over low heat, stirring occasionally, for 8–10 minutes until lightly browned. Add the zucchini (courgettes), season with salt, and cook for 20 minutes until tender. Meanwhile, cook the fusilli in plenty of salted boiling water until al dente. Drain and tip into a warmed serving dish. Remove the zucchini from the heat and stir in the egg yolk, until the zucchini are coated. Pour the zucchini sauce over the pasta, sprinkle with the pecorino, season with pepper, and serve immediately.

FUSILLI WITH MUSHROOMS

FUSILLI AI FUNGHI

Preparation time: *20 min*
Cooking time: *1 hour*
Serves 4

— 3 tablespoons olive oil
— 1 onion, chopped
— 1¾ pounds (800 g) chanterelle
  mushrooms or honey
  fungus, chopped
— 9 ounces (250 g) canned
  tomatoes
— 1 tablespoon chopped fresh
  flat-leaf parsley
— 12 ounces (350 g) fusilli
— ⅓ cup (25 g) grated
  Parmesan cheese
— 2 tablespoons butter
— salt and pepper

Heat the oil in a pan, add the onion and mushrooms, and cook over low heat, stirring occasionally, for 10 minutes. Season with salt and pepper and add the tomatoes with their juice. Simmer for 45 minutes, then remove the pan from the heat, and add the parsley. Meanwhile, cook the fusilli in plenty of salted boiling water until al dente, drain, and tip onto a warmed serving dish. Sprinkle with the Parmesan, add the butter, and toss. Spoon the mushroom sauce on top and serve.

FUSILLI WITH ARUGULA AND PECORINO

FUSILLI ALLA RUCOLA CON PECORINO

Preparation time: *20 min*
Cooking time: *30 min*
Serves 4

— 2 tablespoons olive oil
— 1 onion, chopped
— 3 garlic cloves, chopped
— 2¼ pounds (1 kg) ripe
  tomatoes, coarsely chopped
— 12 ounces (350 g) fusilli
— 3 bunches of arugula (rocket)
— ½ cup (40 g) grated
  pecorino cheese
— salt and pepper

Heat the oil in a shallow pan. Add the onion and garlic and cook over low heat, stirring occasionally, for 5 minutes. Add the tomatoes, season with salt, and simmer for 25 minutes until thickened. Cook the fusilli in plenty of salted boiling water until almost al dente, then about 3 minutes from the end of cooking add the arugula (rocket) to the pan. When the pasta is al dente, drain the pasta and arugula and tip into the pan with the sauce. Toss, transfer to a warmed serving dish, and serve with the pecorino and pepper.

FUSILLI WITH VEGETABLES

Preparation time: *20 min*
Cooking time: *25 min*
Serves 4

— 2 tablespoons olive oil
— 1 garlic clove, finely chopped
— 1 tomato, blanched, peeled, and diced
— 1 zucchini (courgette), diced
— 1 celery heart, diced
— 2 carrots, diced
— 1 yellow bell pepper, seeded and diced
— 12 ounces (350 g) fusilli
— ½ cup (40 g) grated Parmesan cheese
— 1 tablespoon chopped fresh flat-leaf parsley
— salt and pepper

Heat the oil in a pan. Add the garlic and cook over low heat, stirring frequently, for 2–3 minutes. Season with salt and pepper, add the tomato, zucchini (courgette), celery heart, carrots, and yellow bell pepper and cook over low heat, stirring occasionally, for 20 minutes. Meanwhile, cook the fusilli in plenty of salted boiling water until al dente. Drain, tip into a serving dish, sprinkle with the Parmesan, add the vegetables, and stir carefully. Garnish with the parsley and serve immediately.

FUSILLI TIMBALE

TIMBALLO DI FUSILLI

Preparation time: *1 hour*
Cooking time: *1 hour 10 min*
Serves 6

— 4 tablespoons (50 g) butter, plus extra for greasing
— 4 leeks, white parts only, thinly sliced
— ¾ cup (175 ml) dry white wine
— 5 tablespoons milk
— 12 ounces (350 g) fusilli
— 1 cup (80 g) grated Parmesan cheese
— 2 eggs
— 6 fresh sage leaves
— salt and pepper

Preheat the oven to 350°F (180°C/Gas Mark 4). Grease an ovenproof dish with butter. Melt half the butter in a pan, add the leeks, pour in water to a depth of ¾ inch (1.5 cm), and cook over low heat for 10 minutes until softened. Add the wine, increase the heat to medium, and cook until the alcohol has evaporated. Pour in the milk and cook until it has evaporated, then season with salt and pepper to taste. Cook the fusilli in plenty of salted boiling water until al dente, then drain. Cover the base of the prepared dish with a thick layer of fusilli, spoon a little of the leek mixture on top, sprinkle with some of the Parmesan, and dot with some of the remaining butter. Repeat these layers until all the ingredients are used, ending with a layer of fusilli. Beat the eggs with a pinch of salt and pepper, pour over the fusilli, and dot with butter. Garnish with the sage and bake for 40 minutes. Remove the timbale from the oven and let stand for 10 minutes before serving.

GOMITI

Gomiti, meaning "elbows" in Italian, is a short, curved variety of dried pasta belonging to the macaroni family. It can be either *lisce* (smooth) or *rigate* (ridged) and is about ½ inch (1 cm) in diameter and 1½ inches (3.5 cm) long. Gomiti is typically combined with sauces made with sausage, cheese, and vegetables.

PHOTO PAGE 96
Preparation time: *30 min*
Cooking time: *30 min*
Serves 4

— 2 tablespoons olive oil
— 1 small onion, chopped
— 11 ounces (300 g) pumpkin or butternut squash, peeled, seeded, and cut into strips
— ⅔ cup (150 ml) lukewarm water
— 1 head of Treviso or Chioggia radicchio, cut into thin strips
— 1 bunch of fresh flat-leaf parsley, finely chopped
— 12 ounces (350 g) gomiti rigate
— salt and pepper

GOMITI WITH PUMPKIN AND RADICCHIO

GOMITI CON ZUCCA E RADICCHIO

Heat the oil in a shallow pan. Add the onion and cook over low heat, stirring occasionally, for 5 minutes. Increase the heat to medium, add the pumpkin, and cook, stirring occasionally, for 5 minutes until evenly browned. Add the lukewarm water, season with salt and pepper, cover, and simmer for 15 minutes. Stir in the radicchio and three-quarters of the parsley and cook for another 5 minutes. Cook the pasta in plenty of salted boiling water until al dente. Drain, tip into a warmed serving dish, and pour the sauce over the pasta. Sprinkle with the remaining parsley and serve immediately.

GOMITI WITH PUMPKIN AND RADICCHIO (PAGE 95)

MACARONI

Maccheroni was the name given to pasta when it first appeared in the noble courts of southern Italy. Even today, in the south of Italy, the term can refer to all types of durum wheat pasta or to homemade pasta. In northern Italy however, the term generally covers several types of dried, short pasta, which are hollow, cylindrical, and more or less straight, some ridged with closely packed grooves and some with none at all, and with hundreds of names. In the English-speaking world this type of tubular pasta is more often called macaroni. Maccheroncini, or "small macaroni," is a variation on the basic type. Given the variety within the family, macaroni can be matched with virtually any type of sauce and is ideal for oven-baked recipes. It is perhaps most often associated outside Italy with cheese sauces, as in the case of Maccheroni ai Quattro Formaggi (Macaroni with Four Cheeses, see page 100).

Preparation time: *15 min*
Cooking time: *15 min*
Serves 6

— 2 tablespoons olive oil
— 1 garlic clove, finely chopped
— 1 onion, finely chopped
— generous ½ cup (100 g) diced pancetta or bacon
— 1 sprig fresh flat-leaf parsley, finely chopped
— 4 fresh basil leaves, torn
— 1 fresh red chile, seeded and chopped
— 15 ounces (425 g) macaroni
— ½ cup (40 g) grated pecorino cheese
— salt

MACARONI FROM MOLISE

MACCHERONI ALLA MOLISANA

Heat the oil in a shallow pan. Add the garlic and onion, and cook over low heat, stirring occasionally, for 5 minutes. Add the pancetta or bacon, parsley, basil, and chile and cook for a few minutes. Meanwhile, cook the macaroni in plenty of salted boiling water until al dente. Drain and return to the pan. Pour the sauce over the pasta, sprinkle with the pecorino, and mix well. Transfer to a warmed serving dish and serve immediately.

The cuisine of Molise in southern Italy has retained its traditional style based on local produce and hard work. Wheat, meat, fish, pulses, and vegetables are all found in the region's kitchens, but it is wheat that produces the characteristic specialities: delicious pasta, cooked strictly al dente with an abundant sprinkling of diavolino—*red chile—and grated pecorino, alone or mixed with Parmesan.*

MACARONI WITH BELL PEPPERS

MACCHERONI AI PEPERONI

Preparation time: *20 min*
Cooking time: *30 min*
Serves 4

— 2 tablespoons olive oil
— 1 garlic clove
— 4 canned anchovy fillets,
  drained
— 2 yellow bell peppers,
  seeded and cut into strips
— 12 ounces (350 g) macaroni
— chopped fresh oregano,
  to garnish (optional)
— salt and pepper

Heat the oil in a skillet or frying pan. Add the garlic clove and cook over low heat, stirring frequently, for a few minutes until browned. Remove the garlic with a slotted spoon and discard. Add the anchovies and cook, mashing with a wooden spoon, until they have disintegrated. Add the bell pepper strips, season with salt and pepper and cook, stirring occasionally, for 12–15 minutes, until the bell peppers are soft but not mushy. Cook the pasta in plenty of salted boiling water until al dente. Drain, tip into the pan, toss well, and cook for a few minutes more. Serve sprinkled with a little oregano if you like.

WHOLE WHEAT MACARONI WITH CHICORY

MACCHERONI INTEGRALI AL CICORINO

Preparation time: *30 min*
Cooking time: *35 min*
Serves 4

— 3 heads of green chicory
— 11 ounces (300 g) fresh
  tomatoes, blanched, peeled,
  and coarsely chopped, or
  canned chopped tomatoes
— 2 tablespoons olive oil
— 2 garlic cloves
— 1 fresh chile
— 12 ounces (350 g) whole
  wheat macaroni
— 6 torn fresh basil leaves
— ½ cup (40 g) grated
  Parmesan cheese
— salt

Cook the chicory in boiling water for 10 minutes, then drain, reserving the cooking water, and squeeze out the excess liquid. Chop finely. Puree the tomatoes in a food processor. Heat the oil in a shallow pan. Add the garlic cloves and chile and cook over low heat, stirring frequently, for 2–3 minutes. Add the chicory, increase the heat to high, and cook, stirring constantly, for 3 minutes. Add the tomatoes, season with salt, lower the heat, and simmer for 15 minutes. Cook the macaroni in the reserved cooking water, topped up with more boiling water if necessary, until the pasta is al dente. Drain and tip into a warmed serving dish. Remove and discard the garlic cloves and chile from the sauce and pour it over the pasta. Toss well, sprinkle with the basil and Parmesan, and serve immediately.

MACARONI WITH BELL PEPPERS

Preparation time: *10 min*
Cooking time: *30 min*
Serves *4*

— 2 tablespoons butter
— 3 tablespoons olive oil
— 1 garlic clove
— 3⅓ cups (250 g) sliced porcini mushrooms
— 5 ounces (150 g) canned chopped tomatoes, drained
— 1 tablespoon chopped fresh flat-leaf parsley
— 12 ounces (350 g) macaroni
— salt and pepper

MACARONI WITH MUSHROOMS

MACCHERONI AI FUNGHI PORCINI

Heat the butter and oil in a pan, add the garlic clove and porcini, and cook, stirring occasionally, for 5 minutes. Add the tomatoes, season with salt and pepper to taste, cover, and cook over low heat for about 20 minutes. Remove and discard the garlic and stir in the parsley. Cook the macaroni in plenty of salted boiling water until al dente, then drain, toss with the porcini sauce, and serve.

Tip: This sauce can also be made without tomatoes, in which case use 3 tablespoons butter.

Preparation time: *15 min*
Cooking time: *15 min*
Serves *4*

— 3 tablespoons butter
— 5 ounces (150 g) mixed diced mozzarella, caciotta, and Emmenthal cheese
— 12 ounces (350 g) macaroni
— ½ cup (40 g) grated Parmesan cheese
— salt

MACARONI WITH FOUR CHEESES

MACCHERONI AI QUATTRO FORMAGGI

Melt the butter in a heatproof bowl set over a pan of simmering water. Add the mozzarella, caciotta, and Emmenthal and mix but do not melt completely. Season lightly with salt and remove from the heat. Cook the macaroni in plenty of salted boiling water until al dente. Drain, tip into a warmed serving dish, and pour the butter and cheese mixture over it. Sprinkle with the Parmesan and serve immediately.

Preparation time: *20 min,*
plus 1 hour marinating
Cooking time: *10 min*
Serves *4*

— 1¾ cups (200 g) green olives, pitted and chopped
— 5 ounces (150 g) porcini mushrooms in olive oil, drained and sliced
— 2 garlic cloves, chopped
— 1 sprig fresh flat-leaf parsley, chopped
— olive oil, for drizzling
— 12 ounces (350 g) macaroni
— salt and pepper

MACARONI WITH OLIVES
AND MUSHROOMS

MACCHERONI CON OLIVE E FUNGHI

Put the olives, mushrooms, garlic, and parsley into a bowl. Season with salt and pepper and drizzle with olive oil. Let marinate for about 1 hour. Cook the macaroni in plenty of salted boiling water until al dente. Drain, tip into a serving dish, pour the sauce over and serve.

MACARONI WITH PANCETTA

Preparation time: *15 min*
Cooking time: *20 min*
Serves *4*

— 2 tablespoons olive oil
— scant 1 cup (150 g) diced
  smoked pancetta or bacon
— 4 fresh sage leaves
— 1 egg
— 2 tablespoons light
  (single) cream
— 12 ounces (350 g) macaroni
— ⅔ cup (50 g) grated
  Parmesan cheese
— salt and pepper

Heat the oil in a skillet or frying pan. Add the pancetta or bacon and sage leaves and cook over medium–low heat for 8–10 minutes until browned. Beat the egg with the cream in a bowl and season with salt and pepper. Cook the macaroni in plenty of salted boiling water until al dente. Drain, tip into a serving dish, and immediately pour over the egg and cream mixture, mixing thoroughly. Remove and discard the sage leaves, add the pancetta to the pasta, sprinkle with the Parmesan, and serve.

PASTICCIO FROM FERRARA

PASTICCIO ALLA FERRARESE

Preparation time: *30 min*
Cooking time: *1 hour 15 min*
Serves *4*

— 2 squab, cleaned and trussed
— olive oil, for drizzling
— 4 tablespoons (50 g) butter
— 2 eggs, lightly beaten
— 3 cups (250 g) grated
  Parmesan cheese
— 4 tablespoons béchamel
  sauce (see Baked Pumpkin
  Pasta, page 236)
— 10 ounces (275 g) macaroni
— 9 ounces (250 g) ready-made
  pie dough (shortcrust pastry),
  thawed if frozen
— all-purpose (plain) flour,
  for dusting
— salt

Put the squab into a pan, season with salt, drizzle with olive oil, dot with the butter, cover, and cook over medium–low heat, turning occasionally, for 45 minutes. Lift out the birds from the pan and remove and discard the skin. Cut the meat off the bones and cut into strips. Combine the strips of meat, eggs, Parmesan, and béchamel sauce in a bowl. Cook the macaroni in plenty of salted boiling water until al dente. Drain, tip into the bowl and mix well. Preheat the oven to 350°F (180°C/Gas Mark 4). Cut the pastry dough into two pieces, one slightly larger than the other. Roll out the larger piece on a lightly floured surface and use to line the base of a pie dish. Brush the rim with water. Spoon in the macaroni mixture. Roll out the remaining dough on a lightly floured surface and use to cover the pie, pressing the edges together to seal. Crimp the edges with the back of a knife blade. Bake for about 20 minutes until the pastry is golden brown. Serve immediately.

The dish that unites Emilia-Romagna in northern Italy, an area of two combined regions, is pasta with filling. While tortelli (see page 270), served in the various provinces with imaginative fillings, symbolizes this area, Pasticcio is a close and popular relation.

PASTA 'NCASCIATA

PASTA 'NCASCIATA

Preparation time: *1 hour*
Cooking time: *1 hour 15 min*
Serves 6

— 3 eggplants (aubergines),
   sliced
— ½ cup (120 ml) olive oil
— 1 garlic clove
— 1 pound 5 ounces (600 g)
   ripe tomatoes, blanched,
   peeled and diced
— 4 fresh basil leaves
— ⅔ cup (80 g) diced lean beef
— ½ cup (80 g) diced ham
— 3 ounces (80 g) chicken livers,
   trimmed and chopped
— 15 ounces (425 g) macaroni or
   rigatoni
— butter, for greasing
— 4 tablespoons fresh
   bread crumbs
— 3 ounces (80 g) diced
   mozzarella cheese
— 2 hard-cooked eggs, cut
   into wedges
— ⅓ cup (25 g) grated
   pecorino cheese
— salt and pepper

Put the eggplant (aubergine) slices into a colander.
Sprinkle with salt, let drain for 30 minutes, then rinse and
pat dry. Heat 4 tablespoons of the oil in a skillet or frying
pan. Add the eggplant slices in batches, and cook over
medium–low heat for 5–10 minutes on each side until golden
brown. Remove with a spatula and drain on paper towels.
Heat the remaining oil in a shallow pan. Add the garlic clove
and cook over low heat, stirring frequently, for a few minutes
until lightly browned. Remove the garlic with a slotted spoon
and discard. Add the tomatoes, basil leaves, beef, ham, and
chicken livers to the pan, season, cover, and cook over medium
heat for 20 minutes. Cook the pasta in salted boiling water
until al dente. Meanwhile, preheat the oven to 350°F (180°C/
Gas Mark 4). Grease a springform cake pan with butter and
sprinkle with the bread crumbs. Drain the pasta, return to the
pan, and pour the sauce over. Add the mozzarella, eggs, and
eggplant, and stir. Transfer the mixture to the prepared pan,
sprinkle with pecorino and bake for about 20 minutes.
Remove the dish from the oven and let stand for 5 minutes,
then turn out onto a warmed serving dish and serve.

*Traditions are strong in Sicily. It is a place with a baroque heart
not only in the churches and the customs, but also in the kitchen.
Pasta 'Ncasciata, which means "compressed pasta" and includes
meat, chicken livers, tomatoes, mozzarella, pecorino, eggplant and
ham, is a fine example of an age-old dish. This dish can be made
with rigatoni, as pictured opposite.*

MACARONI AU GRATIN

MACCHERONI GRATINATI

Preparation time: *10 min*
Cooking time: *30 min*
Serves 4

— 2 tablespoons butter, softened,
   plus extra for greasing
— 1 quantity béchamel sauce
   (see Baked Pumpkin Pasta,
   page 236)
— ⅔ cup (50 g) grated
   Parmesan cheese
— 2 egg yolks
— 12 ounces (350 g) macaroni
— salt

Preheat the oven to 475°F (240°C/Gas Mark 9). Grease an
ovenproof dish with butter. Combine the béchamel sauce,
Parmesan, butter, and egg yolks. Cook the macaroni in a large
pan of salted boiling water until just al dente, then drain, and
tip into a bowl. Gently stir in half the béchamel sauce mixture
and put in the prepared dish, then spoon the remaining
béchamel sauce mixture on top. Bake for 15–20 minutes until
golden brown. Serve immediately.

MACARONI WITH BELL PEPPERS, OLIVES, AND BASIL

MACCHERONI AI PEPERONI, OLIVE, E BASILICO

Preparation time: *30 min*
Cooking time: *1 hour 30 min*
Serves *4*

— 2 red bell peppers
— 7 ounces (200 g) mozzarella cheese, diced
— 8 black olives, pitted and sliced
— 8 green olives, pitted and sliced
— 4 fresh basil leaves, torn
— olive oil, for drizzling
— 9 ounces (250 g) macaroni
— butter, for greasing
— salt and pepper

Preheat the oven to 350°F (180°C/Gas Mark 4). Put the bell peppers onto a baking sheet and roast, turning twice, for 1 hour. Remove them from the oven, wrap in aluminum foil while still hot, and let cool. When cold, unwrap the bell peppers, peel, seed, and cut the flesh into thin strips. Combine the bell pepper strips, mozzarella, olives, and basil in a bowl, drizzle with olive oil, and season lightly with salt and pepper. Cook the macaroni in plenty of salted boiling water until al dente. Drain the pasta, return to the pan, and add the bell pepper mixture. Mix well, pour into the prepared dish, and bake for 20 minutes.

SMALL MACARONI WITH BEEF AND MUSHROOM RAGU

MACCHERONCINI AL RAGÙ

Preparation time: *20 min*
Cooking time: *35 min*
Serves *4*

— ⅓ cup (20 g) dried mushrooms
— 3 tablespoons olive oil
— ½ onion, chopped
— 1 carrot, chopped
— 2 tablespoons chopped fresh flat-leaf parsley
— 7 ounces (200 g) ground beef
— scant ½ cup (100 ml) white wine
— scant ½ cup (100 ml) warm milk
— 10 ounces (275 g) small macaroni
— ½ cup (40 g) grated Parmesan cheese
— salt and pepper

Put the mushrooms into a heatproof bowl, pour in warm water to cover, and let soak for 20 minutes. Drain and squeeze out the excess liquid, then chop. Heat the oil in a pan. Add the onion, carrot, parsley, ground meat, and mushrooms and cook over medium heat, stirring frequently, until the meat is lightly browned. Pour in the wine and cook until the alcohol has evaporated. Pour in the warm milk and cook, stirring occasionally, for another 15–20 minutes until the meat is cooked through and tender. Season to taste with salt and pepper. Cook the pasta in plenty of salted boiling water until al dente. Drain and tip into a warmed serving dish. Pour the sauce on top and sprinkle with the Parmesan. Serve immediately.

Preparation time: *10 min*
Cooking time: *10 min*
Serves 4

— 1 egg yolk
— scant 1 cup (200 g)
  mascarpone cheese
— pinch of freshly grated nutmeg
— ½ cup (40 g) grated
  Parmesan cheese
— 12 ounces (350 g) small
  macaroni
— salt and pepper

SMALL MACARONI WITH MASCARPONE

MACCHERONCINI AL MASCARPONE

Combine the egg yolk, mascarpone, nutmeg, Parmesan, and a pinch of pepper in a serving dish. Cook the pasta in plenty of salted boiling water until al dente, reserving a few tablespoons of the cooking water. Drain, tip into the dish and toss, adding the reserved cooking water if necessary. Taste and adjust the seasoning, if necessary, and serve immediately.

Preparation time: *15 min*
Cooking time: *20 min*
Serves 4

— 5 ounces (150 g)
  Gorgonzola cheese
— 2 tablespoons butter, softened
— scant 1 cup (200 ml) heavy
  (double) cream
— 12 ounces (350 g) small
  macaroni
— salt and pepper

SMALL MACARONI WITH GORGONZOLA

MACCHERONCINI AL GORGONZOLA

Mash the Gorgonzola in a heatproof bowl with a fork, then work in the butter until the mixture is smooth and creamy. Gradually mix in the cream and season with salt and pepper. Set the bowl over a pan of simmering water and heat through, stirring frequently. Cook the macaroni in plenty of salted boiling water until al dente. Drain, tip into a warmed serving dish, pour the cheese sauce over, and serve immediately.

Preparation time: *20 min*
Cooking time: *30 min*
Serves 4

— 2 tablespoons butter
— 1 onion, chopped
— scant ½ cup (100 ml) dry
  white wine
— 7 ounces (200 g) luganega
  or another Italian sausage,
  skinned and cut into pieces
— 4 fresh basil leaves, torn
— scant ½ cup (100 ml) heavy
  (double) cream
— scant ½ cup (100 ml) milk
— 12 ounces (350 g) small
  macaroni rigati
— ½ cup (40 g) grated
  Parmesan cheese
— salt and freshly ground
  white pepper

SMALL MACARONI WITH SAUSAGE

MACCHERONCINI ALLA SALSICCIA

Melt the butter in a shallow pan. Add the onion and cook over low heat, stirring occasionally, for 5 minutes. Pour in the wine and cook until the alcohol has evaporated. Add the sausage pieces and basil and cook for a few minutes, then pour in the cream and milk, and season with salt. Simmer for about 15 minutes. Meanwhile, cook the pasta in plenty of salted boiling water until al dente. Drain, tip into the pan with the sauce, and toss for a few seconds. Season with white pepper, sprinkle with the Parmesan, and serve immediately.

MEZZE MANICHE

Mezze maniche, meaning "half sleeves" in Italian, is a type of dried pasta originating in central and southern Italy. Hollow and very similar to macaroni and rigatoni, but shorter, it is sometimes called maniche di frate ("monk's sleeves"). The surface of mezze maniche is ridged, which makes it suitable for all kind of sauces. It is also good in cold pasta salads.

⊘ ⓥ ⊗ ⊗

Preparation time: *15 min*
Cooking time: *25 min*
Serves *4*

— 1½ cups (250 g) cooked or canned chickpeas, drained
— 2 tablespoons olive oil
— 1 garlic clove
— 1 sprig fresh rosemary, finely chopped, plus extra to garnish (optional)
— 1 sprig fresh flat-leaf parsley, finely chopped, to garnish (optional)
— 12 ounces (350 g) mezze maniche
— salt and pepper

MEZZE MANICHE WITH CREAMY CHICKPEA SAUCE

MEZZE MANICHE CON CREMA DI CECI

Puree half of the chickpeas in a food processor or blender. Heat the oil in a pan. Add the garlic clove and cook over low heat, stirring frequently, for a few minutes until lightly browned. Remove the garlic with a slotted spoon and discard. Add the pureed chickpeas and the whole chickpeas to the pan, sprinkle with the rosemary, and season with salt and pepper. Cook over low heat, stirring frequently, for 10 minutes. Cook the mezze maniche in plenty of salted boiling water until al dente. Drain, tip into a warmed serving dish, and pour the chickpea sauce over. Garnish with rosemary sprigs or parsley and serve immediately.

MEZZE MANICHE WITH CREAMY CHICKPEA SAUCE

PENNE

These short, diagonally cut tubes have a streamlined shape similar to a quill pen (*penne* means "quills" in Italian). Typical of the region of Calabria in southern Italy, but probably one of the most commonly used of all short pasta types, penne is chewy and substantial and can be *lisce* (smooth) or *rigate* (ridged) on the surface. If not specified in the recipe, you can use either type. Penne can also vary in size, and although it is typically ½ inch (1 cm) in diameter and about 2 inches (5 cm) long, it can also be mezze penne, which is half the size, or pennette, which is even smaller. Penne can be used with almost any ingredient and goes well with meat, fish, and vegetables. It also suits a variety of cooking methods, including frying and baking.

Ⓞ Ⓧ

Preparation time: *1 hour*
Cooking time: *30–40 min*
Serves 4

— 2 small eggplants (aubergines),
  thinly sliced
— ⅔ cup (150 ml) olive oil
— 1 garlic clove, crushed
— 12 ounces (350 g) canned
  chopped tomatoes or
  2¼ cups (500 ml) bottled,
  strained tomatoes
— 9 fresh basil leaves, torn
— 12 ounces (350 g) penne
— scant 1 cup (100 g) grated
  ricotta salata cheese
— salt and pepper

PENNE NORMA

PASTA ALLA NORMA

Put the eggplant (aubergine) slices into a colander, sprinkle with salt, and let drain for 30 minutes, then rinse and pat dry with paper towels. Heat 6 tablespoons of the oil in a large skillet or frying pan. Add the eggplant slices and cook in batches over medium heat for 5–10 minutes on each side until golden brown. Remove with a spatula and drain on paper towels. Meanwhile, heat the remaining oil in a pan. Add the garlic, tomatoes, and 6 of the basil leaves, season with salt and pepper, and cook over low heat, stirring occasionally, for 30 minutes. Remove the pan from the heat and transfer the mixture to a food processor or blender. Process to a puree. Cook the penne in plenty of salted boiling water until al dente. Drain and tip into a warmed serving dish. Sprinkle with half the ricotta, spoon the tomato sauce over it, and arrange the eggplant slices on top. Sprinkle with the remaining ricotta and basil leaves and serve without tossing.

This dish from the city of Catania in Sicily was named in honor of the famous composer Vincenzo Bellini, author of the opera Norma.

Preparation time: *5 min*
Cooking time: *10 min*
Serves 4

— 4 tablespoons (50 g) butter
— 1 onion, thinly sliced
— 12 ounces (350 g) penne
— ½ cup (40 g) grated
  Parmesan cheese
— salt and pepper

Preparation time: *10 min*
Cooking time: *30 min*
Serves 4

— 6 tablespoons oil
— 2 garlic cloves
— ½ fresh chile, seeded
  and chopped
— 1 pound 2 ounces (500 g)
  canned chopped tomatoes,
  drained
— 12 ounces (350 g) penne lisce
— 1 tablespoon chopped fresh
  flat-leaf parsley
— salt

Preparation time: *20 min*
Cooking time: *5 min*
Serves 4

— 4 ripe tomatoes, blanched,
  peeled, and diced
— 4 tablespoons plain yogurt
— olive oil, for drizzling
— 12 ounces (350 g) penne
— ½ cup (50 g) black olives,
  pitted and sliced
— 1 tablespoon chopped fresh
  flat-leaf parsley
— 1 tablespoon chopped
  fresh chervil
— salt and pepper

FRIED PENNE

PENNE IN TEGAME

Melt the butter in a pan, add the onion, then add the penne. Mix well to coat the pasta with butter, then pour in enough boiling water to cover. Add salt and cook until the penne is al dente, adding more boiling water if necessary. Season with pepper, transfer to a warm serving dish, and sprinkle with the Parmesan. Serve immediately.

PENNE ARRABBIATA

PENNE ALL'ARRABBIATA

Heat the oil in a skillet or frying pan, add the garlic cloves and chile, and cook until the garlic browns. Remove the garlic from the pan and discard. Add the tomatoes to the pan, season with salt, and cook for about 15 minutes. Cook the penne in plenty of salted boiling water until al dente, then drain, and tip into the pan. Toss over high heat for a few minutes, then transfer to a warm serving dish. Sprinkle with the parsley and serve immediately.

PENNE WITH OLIVES AND TOMATOES

PENNE CON OLIVE E POMODORI

Put the tomatoes into a large bowl and season with salt and pepper. Gently stir in the yogurt and drizzle with olive oil. Cook the penne in plenty of salted boiling water until al dente. Drain, tip into the bowl, add the olives and chopped herbs, and toss lightly. Serve immediately.

PENNE WITH BLACK OLIVES

PENNE WITH HAM AND MUSHROOMS

Preparation time: *10 min*
Cooking time: *40 min*
Serves 4

— 1 cup (50 g) dried mushrooms
— 2 tablespoons butter
— 2 tablespoons olive oil
— 1 onion
— ⅓ cup (50 g) diced ham
— scant ½ cup (100 ml) dry
    white wine
— 4–5 tablespoons hot vegetable
    broth (stock)
— 3 tablespoons heavy
    (double) cream
— 12 ounces (350 g) penne
— ½ cup (40 g) grated
    Parmesan cheese
— salt and pepper

Put the mushrooms into a bowl, pour in lukewarm water to cover, and let soak for 20 minutes. Drain, squeeze out the excess liquid, and slice. Melt the butter with the oil in a pan. Add the onion and cook over low heat, stirring occasionally, for 8–10 minutes until lightly browned. Add the mushrooms and ham and cook, stirring occasionally, for a few minutes, then pour in the wine, and cook until the alcohol has evaporated. Season with salt and pepper and simmer for 20 minutes, adding enough hot broth (stock) to prevent the mixture from sticking. Stir in the cream and heat through for a few minutes more. Meanwhile, cook the pasta in plenty of salted boiling water until al dente. Drain, tip into a warmed serving dish, and pour the sauce over. Sprinkle with the Parmesan and serve immediately.

PENNE WITH BLACK OLIVES

Preparation time: *15 min*
Cooking time: *20 min*
Serves 4

— 1¼ cups (150 g) black olives,
    pitted and sliced
— ¾ cup (175 ml) heavy
    (double) cream
— 12 ounces (350 g) penne lisce
— ⅓ cup (25 g) grated
    Parmesan cheese
— salt

Put the olives and cream in a pan and cook over low heat for about 15 minutes. Cook the penne in plenty of salted boiling water until al dente, then drain. Spoon half the olive sauce onto the base of a warm serving dish and top with the pasta. Sprinkle with the Parmesan, then spoon the remaining sauce on top. Mix well and serve.

PENNE WITH PEAS AND ARTICHOKES

PENNE AI PISELLI E CARCIOFI

Preparation time: *20 min*
Cooking time: *30 min*
Serves 4

— 2 tablespoons butter
— 2 tablespoons olive oil
— 3 cups (350 g) shelled peas
— 3 young globe artichokes,
  trimmed and thinly sliced
— 12 ounces (350 g) penne
— ½ cup (40 g) grated
  Parmesan cheese
— salt

Melt the butter with the oil in a pan. Add the peas and artichokes and cook over low heat, stirring frequently, for 5 minutes. Season with salt, pour in ⅔ cup (150 ml) water, cover, and simmer for 20–25 minutes until tender. Cook the penne in plenty of salted boiling water until al dente. Drain, tip into a warmed serving dish, and pour the sauce over. Sprinkle with the Parmesan and serve immediately.

PENNE WITH PUMPKIN

PENNE CON LA ZUCCA

Preparation time: *30 min*
Cooking time: *30–35 min*
Serves 4

— 2 tablespoons olive oil
— 1 shallot, chopped
— ⅓ cup (50 g) finely diced
  pancetta or bacon
— 1 pound 2 ounces (500 g)
  pumpkin, peeled, seeded,
  and diced
— scant 1 cup (200 ml) dry
  white wine
— 1 tablespoon butter
— 12 ounces (350 g) penne rigate
— 1 tablespoon chopped fresh
  flat-leaf parsley
— ½ cup (40 g) grated
  Parmesan cheese
— salt and pepper

Heat the oil in a pan. Add the shallot and cook over low heat, stirring occasionally, for 5–8 minutes until lightly browned. Add the pancetta or bacon, increase the heat to medium and cook, stirring frequently, for 4–5 minutes. Add the pumpkin, season with salt and pepper, lower the heat and simmer, gradually stirring in the wine, for about 20 minutes until the pumpkin is pulpy. Remove the pan from the heat and stir in the butter. The sauce should be creamy and moist. Cook the penne in plenty of salted boiling water until al dente. Drain, return to the pan and pour the pumpkin sauce over. Transfer to a warmed serving dish, sprinkle with the parsley and Parmesan and serve immediately.

PENNE WITH TURNIP GREENS

PENNE CON CIME DI RAPA

Preparation time: *12 min*
Cooking time: *18 min*
Serves 4

— 1 pound 2 ounces (500 g)
  turnip greens (tops)
— 4 anchovy fillets
— 3 tablespoons olive oil,
  plus extra for drizzling
— 12 ounces (350 g) penne
— salt and pepper

Cook the turnip greens (tops) in salted, boiling water for 10 minutes, then drain, and chop. Puree the anchovy fillets and the oil in a mini food processor. Cook the penne in plenty of salted boiling water until al dente, then drain and tip into a fairly deep warmed serving dish. Add the turnip greens, drizzle with oil, season with pepper, and stir. Pour in the anchovy puree, mix again, and serve.

SPICED PENNE WITH GOLDEN RAISINS

Preparation time: *15 min*
Cooking time: *20 min*
Serves *4*

— 4 tablespoons butter,
  plus extra for greasing
— scant ½ cup (50 g) golden
  raisins (sultanas)
— 3 hard-boiled eggs, chopped
— 1 cup (250 ml) heavy
  (double) cream
— pinch of ground cinnamon
— 6 tablespoons grated
  Parmesan cheese
— 12 ounces (350 g) penne
— salt and pepper

Preheat the oven to 350°F (180°C/Gas Mark 4) and grease an ovenproof dish with butter. Put the golden raisins (sultanas) into a bowl, pour in warm water to cover, and let soak for 10 minutes, then drain and squeeze out the excess liquid. Melt 3 tablespoons of the butter in a skillet or frying pan. Add the chopped eggs and cook over low heat, stirring gently, for a few minutes. Pour in the cream and add the cinnamon, raisins and half the Parmesan. Cook the penne in plenty of salted boiling water until al dente. Drain, tip into the pan, and toss with the sauce. Transfer the mixture to the prepared dish, sprinkle with the remaining Parmesan, and dot with the remaining butter. Bake for 5–10 minutes, until the top is golden brown. Serve immediately.

PENNE WITH RICOTTA AND PESTO

Preparation time: *5 min*
Cooking time: *5 min*
Serves *4*

— 10 fresh basil leaves
— 1 garlic clove
— ½ cup (120 ml) extra-virgin
  olive oil
— scant ¼ cup (40 g)
  ricotta cheese
— 8 green olives, pitted
  and chopped
— 4 tablespoons grated
  pecorino cheese
— 12 ounces (350 g) penne
— salt

Chop the basil with the garlic and put into a bowl. Season with salt, add the oil, ricotta, olives, and pecorino, and mix well. The sauce should be runny so, if necessary, add more olive oil. Cook the penne in plenty of salted boiling water until al dente, then drain, and toss with the sauce. Serve immediately.

PENNE RIGATE IN TOMATO VODKA SAUCE

PENNE RIGATE IN TOMATO VODKA SAUCE

⊗ ⊘

Preparation time: *10 min*
Cooking time: *20 min*
Serves 4

— 4 tablespoons (50 g) butter
— 1 thick slice cooked ham, diced
— 2 tablespoons tomato paste
  (puree)
— 1 tablespoon chopped fresh
  flat-leaf parsley
— 5 tablespoons heavy
  (double) cream
— 3 tablespoons vodka
— 12 ounces (350 g) penne rigate
— salt and pepper

Melt the butter in a pan, add the ham, tomato paste (puree), and parsley, season with salt and pepper, and cook, stirring occasionally, for about 10 minutes. Stir in the cream and vodka and cook until the vodka has evaporated. Cook the penne in plenty of salted boiling water until al dente, then drain and tip into a warmed serving dish. Pour the sauce over the pasta, toss, and serve.

PENNE RIGATE WITH HERBS

⊗

Preparation time: *25 min*
Cooking time: *30 min*
Serves 4

— 3 fresh anchovies
— 3 tablespoons olive oil
— ½ cup (50 g) green olives,
  pitted and chopped
— 2 garlic cloves, chopped
— 1 bay leaf
— 1 fresh sage leaf, chopped
— 1 fresh pennyroyal or mint
  leaf, chopped
— 1 sprig fresh rosemary,
  chopped
— 1 sprig fresh flat-leaf
  parsley, chopped
— 9 ounces (250 g) canned
  chopped tomatoes
— ½ tablespoon capers, rinsed
— 12 ounces (350 g) penne rigate
— salt and pepper
— grated pecorino cheese,
  to serve

Pinch the heads of the anchovies between your thumb and index finger and pull them off, taking the innards with them. Pinch along the top edge of each anchovy and pull out the backbones. Rinse the fish and pat dry, then chop. Heat the oil in a pan. Add the anchovies, olives, garlic, and herbs and cook over low heat, stirring occasionally, for 5 minutes. Add the tomatoes, season with salt and pepper, cover, and simmer, stirring occasionally, for 15 minutes. Stir in the capers. Cook the penne in plenty of salted boiling water until al dente. Drain, tip into the pan with the sauce, and toss for 1 minute. Transfer to a warmed serving dish and serve immediately, handing the pecorino separately.

PENNE WITH A GRATIN OF CHERRY TOMATOES

PENNE CON POMODORINI GRATINATI

Preparation time: *25 min*
Cooking time: *25 min*
Serves 6

— 2 salted anchovies
— olive oil, for brushing
  and drizzling
— 60 cherry tomatoes, halved
— 1 cup (50 g) fresh bread crumbs
— ½ cup (50 g) grated Gruyère
  or ⅔ cup (50 g) grated
  Parmesan cheese
— 2 garlic cloves, finely chopped
— 1 sprig fresh thyme,
  finely chopped
— 1 sprig fresh marjoram,
  finely chopped
— 3 tablespoons salted capers,
  rinsed and chopped
— 15 ounces (425 g) penne
— 10 fresh basil leaves, torn
— salt and pepper

Pinch the heads of the anchovies between your thumb and index finger and pull them off, taking the innards with them. Pinch along the top edge of each anchovy and pull out the backbones. Put the anchovies into a dish, pour in water to cover, and let soak to remove some of the salt, then drain, pat dry, and chop finely. Preheat the oven to 400°F (200°C/Gas Mark 6) and brush an ovenproof dish with oil. Put the tomatoes into the dish. Combine the bread crumbs, cheese, garlic, thyme, marjoram, capers, and anchovies in a bowl and season with salt and pepper. Spread the mixture over the tomatoes, drizzle with oil, and bake for about 15 minutes until the topping is golden brown. Meanwhile, cook the pasta in plenty of salted boiling water until al dente. Drain and tip into a warmed serving dish. Add the tomato gratin, garnish with the basil, and serve immediately.

PENNETTE WITH BACON AND GREEN OLIVES

PENNETTE ALLA PANCETTA E OLIVE VERDI

Preparation time: *15 min*
Cooking time: *30 min*
Serves 4

— 4 tablespoons olive oil
— 1 small onion, chopped
— 2 ounces (50 g) pancetta
  or bacon, cut into strips
— scant 1 cup (100 g) green
  olives, pitted and halved
— 14 ounces (400 g) canned
  chopped tomatoes
— ½ chile, seeded (optional)
  and chopped
— 12 ounces (350 g)
  pennette rigate
— ⅓ cup (25 g) grated
  pecorino cheese
— ⅓ cup (25 g) grated
  Parmesan cheese
— salt

Heat the oil in a skillet or frying pan. Add the onion, pancetta or bacon, and olives and cook over low heat, stirring occasionally, for 5 minutes. Add the tomatoes and chile and simmer gently, stirring occasionally, for 20 minutes. Cook the penne in plenty of salted boiling water until al dente. Drain, reserving some of the cooking water, tip into the skillet, and toss with the sauce. If the sauce seems too thick, add a little of the pasta cooking water. Transfer to a warmed serving dish, sprinkle with the cheeses and serve immediately.

PENNETTE WITH GORGONZOLA AND GREEN BELL PEPPERS

PENNETTE AL GORGONZOLA E PEPERONI VERDI

Preparation time: *20 min*
Cooking time: *30 min*
Serves *4*

— 2 green bell peppers
— 5 ounces (150 g) mild Gorgonzola cheese, diced
— 2 tablespoons milk
— 12 ounces (350 g) pennette rigate
— salt and pepper

Preheat the oven to 400°F (200°C/Gas Mark 6). Put the bell peppers on a baking sheet and roast, turning occasionally, for about 20 minutes until charred. Remove them from the oven, wrap in aluminum foil while still hot, and let cool. When cold, unwrap the bell peppers, peel, seed, and cut the flesh into thin strips. Melt the Gorgonzola in a small skillet or frying pan over very low heat, stir in the milk, and season with salt and a little pepper. Cook the pennette in plenty of salted boiling water until al dente. Drain and toss with the cheese mixture and bell pepper strips. Serve immediately.

PENNETTE WITH ZUCCHINI

PENNETTE ALLE ZUCCHINE

Preparation time: *20 min*
Cooking time: *30 min*
Serves *4*

— 2 tablespoons butter
— 3 tablespoons olive oil
— 1 shallot, chopped
— scant 2½ cups (300 g) thickly sliced zucchini (courgettes)
— 1 tablespoon chopped fresh marjoram
— 12 ounces (350 g) pennette
— ½ cup (40 g) grated Parmesan cheese
— salt

Melt the butter with the oil in a large skillet or frying pan on low heat. Add the shallot and cook over low heat, stirring occasionally, for 5 minutes. Add the zucchini (courgettes) and cook, stirring and turning frequently, for 15 minutes. Add the marjoram and season to taste with salt. Cook the pennette in plenty of salted boiling water until al dente. Drain, tip into the pan, and toss with the zucchini. Serve immediately, handing the Parmesan separately.

PENNETTE WITH MOZZARELLA, EGG, AND ANCHOVIES

PENNETTE ALLA MOZZARELLA, UOVA, E ACCIUGHE

Preparation time: *10 min*
Cooking time: *15 min*
Serves *4*

— 4 canned anchovy fillets, drained and chopped
— 3 egg yolks
— 7 ounces (200 g) mozzarella cheese, diced
— 12 ounces (350 g) pennette
— salt and pepper

Combine the anchovy fillets, egg yolks, and mozzarella in a bowl and season with salt and pepper. Cook the pennette in plenty of salted boiling water until al dente. Drain, return to the pan, and pour the sauce over. Serve immediately.

Tip: Buy canned anchovy fillets preserved in olive oil. Once opened, transfer any unused anchovies to a small dish, cover, and store in the refrigerator.

PENNETTE WITH CREAMY ARTICHOKE SAUCE

PENNETTE ALLA CREMA DI CARCIOFI

Preparation time: *25 min*
Cooking time: *30 min*
Serves 4

— juice of ½ lemon
— 4 globe artichokes
— 2 tablespoons olive oil
— 1 garlic clove, crushed
— 12 ounces (350 g) pennette
— ⅔ cup (50 g) grated
  Parmesan cheese
— 3–4 tablespoons milk
— salt and pepper

Half fill a bowl with water and add the lemon juice. Trim the artichokes and remove tough leaves and chokes, if necessary. Cut into slices and immediately put into the acidulated water to prevent discoloration. Heat the oil in a shallow pan. Add the garlic and cook over low heat, stirring occasionally, for a few minutes until lightly browned. Drain the artichokes, add to the pan, and season with salt. Cover and cook over medium heat for about 20 minutes until tender. Cook the pasta in plenty of salted boiling water until al dente. Meanwhile, transfer half the artichokes to a food processor or blender, add the Parmesan, and process, adding the milk if necessary to obtain a creamy consistency. Drain the pasta, tip it into a warmed serving dish, pour the processed artichokes over and add the remaining sliced artichokes. Season with pepper and serve immediately.

PENNETTE WITH CHERRY TOMATOES AND GREEN BEANS

PENNETTE CON POMODORINI E FAGIOLINI

Preparation time: *40 min*
Cooking time: *35 min*
Serves 4

— 4 canned anchovy fillets,
  drained
— 3½ ounces (100 g) bread,
  crusts removed
— 1 bunch of fresh basil
— 2 tablespoons olive oil,
  plus extra for brushing
— 1⅓ cups (200 g) green
  beans, trimmed
— 2 garlic cloves
— 7 ounces (200 g) cherry
  tomatoes, halved
— pinch of chili powder
— 12 ounces (350 g) whole
  wheat pennette
— salt and pepper

Put the anchovies into a bowl, add water to cover, and soak for 10 minutes to remove some of the salt. Meanwhile, tear the bread into pieces and put into a food processor or blender with the basil. Process until combined. Brush a small, shallow nonstick skillet or frying pan with oil and heat gently. Add the bread mixture, flatten, and cook, turning once, until golden brown on both sides. Remove the pan from the heat. Cook the beans in salted boiling water for 10–15 minutes until tender. Drain, reserving the cooking water, and cut into short lengths. Meanwhile, drain the anchovies, pat dry, and chop. Chop the toasted bread. Heat the oil in a large pan. Add the garlic cloves and cook over low heat, stirring frequently, for a few minutes until lightly browned. Remove the garlic with a slotted spoon and discard. Add the anchovies, tomatoes, beans, and chili powder to the pan, season with salt and pepper, and cook, stirring occasionally, for 10 minutes. Cook the pennette in the reserved cooking water, topped up with more boiling water if necessary, until al dente. Drain, tip into the pan with the vegetables, and toss over the heat for a minute. Add the bread, stir, transfer to a warmed serving dish. Serve immediately.

PENNETTE WITH ONION SAUCE

PENNETTE ALLA SALSA DI CIPOLLE

Preparation time: *10 min*
Cooking time: *25 min*
Serves 4

— 2 tablespoons olive oil
— 11 ounces (300 g) onions, thinly sliced
— ⅔ cup (150 ml) vegetable broth (stock)
— 12 ounces (350 g) pennette lisce
— 3 eggs
— ½ cup (40 g) grated Parmesan cheese
— salt and pepper

Heat the oil in a pan. Add the onions and cook over low heat, stirring occasionally, for 5 minutes. Pour in the broth (stock), cover, and simmer, stirring occasionally, for 20 minutes until the onions have almost disintegrated. Meanwhile, cook the pennette in plenty of salted boiling water until al dente. Drain, tip into the pan of onions, increase the heat to high, and toss for a few minutes. Beat the eggs with a pinch of salt and pepper in a serving dish, add the pasta, sprinkle with the Parmesan, toss again, and serve immediately.

PENNETTE WITH BELL PEPPER SAUCE

PENNETTE ALLA SALSA DI PEPERONI

Preparation time: *25 min*
Cooking time: *1 hour 20 min*
Serves 4

— 1 red bell pepper
— 4 tablespoons olive oil
— 1 shallot, chopped
— 2 garlic cloves
— 1 green bell pepper, seeded and diced
— 1 yellow bell pepper, seeded and diced
— 9 ounces (250 g) robiola cheese
— 2–3 tablespoons hot water
— 12 ounces (350 g) pennette
— ½ cup (40 g) grated Parmesan cheese
— 6 fresh basil leaves
— salt and pepper

Preheat the oven to 350°F (180°C/Gas Mark 4). Put the red bell pepper on a baking sheet and roast, turning occasionally, for 1 hour. Remove from the oven and when cool enough to handle peel, seed, and dice the flesh. Heat 2 tablespoons of the oil in a pan. Add the shallot and red bell pepper, season with salt, and cook over low heat, stirring occasionally, for 5 minutes, then remove the pan from the heat.

Heat the remaining oil in another pan. Add the garlic cloves and cook over low heat, stirring frequently, for a few minutes until lightly browned. Remove the garlic with a slotted spoon and discard. Reserve 2 tablespoons of the green and yellow bell peppers, add the remainder to the pan, and cook, stirring occasionally, for 10 minutes. Beat the robiola into the red bell pepper mixture, adding enough of the water to obtain a creamy mixture. Stir the mixture into the pan with the other bell peppers and cook, stirring constantly, for a few minutes.

Cook the pennette in plenty of salted boiling water until al dente. Drain, tip into the pan with the sauce, and toss over the heat for a minute. Transfer to a warmed serving dish, sprinkle with Parmesan, and garnish with the reserved bell peppers and basil leaves.

PIPE

Pipe is a type of dried pasta made of durum wheat semolina flour. Like the smaller pipette, its shape is similar to a short, hollow cylinder with a ridged surface, which has been curled into a half-moon shape. The internal cavity is ideal to catch and retain the sauce, and pipe is also good in soups and pasta salads.

Preparation time: 20 *min*
Cooking time: 20–25 *min*
Serves 4

— 4 tablespoons olive oil
— 9 ounces (250 g) tomatoes, blanched, peeled, and diced
— 1 bunch of arugula (rocket), chopped
— 12 ounces (350 g) pipe
— 2 small diced mozzarella cheeses, about 5 ounces (150 g) each
— salt

PIPE WITH ARUGULA

PIPE ALLA RUCOLA

Heat the oil in a skillet or frying pan. Add the tomatoes and cook over medium heat, stirring occasionally, for 4–5 minutes. Add the arugula (rocket) and season with salt. Lower the heat, cover, and cook for 5 minutes. Cook the pasta in plenty of salted boiling water until al dente. Drain, tip into the pan, and toss well. Add the mozzarella, toss again, and remove from the heat as soon as the cheese starts to become stringy. Transfer to a warm serving dish and serve immediately.

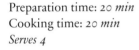

Preparation time: 20 *min*
Cooking time: 20 *min*
Serves 4

— 5 ounces (150 g) pumpkin flowers
— pinch of saffron threads, lightly crushed
— 1 tablespoon lukewarm water
— 2 tablespoons butter
— ⅔ cup (120 g) diced smoked pancetta or bacon
— 2 tablespoons heavy (double) cream
— 12 ounces (350 g) pipette
— salt

PIPETTE WITH PUMPKIN FLOWERS AND PANCETTA

PIPETTE AI FIORI DI ZUCCA E PANCETTA

Remove and discard the pistils from the pumpkin flowers and cut into thin strips. Stir the saffron into the lukewarm water in a small bowl and set aside. Melt the butter in a shallow pan. Add the pancetta or bacon and cook over medium heat, stirring occasionally, for 4–5 minutes until lightly browned. Pour in the cream, lower the heat, add the saffron with its soaking water, and mix well. Cook the pipette in plenty of salted boiling water until al dente. Drain, return to the pan, and add the saffron sauce and the strips of pumpkin flowers. Transfer the pasta to a warmed serving dish and serve immediately.

RIGATONI

Rigatoni is a type of dried pasta made of durum wheat semolina flour that is long, wide, and tubular (like macaroni, but slightly bigger), varying in length from 1¾–3¼ inches (4–8 cm). The name means "ridged" or "those with lines," after the Italian word for "line," *riga*. Rigatoni is suitable for virtually any kind of sauce thanks to its length and cavity, but particularly complements those containing meat because of its ridges. In the regions of Campania and Puglia, it is also commonly used in baked pasta dishes.

RIGATONI WITH CREAM, PESTO, AND TOMATOES

RIGATONI PANNA, PESTO, E POMODORO

Preparation time: *10 min*
Cooking time: *20 min*
Serves 4

— scant 1 cup (200 ml) heavy (double) cream
— 11 ounces (300 g) fresh tomatoes, thinly sliced, or canned chopped tomatoes, drained
— 2 tablespoons pesto (see Trenette with Pesto, page 206)
— 12 ounces (350 g) rigatoni
— ½ cup (40 g) grated Parmesan cheese
— salt

Pour the cream into a pan, add the tomatoes, and cook over low heat for 10 minutes. Remove the pan from the heat and stir in the pesto. Meanwhile, cook the rigatoni in plenty of salted boiling water until al dente, then drain and tip into a warm serving dish. Sprinkle the pasta with the Parmesan, spoon the sauce over and serve immediately.

BAKED RIGATONI

RIGATONI AL FORNO

Preparation time: *40 min*
Cooking time: *45 min*
Serves 4

— 3 tablespoons butter
— ⅓ cup (40 g) all-purpose (plain) flour
— 2¼ cups (500 ml) lukewarm milk
— 7 ounces (200 g) diced fontina or other semi-soft cheese
— 12 ounces (350 g) plain or wholewheat rigatoni
— ½ cup (50 g) grated Gruyère cheese
— salt and pepper

To make the béchamel sauce, melt the butter in a pan. Stir in the flour and cook over medium heat, stirring constantly, for 2–3 minutes until golden brown. Gradually stir in the milk, a little at a time. Bring to a boil, stirring constantly, lower the heat, and simmer gently, stirring constantly, for 20 minutes until thickened and smooth. Remove the pan from the heat and stir in the fontina. Season lightly with salt and pepper. Cook the rigatoni in plenty of salted boiling water until al dente. Meanwhile, preheat the oven to 350°F (180°C/Gas Mark 4). Drain the pasta and mix with the béchamel sauce. Tip into an ovenproof dish, sprinkle with the Gruyère, and bake for about 20 minutes until golden brown. Serve immediately.

RIGATONI WITH MEATBALLS

PHOTO PAGE 125
Preparation time: *30 min*
Cooking time: *1 hour*
Serves 4

— 11 ounces (300 g) ground
   (minced) meat of your choice
— 1 sprig fresh flat-leaf parsley,
   chopped
— ½ garlic clove, chopped
— 1 egg, lightly beaten
— all-purpose (plain) flour,
   for dusting
— 3 tablespoons olive oil
— 1 onion, thinly sliced
— 1 celery stalk, chopped
— 1 carrot, chopped
— 1 small sprig fresh
   rosemary, chopped
— 1¾ cups (400 ml) pureed
   canned tomatoes (passata)
— 12 ounces (350 g) rigatoni
— ⅓ cup (25 g) grated
   Parmesan cheese
— salt and pepper

RIGATONI CON POLPETTINE

Combine the ground (minced) meat, parsley, and garlic in a bowl, then stir in the egg, and season with salt and pepper. Shape the mixture into small meatballs, dust with flour, and set aside. Heat the oil in a pan, add the onion, celery, carrot, and rosemary and cook over low heat, stirring occasionally, for 5 minutes. Then add the meatballs, and increase the heat to medium. Cook until the meatballs are lightly browned all over, add the pureed canned tomatoes (passata) and season with salt. Lower the heat, cover, and simmer, stirring occasionally, for about 40 minutes. Cook the rigatoni in plenty of salted boiling water until al dente, then drain and tip into the pan with the meatballs. Mix well and heat through for 2 minutes. Transfer to a warm serving dish and sprinkle with the Parmesan.

RIGATONI WITH BLACK OLIVE AND TOMATO SAUCE

Preparation time: *15 min*
Cooking time: *20 min*
Serves 4

— 2 tablespoons olive oil
— 4 tomatoes, blanched,
   peeled, and diced
— scant ¼ cup (50 g) black
   olive paste
— ½ cup (40 g) grated
   pecorino cheese
— 12 ounces (350 g) rigatoni
— torn fresh basil, to garnish
— salt and pepper

RIGATONI ALLA PASTA D'OLIVE

Heat the olive oil in a pan. Add the tomatoes and cook over medium heat, stirring occasionally, for 5 minutes. Meanwhile mix the olive paste with 3 tablespoons water in a bowl. Add the pecorino and diluted olive paste to the pan and season to taste with salt and pepper. Cook the pasta in plenty of salted boiling water until al dente. Drain and toss with the sauce. Garnish with the basil and serve immediately.

Tip: Instead of washing the basil leaves, clean them with a damp cloth. It is also better to tear them by hand than to chop them with a knife.

RUOTE

A type of dried pasta made from durum wheat semolina flour, ruote is so called because it looks like a wagon wheel, and *ruote* literally means "wheels" in Italian. It is ridged along its external circumference, which makes it suitable for most sauces, but mainly those with vegetables. Ruote also works well in cold pasta salads.

PHOTO PAGE 128
Preparation time: *20 min*
Cooking time: *30 min*
Serves 4

— pinch of saffron threads
— 3 tablespoons butter
— 1 small onion, thinly sliced
— 4½ cups (400 g) shelled baby peas (petits pois)
— 12 ounces (350 g) ruote
— salt

RUOTE WITH SAFFRON AND PEAS

RUOTE ALLO ZAFFERANO E PISELLI

Put the saffron into a bowl, add 3 tablespoons warm water, and let steep. Melt the butter in a skillet or frying pan. Add the onion and cook over low heat, stirring occasionally, for 5 minutes. Stir in the saffron and its soaking water. Blanch the peas in salted boiling water for 3 minutes, then drain, add to the pan, and cook, stirring occasionally, for another 10 minutes. Cook the pasta in plenty of salted boiling water until al dente. Drain, tip into the pan, and toss well. Serve immediately.

Preparation time: *20 min*
Cooking time: *30 min*
Serves 4

— 4 tablespoons olive oil
— 10 fresh basil leaves, torn, plus extra to garnish
— 2 garlic cloves, finely chopped
— 1 pound 5 ounces (600 g) zucchini (courgettes), diced
— 11 ounces (300 g) tomatoes, blanched, peeled, seeded, and coarsely chopped
— 12 ounces (350 g) ruote
— salt and pepper

RUOTE WITH ZUCCHINI AND TOMATOES

RUOTE ALLE ZUCCHINE E POMODORI

Heat half the oil with half the basil and half the garlic in a shallow pan. Add the zucchini (courgettes) and cook, stirring occasionally, for 10 minutes until lightly browned. Meanwhile, heat the remaining oil in another shallow pan. Add the remaining garlic and the tomatoes, season with salt and pepper, and cook over medium–high heat, stirring occasionally, for 5 minutes. Tip the zucchini into the pan of tomatoes, add the remaining basil, and cook for another 2–3 minutes. Cook the pasta in plenty of salted boiling water until al dente. Drain, return to the pan, and pour the sauce over. Transfer to a warmed serving dish, garnish with extra basil leaves, and serve immediately.

RUOTE WITH SAFFRON AND PEAS (PAGE 127)

SEDANI

A type of short, dried pasta from the macaroni family, sedani is made of durum wheat semolina flour. It has a cylindrical, hollow, and slightly bent shape, with a ridged surface. The name comes from the Italian word for "celery," *sedano*, which it resembles. Sedani is also sometimes called maccheroncini, or small macaroni. Its versatile shape combines well with simple sauces made with tomatoes, cream, or vegetables. Sedani also works well in baked dishes.

Ⓐ

Preparation time: *50 min*
Cooking time: *1 hour 25 min*
Serves 4

— 1 cauliflower
— 5 tablespoons butter
— 6 ounces (180 g) scamorza
  cheese, diced
— 3 ounces (80 g) fontina
  cheese, diced
— ½ cup (40 g) grated
  Parmesan cheese
— 12 ounces (350 g) sedani
  or other short pasta
— olive oil, for drizzling
— 1 quantity béchamel sauce
  (see Baked Rigatoni, page 124)
— salt

PASTA WITH CAULIFLOWER

PASTA E CAVOLFIORE

Cook the cauliflower in lightly salted boiling water for 10–12 minutes until just tender but still firm. Drain and let cool, then cut into florets. Melt 3 tablespoons of the butter in a skillet or frying pan. Add the cauliflower florets and cook over medium–low heat, stirring occasionally, for 5–8 minutes until lightly golden. Add the scamorza, fontina, and Parmesan, stir well, and turn off the heat. Cover the pan until all the cheese has melted.

Cook the sedani in plenty of salted boiling water until al dente. Meanwhile, preheat the oven to 350°F (180°C/Gas Mark 4). Drain the pasta, return to the pan, and drizzle with oil. Dice the remaining butter, add to the pasta along with the cauliflower florets, and stir to mix. Transfer the mixture to an ovenproof dish, pour the béchamel over to cover, and bake for about 20 minutes until golden brown. Serve immediately.

TORTIGLIONI

A type of dried pasta from the macaroni family, tortiglioni is tubular and similar to rigatoni, but slightly longer. Originating in Naples in southern Italy, it has a slightly curved shape and unmistakable spiral grooving. A particularly versatile and original shape, tortiglioni is best combined with full-bodied sauces such as those with meat, cream, and mushrooms, and is also good for making baked pasta dishes.

TORTIGLIONI WITH MUSHROOMS AND EGGPLANT

TORTIGLIONI CON FUNGHI E MELANZANE

Preparation time: *15 min*
Cooking time: *20 min*
Serves *4*

— 2 tablespoons olive oil
— 1 onion, thinly sliced
— 1 garlic clove
— 2¾ cups (200 g) chopped mushrooms
— 1 eggplant (aubergine), diced
— scant ½ cup (100 ml) heavy (double) cream
— 12 ounces (350 g) tortiglioni
— ½ cup (40 g) grated Parmesan cheese
— salt and pepper

Heat the oil in a pan, add the onion and garlic, and cook over low heat until the garlic has browned. Remove and discard the garlic, add the mushrooms and eggplant (aubergine) to the pan and cook, stirring frequently, until light golden brown. Stir in the cream, season with salt and pepper, cover, and cook over low heat for another 10 minutes. Meanwhile, cook the tortiglioni in plenty of salted boiling water until al dente, then drain, tip into the pan of sauce, and cook for 1 minute. Transfer to a warm serving dish and sprinkle with the Parmesan.

FRESH PASTA

FRESH PASTA

With the exception of a few types of pasta from southern Italy, the soft wheat flour used in fresh pasta is the key to the difference in taste, nutritional value, and texture between fresh and dried pasta. The gluten in soft wheat flour is supple and elastic and does not retain the starches released in water, so it offers lower resistance to cooking. When eggs are used in the dough they improve the consistency of the pasta, the proteins are increased in proportion to the starches, there are more vitamins, fats, and mineral salts, and above all the cooking improves. Egg pasta is used for making tagliatelle, maltagliati, and pasta with fillings, such as lasagna, cannelloni, tortellini, and ravioli. Historically, egg pasta was eaten only on special occasions and at wealthy tables. For everyday pasta, it was more usual just to mix flour and water, as still seen today in some regional dishes such as Orecchiette (see page 154).

REGIONAL TASTES

Every city, town, region, and village in Italy has its own method of making pasta: the shape, sauce, filling, and even the dough varies, and each is enriched with personal touches. For example, on the Po river plain in the north, where the climate suits the cultivation of soft wheat, they tend to use more eggs, whereas in central Italy, where the wheat becomes semihard, fewer eggs are used, and in the southern regions such as Puglia, Basilicata, and Calabria, no eggs are used at all. In these regions, durum wheat semolina flour is used for fresh pasta, such as orecchiette and cavatelli. In addition to the quality of the ingredients, good results depend on a number of factors, ranging from the way in which the dough is handled to the warmth of the cook's hands, which can affect the drying of the pasta.

LASAGNA AS BASIC PASTA

Lasagna can rightly be considered the basis for all fresh pasta. It was held in high esteem by medieval cooks—as one of the first known pasta dishes, it was traditionally cooked in water and broth (stock), and served sprinkled with plenty of cheese and spices. In the Middle Ages, Italian cooks paid considerable attention to the shape of the pasta, and many new types of pasta made an appearance in addition to the classics. Around the sixteenth century, a sweeter version of fresh pasta developed, when sugar was added to the basic mixture, and eggs were used more frequently and in larger quantities.

FILLED PASTA

Fresh pasta is often used to make filled pasta, the idea of which is inherited from the Latin *laganum*—the ancestor of modern pasta—whose overlapping sheets separated layers of ground (minced) meat. In the Middle Ages, until the fifteenth century, filled pasta meant a miniature pie, a tortello, also known as raviolo, which was fried in a pan and resembled larger pies that were cooked in the dry heat of the oven. The variety of fillings using more or less sophisticated ingredients can be roughly divided into two groups: Those without and those with meat. The first type was documented in works from the early Middle Ages—a cookbook by an anonymous Venetian describes one of the first examples of ravioli di magro based on vegetables and fresh cheese. The composition of pasta with fillings was perfected from the fifteenth century onward and the range of ingredients was extended to include meat. In his *Libro de Arte Coquinaria*, Maestro Martino includes the recipe ravioli in tempo di carne, which has a filling of pork or veal, seasoned cheese, aromatic herbs, spices, and capon breast. Martino points out that it is also excellent made with pheasant, partridge, and other game. From the two families of ravioli and tortellini, filled pasta gradually developed into the diverse shapes and flavors we know today.

COOKING INSTRUCTIONS

QUANTITY	The recommended quantity to serve 4 is 1¾ cups (200 g) flour and 2 eggs plus a pinch of salt, which produces 10 ounces (275 g) fresh pasta, about 2¾ ounces (70 g) per serving.
OLIVE OIL	When boiling sheets of pasta for lasagna, add 1 tablespoon olive oil to the cooking water to prevent them sticking together.
COOKING AND PREPARATION TIME	Fresh pasta cooks faster than dried pasta. When boiling filled pasta remember that the filling adds flavor so the quantity of salt in the water should be reduced. The times indicated for the recipes have been calculated as an average as they vary according to the type of heat, quality of the ingredients, and the skill of the cook.
SAUCE AND CHEESE	Fresh pasta absorbs more sauce than dried pasta, although the same rules still apply. If you require cheese, always use fresh and grate it just before sprinkling it on the pasta. Do not overdo the quantity. Those who wish may add more at the table from the cheese dish. And always keep serving dishes warm.
STORAGE	You can keep homemade fresh pasta for about 15 days and up to a month in the freezer, provided it has been fully air-dried, laid out on a board covered with lightly floured white cloths, for about 24 hours.

BASIC RECIPES FOR FRESH PASTA

FRESH PASTA DOUGH

PASTA ALL'UOVO

Preparation time: *30 min,*
plus 15 min resting
Serves 4

— 1¾ cups (200 g) all-purpose
  (plain) flour, preferably Italian
  type 00, plus extra for dusting
— 2 eggs, lightly beaten
— salt

Sift the flour and a pinch of salt into a mound on a counter.
Make a well in the middle and add the eggs. Using your
fingers, gradually incorporate the flour into the eggs, then
knead for about 10 minutes. If the mixture is too soft,
add a little extra flour; if it is too firm, add a little water.
Shape the dough into a ball and let rest for 15 minutes.
Roll out on a lightly floured counter or use a pasta machine
to make a thin sheet, and cut out shapes such as fettuccine,
lasagna, maltagliati, orecchiette, pappardelle, stracci,
tagliatelle, taglierini, trenette, and trofie.

GREEN PASTA DOUGH

PASTA VERDE

Preparation time: *30 min,*
plus 15 min resting
Serves 4

— 1¾ cups (200 g) all-purpose
  (plain) flour, preferably Italian
  type 00, plus extra for dusting
— 2 eggs, lightly beaten
— generous 1 cup (100 g)
  cooked spinach, squeezed
  dry and chopped
— salt

Sift the flour and a pinch of salt into a mound on a counter.
Make a well in the middle and add the eggs and spinach.
Using your fingers, gradually incorporate the flour into the
eggs, then knead for about 10 minutes. If the spinach is very
damp, add more flour, a little at a time. Shape the dough into
a ball and let rest for 15 minutes, then roll out on a lightly
floured counter or use a pasta machine to make a fairly thin
sheet. This pasta may be used for lasagna, tagliatelle,
tortellini, and ravioli.

RED PASTA DOUGH

PASTA ROSSA

Preparation time: *30 min,*
plus 15 min resting
Serves 4

— 1¾ cups (200 g) all-purpose
  (plain) flour, preferably Italian
  type 00, plus extra for dusting
— 2 eggs
— scant 1 cup (200 ml) beet
  (beetroot) juice
— salt

Sift the flour into a mound on a counter and make a well in
the middle. Break the eggs into the well and add a pinch of
salt and the beet (beetroot) juice. Using your fingers, gradually
incorporate the flour into the egg mixture, then knead for 10
minutes, adding more flour, a little at a time, if the beet juice
makes the dough too wet. Let the pasta rest for 15 minutes,
then roll out on a lightly floured counter or use a pasta
machine to make a fairly thin sheet. This pasta can be used for
lasagna, tagliatelle, and ravioli with a spinach and ricotta
filling. The most suitable sauces are the classic ones: meat,
melted butter, and cheese.

CUT PASTA

BIGOLI WITH ANCHOVIES

BIGOLI

Bigoli is a handmade version of spaghetti that is thick, with a tubular shape and an uneven surface. It comes from the city of Mantua in Lombardy and from the Veneto region in northern Italy. It is produced using a press fitted with a special mold, known as the *bigolaro,* and the original dough is made with soft wheat flour, butter, and eggs (traditionally duck eggs). Bigoli is particularly well-suited to strong sauces.

Preparation time: *35 min*
Cooking time: *20 min*
Serves 4

For the bigoli:
— 3½ cups (400 g) all-purpose (plain) flour, preferably Italian type 00
— 3 eggs, lightly beaten

For the sauce:
— 6 tablespoons butter
— 4 onions, thinly sliced
— ½ teaspoon dried thyme
— ¼ cup (25 g) grated Gruyère cheese
— salt and pepper

BIGOLI WITH ONIONS

BIGOLI ALLE CIPOLE

To make the bigoli, sift the flour with a pinch of salt into a mound on a counter, make a well in the middle, and add the eggs. Using your fingers, gradually incorporate the flour into the eggs, with enough water to make an elastic dough, then knead for about 10 minutes. Press the dough through the *bigolaro,* a little at a time. To make the sauce, melt the butter in a shallow pan. Add the onions and cook over low heat, stirring occasionally, for 20 minutes. Add the thyme and season with salt and pepper. Remove from the heat and keep warm. Cook the bigoli in plenty of salted boiling water for 2–3 minutes until al dente. Drain, tip into the pan with the sauce, toss, sprinkle with the Gruyère, and season with pepper.

Preparation time: *35 min plus soaking*
Cooking time: *40 min*
Serves 4

— 3½ ounces (100 g) salted anchovies
— 2 tablespoons olive oil
— 3 garlic cloves
— 1 fresh chile
— 1 tablespoon fresh flat-leaf parsley, chopped
— 2 tablespoons bread crumbs
— 10 ripe tomatoes, blanched, peeled, and coarsely chopped
— pinch of dried oregano
— 12 ounces (350 g) fresh bigoli (see Bigoli with Onions, above)
— salt

BIGOLI WITH ANCHOVIES

BIGOLI ALLE ACCIUGHE

Pull off the heads of the anchovies, taking the innards with them. Pinch along the top edge of each anchovy and pull out the backbones. Put them into a dish, pour in water to cover and leave to soak to remove some of the salt. Drain and pat dry. Heat the oil in a saucepan. Add 2 garlic cloves and the chile and cook over a low heat, stirring frequently, for a few minutes until the garlic is golden brown. Remove with a slotted spoon and discard. Add the anchovies, half the parsley, and the bread crumbs and cook over a low heat, stirring occasionally, for 10 minutes. Stir in the tomatoes and oregano and season to taste with salt, then simmer for a further 15 minutes. Meanwhile, chop half the remaining garlic clove. Cook the pasta in plenty of salted boiling water until al dente. Drain and tip into a warmed serving dish. Stir the remaining parsley and chopped garlic into the sauce, pour it over the pasta and serve immediately.

FETTUCCINE

A type of fresh egg pasta, fettuccine is frequently served in central and southern Italy. Its name means "small ribbons" in Italian. This type of pasta is similar to tagliatelle, but a little wider—½ inch (1 cm)—and a little thicker—⅛ inch (3 mm). The names are often used interchangeably, however, particularly in the south of Italy where tagliatelle is sometimes known as fettuccine. The flat, elongated shape of fettuccine is best suited to sauces based on meat, sausage, mushrooms, and tomatoes.

⊗ ⊕

Preparation time: *1 hour, plus 1 hour resting*
Cooking time: *8 min*
Serves 4

— 1 quantity Fresh Pasta Dough (see page 139)
— 1 cup (80 g) grated Parmesan cheese
— pinch of freshly grated nutmeg
— 4 tablespoons (50 g) butter
— 1 Bianco d'Alba truffle, shaved
— salt and pepper

FETTUCCINE FROM ALBA

FETTUCCINE D'ALBA

Roll out the pasta dough on a lightly floured counter into a thin sheet. Cut into strips about ½-inch (1 cm) wide and let dry on floured dish towels. Combine the Parmesan, nutmeg, and a pinch each of salt and pepper in a serving dish and put in a warm place. Cook the fettuccine in plenty of salted boiling water for 2–3 minutes until al dente. Drain, tip into the dish, add the butter, and toss gently. Sprinkle with the truffle shavings and serve immediately.

The Piedmont region of northern Italy is famous for its tasty first courses where the palate is indulged at the start of the meal with unforgettable flavors. The abundant use of truffles, a celebrated local product, gives a special touch and aroma to even the simplest dishes. The Bianco d'Alba truffle is the most precious of the ten species harvested in Italy, with large examples commanding record prices.

FETTUCCINE WITH CHICKEN AND ALMONDS

Preparation time: *20 min*
Cooking time: *30 min*
Serves 4

— 2 tablespoons butter
— 1 shallot, chopped
— 5 ounces (150 g) skinless, boneless chicken breast, chopped
— scant ½ cup (100 ml) dry white wine
— ⅓ cup (40 g) almonds, chopped
— scant 1 cup (200 ml) heavy (double) cream
— 10 ounces (275 g) fresh fettuccine (see Fettuccine from Alba, page 144)
— ⅓ cup (25 g) grated Parmesan cheese
— salt and pepper

FETTUCCINE AL POLLO E MANDORLE

Melt the butter in a small pan. Add the shallot and cook over low heat, stirring occasionally, for 5 minutes. Add the chicken, stir well, and cook for a few minutes. Pour in the wine and cook until the alcohol has evaporated, then add the almonds and stir in the cream. Simmer over low heat, stirring occasionally, for about 10 minutes, then season with salt and pepper. Cook the fettuccine in plenty of salted boiling water for 2–3 minutes until al dente. Drain, tip into a warmed serving dish, pour the chicken sauce over it and sprinkle with the Parmesan. Serve immediately.

FETTUCCINE WITH SAUSAGE IN BALSAMIC VINEGAR

Preparation time: *15 min*
Cooking time: *30 min*
Serves 4

— 2 tablespoons butter
— 1 onion, chopped
— 3 ounces (80 g) Italian sausage, skinned and chopped
— 7 ounces (200 g) canned chopped tomatoes
— 10 ounces (275 g) fresh fettuccine (see Fettuccine from Alba, page 144)
— 1 tablespoon balsamic vinegar
— chopped fresh marjoram, to garnish
— salt and pepper

FETTUCCINE CON SALSICCIA ALL'ACETO BALSAMICO

Melt the butter in a pan. Add the onion and sausage and cook over low heat, stirring frequently, for 10 minutes. Add the tomatoes, season with salt and pepper, stir well, and simmer for 10 minutes. Cook the fettuccine in plenty of salted boiling water for 2–3 minutes until al dente. Drain, tip into the pan with the sauce, and toss over the heat for 30 seconds. Drizzle with the balsamic vinegar, garnish with the marjoram, and serve immediately.

Tip: There are many surprising ways of using balsamic vinegar. The most traditional include sprinkled on flakes of Parmesan, risotto, escalopes or a fresh salad. It can also be served "in spoonfuls" as an unusual aperitif or, for a more sophisticated palate, with strawberries and ice cream.

FETTUCCINE WITH CHICKEN AND ALMONDS

FETTUCCINE WITH BASIL

FETTUCCINE CON BASILICO

Preparation time: *15 min*
Cooking time: *40 min*
Serves 4

— ¼ cup (15 g) dried mushrooms
— 2 tablespoons butter
— generous ½ cup (100 g) chopped prosciutto
— 20 fresh basil leaves
— 10 ounces (275 g) fresh fettuccine (see Fettuccine from Alba, page 144)
— ½ cup (40 g) grated Parmesan cheese
— salt and pepper

Put the mushrooms into a bowl, pour in warm water to cover, and let soak for 15 minutes, then drain, squeeze out the excess liquid, and chop. Melt the butter in a shallow pan. Add the prosciutto, mushrooms, and basil and cook over low heat, stirring occasionally for 5 minutes. Season with salt and pepper and simmer for 30 minutes. Cook the fettuccine in plenty of salted boiling water for 2–3 minutes until al dente. Drain, tip into a warmed serving dish, and pour the basil sauce over. Sprinkle with the Parmesan and serve immediately.

FETTUCCINE WITH ASPARAGUS AND CHEESE

FETTUCCINE CON ASPARAGI E FORMAGGIO

Preparation time: *15 min*
Cooking time: *20 min*
Serves 4

— 3 tablespoons butter
— 1 small shallot, chopped
— 40 asparagus tips
— 10 ounces (275 g) fresh fettuccine (see Fettuccine from Alba, page 144)
— ⅓ cup (40 g) grated Gruyère cheese
— ½ cup (80 g) chopped ham
— salt and freshly ground white pepper

Melt the butter in a shallow pan. Add the shallot and cook over low heat, stirring occasionally, for 5 minutes. Add the asparagus tips, cover, and cook over low heat for about 10 minutes until tender. Season with salt and white pepper. Cook the fettuccine in plenty of salted boiling water for 2–3 minutes until al dente. Drain, tip into a warmed serving dish, and add the asparagus mixture. Sprinkle with the Gruyère and chopped ham and serve immediately.

FETTUCCINE IN BROWN BUTTER

FETTUCCINE AL BURRO BRUNO

Preparation time: *10 min*
Cooking time: *7 min*
Serves 4

— 10 ounces (275 g) fresh fettuccine (see Fettuccine from Alba, page 144)
— 4 tablespoons (50 g) butter
— 4–5 tablespoons meat juices
— ⅔ cup (50 g) grated Parmesan cheese
— salt

Cook the fettuccine in plenty of salted boiling water for 2–3 minutes until al dente. Meanwhile, melt the butter in a skillet or frying pan over low heat and stir in the meat juices, which should be fairly concentrated. Drain the pasta, add to the pan, toss well, and transfer to a warmed serving dish. Sprinkle with the Parmesan and serve.

Traditionally, this dish is prepared using the leftover juices from a dish of roast meat, such as veal, cooked the day before.

FETTUCCINE WITH HAM

FETTUCCINE AL PROSCIUTTO COTTO

Preparation time: *15 min*
Cooking time: *20 min*
Serves 4

— 4 tablespoons (50 g) butter
— 1 onion, very thinly sliced
— 5 ounces (150 g) ham, diced
— 3 eggs
— 3 tablespoons grated Parmesan cheese, plus extra to serve
— pinch of freshly grated nutmeg
— 2 tablespoons heavy (double) cream
— 10 ounces (275 g) fresh fettuccine (see Fettuccine from Alba, page 144)
— salt and pepper

Melt half the butter in a pan. Add the onion and ham and cook over low heat, stirring occasionally, for 10 minutes. Meanwhile, beat the eggs with the Parmesan, nutmeg, and cream in a large serving dish and season with salt and pepper. Cook the fettuccine in plenty of salted boiling water for 2–3 minutes until al dente. Drain, but not completely, tip into the dish, and stir. Add the ham mixture and remaining butter if the pasta is a little dry. Sprinkle with Parmesan, season with pepper, and serve immediately.

FETTUCCINE WITH ORANGE BLOSSOM

FETTUCCINE CON FIORI D'ARANCIA

Preparation time: *15 min*
Cooking time: *30 min*
Serves 4

— 4 tablespoons olive oil
— 7 ounces (200 g) ground (minced) meat of your choice
— 2½ ounces (65 g) Italian sausages, chopped
— 1 garlic clove
— ½ onion, chopped
— 4 fresh tomatoes, blanched, peeled, and chopped, or canned peeled tomatoes
— 10 fresh basil leaves, torn
— 2 ounces (50 g) orange blossom, plus extra to garnish
— 14 ounces (400 g) fresh fettuccine (see Fettuccine from Alba, page 144)
— salt and pepper

Heat the oil in a skillet or frying pan. Add the ground (minced) meat, sausages, garlic clove, and chopped onion and cook over medium–low heat, stirring occasionally, for 6–8 minutes until the meat is lightly browned. Remove and discard the garlic as soon as it browns. Meanwhile, if using canned tomatoes, process them with a little water in a food processor or blender. Add the fresh tomatoes or pureed canned tomatoes and the basil to the pan and cook over low heat, stirring occasionally, for 10–15 minutes until the meat is cooked through and the sauce has thickened. Gently stir in the orange blossom. Cook the pasta in plenty of salted boiling water for 2–3 minutes until al dente. Drain, tip into a warmed serving dish, top with the sauce, and garnish with a little orange blossom. Serve immediately.

MACCHERONI ALLA CHITARRA

A specialty of the Abruzzo region in central Italy, maccheroni alla chitarra is a type of fresh pasta that gains its name from the method of production. Invented during the second half of the nineteenth century, the *chitarra*, or "guitar," is a device consisting of a wooden frame with metal threads, spaced approximately ⅛–⅓ inch (3–4 mm) apart. Sheets of fresh pasta about ¼ inch (5 mm) thick are placed on top of the threads, and then pushed through using a rolling pin. This produces long pasta similar to spaghetti but with a square section. Maccheroni alla chitarra is commonly combined with meat sauces, such as chicken livers (see below).

MACCHERONI ALLA CHITARRA WITH CHICKEN LIVERS

MACCHERONI ALLA CHITARRA CON FEGATINI

Preparation time: *15 min*
Cooking time: *30 min*
Serves 6

— 6 tablespoons (80 g) butter
— 3 tablespoons olive oil
— 1 onion, chopped
— 12 ounces (350 g) chicken livers, trimmed and chopped
— 4 tablespoons meat broth (stock)
— 14 ounces (400 g) fresh maccheroni alla chitarra (see Maccheroni alla Chitarra with Tomato Sauce, below)
— 3 tablespoons grated Parmesan cheese
— salt

Heat the butter and oil in a skillet or frying pan, add the onion, and cook over low heat, stirring occasionally, for 5 minutes. Add the chicken livers and cook, stirring occasionally, until browned. Add the broth (stock) and cook until it has evaporated, then season with salt. Cook the maccheroni in plenty of salted boiling water for 2–3 minutes until al dente, drain, and toss with the sauce. Sprinkle with the Parmesan and serve.

MACCHERONI ALLA CHITARRA WITH TOMATO SAUCE

MACCHERONI ALLA CHITARRA CON SUGO DI POMODORO

Preparation time: *40 min, plus 1 hour resting*
Cooking time: *15 min*
Serves 6

— 1½ quantity Fresh Pasta Dough (see page 139)
— 6 tablespoons olive oil
— 1 pound 2 ounces (500 g) tomatoes, blanched, peeled, and diced
— pinch of chili powder
— salt

Roll out the pasta dough on a lightly floured counter into a sheet ⅛ inch (3 mm) thick. Place on the chitarra and roll over it with a rolling pin so that the wires cut the pasta into long square-section ribbons. For the sauce, heat the olive oil in a skillet or frying pan, add the tomatoes, and cook, stirring occasionally, for 10 minutes. Season with salt and chili powder. Cook the maccheroni in plenty of salted boiling water for 2–3 minutes until al dente, drain, toss with the tomato sauce, and serve immediately.

Preparation time: *25 min*
Cooking time: *40 min*
Serves 4

— 14 ounces (400 g)
  asparagus, trimmed
— 3 tablespoons olive oil
— 1½ ounces (40 g) pancetta
  or bacon, cut into strips
— 1 shallot, chopped
— scant 1 cup (200 ml) dry
  white wine
— 10 ounces (275 g) fresh
  maccheroni alla chitarra
  (see Maccheroni alla Chitarra
  with Tomato Sauce, opposite)
— 2 tomatoes, diced
— ½ cup (40 g) grated
  Parmesan cheese
— salt and pepper

MACCHERONI ALLA CHITARRA WITH PANCETTA AND ASPARAGUS

MACCHERONI ALLA CHITARRA CON PANCETTA E ASPARAGI

Tie the asparagus into a bundle and put into a tall pan or asparagus pan. Pour in boiling water to reach to just below the tips, add a pinch of salt, cover, and cook for 10 minutes until tender. Remove from the pan and cut into short lengths. Heat the oil in a pan. Add the pancetta or bacon and cook over medium–low heat, stirring occasionally, for 4–5 minutes. Add the shallot and cook, stirring occasionally, for 5 minutes. Pour in the wine and cook until the alcohol has evaporated. Add the asparagus, season with salt and pepper, and simmer for 10 minutes. Cook the pasta in plenty of salted boiling water for 2–3 minutes until al dente. Drain, tip into the pan with the sauce, and toss. Add the tomatoes and toss over the heat for 1 minute. Sprinkle with the Parmesan and serve immediately.

Preparation time: *45 min*
Cooking time: *1 hour 20 min*
Serves 4

— 5 tablespoons (65 g) butter
— 2 tablespoons olive oil
— 1¾ pounds (800 g) boneless
  veal rump roast
— 2 teaspoons chopped
  fresh rosemary
— scant 1 cup (200 ml) dry
  white wine
— 12 ounces (350 g) fresh
  maccheroni alla chitarra
  (see Maccheroni alla Chitarra
  with Tomato Sauce, opposite)
— ½ cup (40 g) grated
  Parmesan cheese
— salt

MACCHERONI ALLA CHITARRA WITH ROASTED VEAL AND ROSEMARY SAUCE

MACCHERONI ALLA CHITARRA CON SALSA DI VITELLO ARROSTO E ROSEMARINO

Preheat the oven to 350°F (180°C/Gas Mark 4). Melt the butter with the oil in a roasting pan. Season the piece of veal with salt, sprinkle with the rosemary, and add to the pan. Cook over low heat, turning frequently, for 10 minutes. Pour in the wine and cook until the alcohol has evaporated. Transfer the pan to the oven and roast for 1 hour until tender. Cook the pasta in plenty of salted boiling water for 2–3 minutes until al dente. Drain and tip into a warmed serving dish. Remove the pan from the oven and transfer the meat to a dish (keep warm and serve as the second course). Pour the roasting juices over the pasta, sprinkle with Parmesan, and serve immediately.

MALTAGLIATI

A type of fresh pasta made from the trimmings of lasagna and other homemade pasta, *maltagliati* means "badly cut" in Italian. It originated in the Emilia-Romagna region in northern Italy and has since spread throughout the country. Further north, in the city of Mantua in Lombardy, the dough is often cut into long narrow triangles, while in Emilia-Romagna and the Veneto region in the northeast, it is cut into small diamond shapes. It is commonly served in broth or as an ingredient of bean soups. It also goes well with vegetable sauces. Another type of pasta, made from durum wheat semolina flour and cut into short penne-like shapes, also goes by the name maltagliati, and is served with meat, tomato, and chunky vegetable sauces.

Preparation time: *40 min, plus 1 hour cooling*
Cooking time: *1 hour 5 min*
Serves *4*

— 2 red bell peppers
— 5 tablespoons olive oil
— 14 ounces (400 g) fresh maltagliati (see Maltagliati with Pumpkin, below)
— salt

MALTAGLIATI WITH BELL PEPPERS

MALTAGLIATI AI PEPERONI

Preheat the oven to 400°F (200°C/Gas Mark 6). Put the bell peppers onto a baking sheet and roast for 1 hour, turning twice. Remove from the oven, wrap in aluminum foil, and let cool for 1 hour. Unwrap the bell peppers, peel and seed them, then cut the flesh into large strips. Purée the bell pepper strips, oil, and a pinch of salt in a food processor or blender. Transfer the puree to a pan and heat gently. Cook the maltagliati in plenty of salted boiling water for 2–3 minutes until al dente. Drain, tip into a warmed serving dish, and pour the hot sauce over. Serve immediately.

Preparation time: *1 hour 10 min, plus 1 hour resting*
Cooking time: *35 min*
Serves *6*

— 1½ quantity Fresh Pasta Dough (see page 139)
— 3 tablespoons olive oil
— scant ½ cup (100 g) butter
— 1 pound 2 ounces (500 g) pumpkin, peeled, seeded, and diced
— pinch of freshly grated nutmeg
— ⅔ cup (50 g) grated Parmesan cheese
— salt and pepper

MALTAGLIATI WITH PUMPKIN

MALTAGLIATI CON LA ZUCCA

Roll out the pasta dough on a lightly floured counter into a thin sheet. Cut into wide, irregular pieces and let dry on floured dish towels. Heat the oil and 6 tablespoons (80 g) of the butter in a pan, add the pumpkin, and cook over low heat, stirring occasionally, for 5 minutes. Add a little water, season with salt, and simmer, stirring frequently, until the pumpkin is tender. Meanwhile, cook the pasta in plenty of salted boiling water for 2–3 minutes until just al dente. Drain, stir into the pumpkin, and add the remaining butter, the nutmeg, and a little pepper. Mix well, sprinkle with the Parmesan, and serve.

MALTAGLIATI WITH BELL PEPPERS

ORECCHIETTE

Orecchiette, meaning "small ears," is a signature dish from the Puglia region in southern Italy. It is made with a very firm dough made of durum wheat semolina flour, either by hand or commercially produced. These small shapes have a rough exterior and a smooth interior, which is created by pressing down lightly with the thumb on small balls of pasta. Locals in Puglia assert that it is based on *trulli*, cylindrical houses with conical roofs that are found in the region. Orecchiette varies slightly in consistency and shape from one area to another, according to the type of flour used, and has various regional names: ricchietelle in Foggia, strascinati in Bari, chiangarelle in Taranto, and stacchiodde in Brindisi. The rough exterior makes it perfect for holding sauce, and the most traditional recipe is Orecchiette con Cime di Rapa (Orecchiette with Turnip Greens, see opposite).

Preparation time: *40 min,*
plus 1 hour resting
Serves *4*

— 1¾ cups (200 g) all-purpose (plain) flour, preferably Italian type 00
— generous ½ cup (100 g) durum wheat semolina flour
— warm water
— salt

ORECCHIETTE (BASIC RECIPE)

ORECCHIETTE (RICETTA BASE)

Combine the flour, semolina flour, and a pinch of salt and heap into a mound on the counter. Make a well in the middle, add a little warm water, and mix to a firm, elastic dough. Knead well, then shape into long rolls 1 inch (2.5 cm) in diameter. Cut into sections and drag them slowly over the counter, one at a time, using the tip of a knife to form small shells. Put each shell upside down on the tip of your thumb and press it down on the counter to accentuate its curvature.

Preparation time: *15 min*
Cooking time: *35 min*
Serves *4*

— 4 tablespoons olive oil
— 1 garlic clove
— 2 eggplants (aubergines), diced
— 20 fresh basil leaves, chopped
— 10 ounces (275 g) orecchiette (see above)
— salt

ORECCHIETTE WITH EGGPLANT AND BASIL

ORECCHIETTE ALLE MELANZANE E BASILICO

Heat the oil with the garlic clove in a skillet or frying pan. Add the eggplants (aubergines) and cook over medium–low heat, stirring frequently, for 5–8 minutes, until lightly browned. Add the chopped basil and season to taste with salt. Lower the heat, cover, and cook for 20 minutes, then remove and discard the garlic clove. Cook the orecchiette in plenty of salted boiling water for 2–3 minutes until al dente. Drain, tip into the pan, and toss well. Serve immediately.

ORECCHIETTE WITH VEAL, TOMATO, AND CHILE SAUCE

ORECCHIETTE AL VITELLO, POMODORI, E PEPERONCINO

Preparation time: *18 min*
Cooking time: *35 min*
Serves 4–6

— 3 tablespoons olive oil
— 1 onion, finely chopped
— 14 ounces (400 g) ground (minced) veal
— scant 1 cup (200 ml) dry white wine
— 14 ounces (400 g) tomatoes, blanched, peeled, and diced
— 1 dried red chile, crumbled
— grated zest of ½ lemon
— 14 ounces (400 g) orecchiette (see opposite)
— ½ cup (40 g) grated pecorino cheese
— salt and pepper

Heat the oil in a large shallow pan. Add the onion and cook over low heat, stirring occasionally, for 5 minutes. Add the meat and cook, stirring frequently, for 5–8 minutes until lightly browned. Pour in the wine and cook until the alcohol has evaporated. Stir in the tomatoes, chile, and lemon zest, season with salt and pepper, cover, and simmer for 20 minutes. Cook the orecchiette in plenty of salted boiling water for 2–3 minutes until al dente. Drain, tip into the pan with the sauce, and toss over the heat for 2 minutes. Transfer to a warmed serving dish, sprinkle with the pecorino, and serve immediately.

Tip: Earthenware pans, lined with enamel and with a tight-fitting lid, are the ideal choice for cooking a meat sauce. By maintaining even heat they allow prolonged cooking of the food and enhance its flavor.

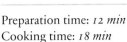

ORECCHIETTE WITH TURNIP GREENS

ORECCHIETTE CON CIME DI RAPA

Preparation time: *12 min*
Cooking time: *18 min*
Serves 4

— 12½ ounces (360 g) orecchiette (see opposite)
— 14 ounces (400 g) turnip greens (tops)
— olive oil, for drizzling
— salt and pepper

Cook the orecchiette in a large pan of salted boiling water for 10 minutes, then add the turnip greens (tops) and cook for another 5 minutes until tender. Drain, transfer to a warm serving dish, drizzle with plenty of olive oil, and season with pepper. Alternatively, heat 4 tablespoons olive oil with 2 garlic cloves, add the drained orecchiette mixture, cook for a few minutes, then discard the garlic and serve immediately.

ORECCHIETTE WITH BROCCOLI

ORECCHIETTE WITH BROCCOLI

ORECCHIETTE CON BROCCOLI

Preparation time: *12 min*
Cooking time: *20 min*
Serves 4

— 1¾ pounds (800 g) broccoli, cut into florets
— 2 tablespoons olive oil
— 1 garlic clove, chopped
— 1 fresh chile, seeded and chopped
— 10 ounces (275 g) orecchiette (see page 154)
— grated Parmesan or pecorino cheese, to serve
— salt

Cook the broccoli in boiling salted water for 8 minutes, then drain. Heat the olive oil in a pan, add the garlic and chile, and cook for 3 minutes, then add the broccoli, and cook over low heat, stirring occasionally, for 5 minutes until tender. Meanwhile, cook the orecchiette in plenty of salted boiling water for 2–3 minutes until al dente, then drain, and toss with the broccoli. Serve with Parmesan or pecorino.

Tip: Alternatively, the broccoli may be cooked with the orecchiette. In this case, drain everything, then drizzle with olive oil, and sprinkle with grated pecorino. This recipe also works well with short dried pasta, such as rigatoni.

ORECCHIETTE WITH CHICKEN

ORECCHIETTE AL PETTO DI POLLO

Preparation time: *20 min*
Cooking time: *30 min*
Serves 4

— 3 tablespoons olive oil
— 2 garlic cloves
— 2 young globe artichokes, trimmed and thinly sliced
— 9 ounces (250 g) skinless, boneless chicken breast, diced
— scant 1 cup (200 ml) dry white wine
— 1 vegetable bouillon (stock) cube
— 10 ounces (275 g) orecchiette (see page 154)
— 1 sprig fresh flat-leaf parsley, chopped
— ½ cup (40 g) grated Parmesan cheese
— 1 tablespoon butter
— salt and pepper

Heat the oil in a shallow pan. Add the garlic cloves and cook over low heat, stirring frequently, for a few minutes until lightly browned. Remove the garlic with a slotted spoon and discard. Increase the heat to medium, add the artichokes and chicken and cook, stirring occasionally, for 10 minutes. Pour in the wine and cook until the alcohol has evaporated. Crumble in the bouillon (stock) cube, season with salt and pepper, stir, and simmer for another 5 minutes. Cook the orecchiette in plenty of salted boiling water for 2–3 minutes until al dente. Drain, tip into the pan with the sauce, and sprinkle with the parsley and Parmesan. Add the butter, toss, transfer to a warmed serving dish, and serve.

ORECCHIETTE WITH OVEN-ROASTED TOMATOES

ORECCHIETTE CON POMODORI AL FORNO

Preparation time: *15 min*
Cooking time: *50 min*
Serves 4

— 1 pound 5 ounces (600 g) vine tomatoes, halved and seeded
— 1 sprig fresh flat-leaf parsley
— 1 garlic clove
— pinch of dried oregano
— olive oil, for drizzling
— 10 ounces (275 g) orecchiette (see page 154)
— ½ cup (40 g) grated pecorino cheese
— salt and pepper

Preheat the oven to 350°F (180°C/Gas Mark 4). Put the tomatoes into an ovenproof dish, cut sides up. Chop the parsley and garlic clove together and sprinkle them over the tomatoes with the oregano. Season with salt and pepper and drizzle with olive oil. Roast for 30–40 minutes. Cook the orecchiette in plenty of salted boiling water for 2–3 minutes until al dente. Drain, tip into the dish of tomatoes, and stir well. Sprinkle with the grated pecorino, season with pepper, and transfer to a warmed serving dish. Serve immediately.

ORECCHIETTE WITH SPECK

ORECCHIETTE ALLO SPECK

Preparation time: *18 min*
Cooking time: *25 min*
Serves 4

— 2 tablespoons olive oil
— 1 onion, finely chopped
— 4 zucchini (courgettes), thickly sliced
— 3½ ounces (100 g) speck or smoked bacon, cut into strips
— 4 tablespoons heavy (double) cream
— 10 ounces (275 g) orecchiette (see page 154)
— salt and pepper

Heat the oil in a shallow pan. Add the onion and cook over low heat, stirring occasionally, for 5 minutes. Add the zucchini (courgettes), season with salt and pepper, and cook, stirring occasionally, for 15 minutes. Add the speck or bacon, stir in the cream, and cook for a few minutes more until the speck is tender. Taste and adjust the seasoning if necessary, remove from the heat, and keep warm. Cook the orecchiette in plenty of salted boiling water for 2–3 minutes until al dente. Drain, tip into a warmed serving dish, and pour the sauce over. Serve immediately.

ORECCHIETTE WITH TOMATO AND RICOTTA

ORECCHIETTE CON POMODORO E RICOTTA

Preparation time: *45 min*
Cooking time: *40 min*
Serves 4

— 4 tablespoons olive oil
— 9 ounces (250 g) canned tomatoes
— 6 fresh basil leaves
— 12½ ounces (360 g) orecchiette (see page 154)
— ½ cup (50 g) grated firm ricotta cheese
— salt

Heat the oil in a small pan, add the tomatoes and a pinch of salt, and simmer for about 30 minutes. Mash the tomatoes with a fork, add the basil, turn off the heat, and cover. Cook the orecchiette in plenty of salted boiling water for 2–3 minutes until al dente, drain well, and transfer to a warmed serving dish. Pour the tomato sauce over the pasta and sprinkle with the ricotta.

ORECCHIETTE WITH OVEN-ROASTED TOMATOES

PAPPARDELLE

Wide ribbons of fresh pasta similar to large tagliatelle, pappardelle ranges in width from 1 inch (2.5 cm) up to 2¼ inches (6 cm). Traditionally, pappardelle is made from large sheets of dough and cut into strips using a pasta wheel. It has its origins in central and northern Italy, and the name itself is of Tuscan origin. In Bologna, in northern Italy, pappardelle is often called larghissime, "very wide." Available both dried and fresh, it sometimes has serrated edges and is typically served with rich meat, mushroom, and organ meat (offal) sauces. In Tuscany, it is mainly served with hare, duck, or wild boar sauces, while in the Veneto region in northern Italy it is generally accompanied by a veal sauce.

Preparation time: *40 min,*
plus 1 hour resting
Serves 4–6

— 3½ cups (400 g) all-purpose (plain) flour, plus extra for dusting
— 4 eggs
— salt

PAPPARDELLE (BASIC RECIPE)

PAPPARDELLE (RICETTA BASE)

Sift the flour into a mound on a counter and make a well in the middle. Break the eggs into the well and add a pinch of salt. Using your fingers, gradually incorporate the flour into the eggs. Knead thoroughly, shape into a ball, cover with a clean dish towel and let rest for 1 hour. Roll out the dough on a lightly floured counter into a fairly thin sheet. Cut into strips about 1¼ inches (3 cm) wide.

Preparation time: *10 min*
Cooking time: *15 min*
Serves 4

— 3 tablespoons butter
— ¾ cup (80 g) coarsely chopped walnuts
— 1 tablespoon pink peppercorns, crushed
— 1 tablespoon chopped fresh flat-leaf parsley
— 10 ounces (275 g) pappardelle (see above)
— salt

PAPPARDELLE IN WALNUT SAUCE

PAPPARDELLE ALLE NOCI

Melt the butter in a skillet or frying pan. Add the walnuts and peppercorns and cook over low heat, stirring constantly, for a few minutes. Remove the pan from the heat and stir in the parsley. Cook the pasta in plenty of salted boiling water for 2–3 minutes until al dente. Drain, tip into the pan, and toss well. Transfer to a warmed serving dish and serve immediately.

PAPPARDELLE WITH CAULIFLOWER AND GORGONZOLA

PAPPARDELLE CON CAVOLFIORI ALLA CREMA DI GORGONZOLA

Preparation time: *25 min*
Cooking time: *25 min*
Serves 4

— 7 ounces (200 g) cauliflower,
  cut into florets
— 1½ tablespoons butter
— 5 ounces (150 g) Gorgonzola
  cheese, diced
— 3–4 tablespoons milk
  (optional)
— 2–3 tablespoons olive oil
— 1 garlic clove
— 1 tablespoon chopped
  fresh thyme
— 10 ounces (275 g) pappardelle
  (see opposite)
— ⅓ cup (25 g) grated
  Parmesan cheese
— salt and pepper

Parboil the cauliflower in salted boiling water for 10 minutes, then drain, reserving the cooking water. Melt the butter with the Gorgonzola in a small pan over very low heat, stirring constantly and adding a few tablespoons of milk if necessary. Do not let the mixture boil. Remove the pan from the heat. Heat the oil in a shallow pan. Add the garlic clove and cook over low heat, stirring frequently, for a few minutes until lightly browned. Remove the garlic with a slotted spoon and discard. Add the cauliflower to the pan and cook, stirring occasionally, for 5 minutes. Sprinkle with the thyme and season with salt and pepper. Cook the pappardelle in the reserved cooking water, topped up with more boiling water if necessary, for 2–3 minutes until al dente. Drain, tip into the pan with the cauliflower, and stir. Stir in the Gorgonzola mixture, remove from the heat, and serve sprinkled with the grated cheese.

PAPPARDELLE WITH CHICKEN LIVERS

PAPPARDELLE AI FEGATINI DI POLLO

Preparation time: *15 min*
Cooking time: *30 min*
Serves 4

— 2 tablespoons butter
— 2 tablespoons olive oil
— 1 carrot, chopped
— 1 onion, chopped
— 1 celery stick, chopped
— 7 ounces (200 g) chicken
  livers, trimmed and chopped
— scant ½ cup (100 ml) dry
  Marsala wine
— 1 tablespoon tomato paste
— 2 tablespoons water
— 10 ounces (275 g) pappardelle
  (see opposite)
— ⅔ cup (50 g) grated
  Parmesan cheese
— salt

Melt the butter with the oil in a pan. Add the carrot, onion, and celery and cook over low heat, stirring occasionally, for 10 minutes. Add the chicken livers, drizzle with the Marsala, and cook until the alcohol has evaporated. Mix the tomato paste with 2 tablespoons water and stir into the pan. Season with salt and simmer for 10 minutes. Cook the pappardelle in plenty of salted boiling water for 2–3 minutes until al dente. Drain, tip into a warmed serving, dish and pour the sauce over. Sprinkle with the Parmesan and serve immediately.

PAPPARDELLE ARETINA

PAPPARDELLE ALL'ARETINA

Preparation time: *30 min*
Cooking time: *1 hour 50 min*
Serves 4

— 2 tablespoons olive oil
— generous ½ cup (100 g)
    chopped prosciutto
— 1 onion, chopped
— 1 celery stalk, chopped
— 1 carrot, chopped
— 2¼-pound (1-kg) duckling,
    liver reserved, cut into
    serving pieces
— scant 1 cup (200 ml) dry
    white wine
— 7 ounces (200 g) canned
    chopped tomatoes
— 1 sprig fresh sage
— 1 sprig fresh basil
— 10 ounces (275 g)
    pappardelle (see page 160)
— 2 tablespoons butter, chilled
— ½ cup (40 g) grated
    Parmesan cheese
— salt and pepper

Heat the oil in a shallow pan. Add the prosciutto, onion, celery, and carrot and cook over low heat, stirring occasionally, for 5 minutes. Add the pieces of duckling and cook, stirring frequently, until lightly browned all over. Pour in the wine and cook until the alcohol has evaporated. Stir in the tomatoes, add the sage and basil, and season with salt and pepper. Cover and simmer, stirring occasionally, for about 1½ hours until the meat is tender. Ten minutes before the end of cooking, add the liver. Remove the pieces of duckling from the pan and keep warm. Pass the sauce through a strainer into a bowl, pressing with the back of a wooden spoon. Cook the pappardelle in plenty of salted boiling water for 2–3 minutes until al dente. Drain and return to the pan, then pour the sauce over, add the butter, and toss. Sprinkle with Parmesan, transfer to a warmed serving dish, and serve immediately. Serve the duckling separately.

PAPPARDELLE WITH BEEF RAGU

PAPPARDELLE AL RAGÙ DI MANZO

Preparation time: *30 min*
Cooking time: *45 min*
Serves 4

— 4 tablespoons (50 g) butter
— 2 tablespoons olive oil
— ½ onion, chopped
— ½ carrot, chopped
— 1 celery stalk, chopped
— 2½ tablespoons diced
    pancetta or bacon
— 7 ounces (200 g) ground
    (minced) beef or pork
— pinch of freshly grated nutmeg
— scant 1 cup (200 ml) red wine
— 9 ounces (250 g) canned
    chopped tomatoes
— 3½ ounces (100 g) chicken
    livers, trimmed and chopped
— 10 ounces (275 g) pappardelle
    (see page 160)
— ½ cup (40 g) grated
    Parmesan cheese
— salt and pepper

Melt half the butter with the oil in a shallow pan. Add the onion, carrot, celery, and pancetta or bacon and cook over low heat, stirring occasionally, for 10 minutes. Stir in the ground (minced) meat, season with salt and pepper, and add the nutmeg. Cook over low heat, stirring frequently, for 5–8 minutes until the meat is lightly browned. Pour in the wine and cook until the alcohol has evaporated, then add the tomatoes. Cover and simmer over low heat, stirring occasionally and adding a little hot water if the sauce is too thick, for 15 minutes. Melt the remaining butter in a small skillet or frying pan. Add the chicken livers and cook over low heat, stirring frequently, for 10 minutes, then season with salt and pepper. Cook the pappardelle in plenty of salted boiling water for 2–3 minutes until al dente. Drain, tip into a warmed serving dish, pour the sauce over, and add the chicken livers. Toss well, sprinkle with the Parmesan, and serve immediately.

PAPPARDELLE WITH RABBIT SAUCE

GARLIC PAPPARDELLE

Preparation time: *1 hour 10 min, plus 1 hour resting*
Cooking time: *40 min*
Serves *4*

— 3 garlic cloves
— 2¾ cups (300 g) all-purpose (plain) flour, preferably Italian type 00, plus extra for dusting
— ½ cup (50 g) durum wheat semolina flour
— 3 eggs
— salt

For the sauce:
— 3 tablespoons olive oil
— 1 large eggplant (aubergine), diced
— 9 ounces (250 g) canned chopped tomatoes
— 1 tablespoon chopped fresh flat-leaf parsley
— 1 cup (80 g) grated Parmesan cheese
— salt and pepper

First make the pasta dough. Cook the garlic cloves in boiling water for 15–20 minutes until softened. Drain, peel, and mash in a bowl until smooth. Sift together both types of flour into a mound on a counter and make a well in the middle. Break the eggs into the well and add the mashed garlic and a pinch of salt. Using your fingers, gradually incorporate the flour into the eggs. Knead thoroughly, shape into a ball, cover with a clean dish towel, and let rest for 1 hour. Meanwhile, make the sauce. Heat the oil in a pan. Add the eggplant (aubergine) and cook over low heat, stirring frequently, for 10 minutes until almost cooked through. Add the tomatoes, season with salt and pepper, and stir in the parsley. Simmer, stirring occasionally, for 10 minutes, then remove the pan from the heat. Roll out the dough on a lightly floured counter into a thin sheet. Cut into 1¼-inch (3-cm) wide strips. Cook the pappardelle in plenty of salted boiling water for 2–3 minutes until al dente. Drain, tip into the pan with the sauce, and toss well. Transfer to a warmed serving dish, sprinkle with the Parmesan, and serve.

PAPPARDELLE WITH RABBIT SAUCE

Preparation time: *20 min*
Cooking time: *40 min*
Serves *4*

— 3 tablespoons olive oil
— 1 onion, finely chopped
— 1 celery stalk, finely chopped
— 1 sprig fresh flat-leaf parsley, finely chopped
— 1 garlic clove, finely chopped
— 1 pound 2 ounces (500 g) boneless rabbit, ground
— scant ½ cup (100 ml) dry white wine
— 1½ cups (350 ml) pureed canned tomatoes (passata)
— 4–5 tablespoons vegetable broth (stock)
— 10 ounces (275 g) pappardelle (see page 160)
— salt and pepper

Heat the oil in a shallow pan. Add the onion, celery, parsley, and garlic and cook over very low heat, stirring occasionally, for 5 minutes. Season with salt and pepper and cook, stirring occasionally, for another 10 minutes. Add the rabbit meat and cook, stirring frequently, for 5 minutes, then pour in the wine and cook until the alcohol has evaporated. Stir in the pureed canned tomatoes (passata) and simmer for 20 minutes, stirring in a little broth (stock) if the sauce is too thick. Cook the pappardelle in plenty of salted boiling water for 2–3 minutes until al dente. Drain, tip into a warmed serving dish, pour the sauce over, and serve.

PAPPARDELLE WITH SCALLOPS

PAPPARDELLE ALLE CAPPESANTE

Preparation time: *18 min*
Cooking time: *25 min*
Serves 4

— 2 tablespoons olive oil
— 1 shallot, finely chopped
— 1 sprig fresh tarragon, finely chopped
— 12 scallops, shelled
— scant 1 cup (200 ml) dry white wine
— 7 ounces (200 g) canned chopped tomatoes
— 10 ounces (275 g) pappardelle (see page 160)
— 1 tablespoon finely chopped fresh flat-leaf parsley
— salt and pepper

Heat the oil in a pan. Add the shallot and tarragon and cook over low heat, stirring occasionally, for 5 minutes. Add the scallops, drizzle with the wine, and cook until the alcohol has evaporated. Simmer for 10 minutes, then add the tomatoes, season with salt and pepper, and simmer for another 5 minutes. Cook the pasta in plenty of salted boiling water for 2–3 minutes until al dente. Drain, tip into a warmed serving dish, and pour the sauce over. Sprinkle with the parsley and serve immediately.

PAPPARDELLE EN CROÛTE

PAPPARDELLE IN CROSTA

Preparation time: *50 min*
Cooking time: *55 min*
Serves 6

— 1¼ cups (150 g) baby peas (petits pois)
— 1 quantity béchamel sauce (see Baked Rigatoni, page 124)
— scant 1 cup (100 g) grated Gruyère cheese
— 5 ounces (150 g) ham in a single slice, diced
— pinch of freshly grated nutmeg
— 1 tablespoon chopped fresh flat-leaf parsley
— 12 ounces (350 g) pappardelle (see page 160)
— butter, for greasing
— 14 ounces (400 g) ready-made pie dough (shortcrust pastry), thawed if frozen
— all-purpose (plain) flour, for dusting
— 1 egg yolk
— 1 tablespoon milk
— salt and pepper

Cook the peas in lightly salted boiling water for about 10 minutes until tender. Meanwhile, gently heat the béchamel sauce in another pan, stirring occasionally. Drain the peas and stir into the sauce along with the Gruyère, ham, nutmeg, and parsley. Season with pepper and remove from the heat. Cook the pappardelle in plenty of salted boiling water for 2–3 minutes until al dente. Drain, return to the pan, pour in the béchamel mixture, and stir. Preheat the oven to 400°F (200°C/Gas Mark 6) and grease a baking pan with butter. Roll out the pie dough on a lightly floured counter and cut out 2 circles, one large enough to line the baking pan, the other large enough to cover the top. Use the larger round to line the base and sides of the prepared pan, then spoon in the pasta mixture. Cover with the smaller round, brushing the edge with water and pressing to seal. Beat the egg yolk with the milk in a small bowl and brush the surface of the pie with the mixture, then prick with a toothpick or cocktail stick. Bake for about 20 minutes until golden. Remove from the oven and serve.

STRACCI

Typical of the Piedmont and Liguria regions in the northwest of Italy, stracci, meaning "rags," is a type of homemade pasta that is long and flat, similar to lasagna but narrower. The shapes are cut irregularly and the dough is often made softer with oil and milk. Spinach is sometimes added to make it green. Stracci is most often combined with seafood sauces.

Ⓐ

Preparation time: *30 min*
Cooking time: *30 min*
Serves 6

— 2 tablespoons butter
— 1 onion, chopped
— 1 celery stalk, cut into
  1¼-inch (3-cm) batons
— ½ fennel bulb, cut into
  1¼-inch (3-cm) batons
— 5 tablespoons olive oil
— 1 garlic clove
— 2 sprigs fresh flat-leaf
  parsley, chopped
— 1 zucchini (courgette), cut
  into 1¼-inch (3-cm) batons
— ½ eggplant (aubergine), cut
  into 1¼-inch (3-cm) batons
— 2 lobsters
— 3 tomatoes, blanched,
  peeled, and diced
— 12 ounces (350 g) fresh stracci
  (see Stracci with Zucchini
  Sauce, page 170)
— salt and pepper

STRACCI WITH LOBSTER

STRACCI AGLI ASTICI

Melt the butter in a pan, add the onion and cook over low heat, stirring occasionally, for 5 minutes until softened. Parboil the celery and fennel for a few minutes, then drain. Heat 3 tablespoons of the oil in a pan, add the garlic and parsley, and cook for a few minutes. Add the onion, zucchini (courgette), eggplant (aubergine), celery, and fennel, season with salt and pepper, and cook, stirring frequently, for about 10 minutes until tender.

Meanwhile, prepare the lobsters. Plunge them into a pan of boiling salted water, cover, bring back to a boil, and cook for 10 minutes. Remove from the pan and leave to cool. Put each lobster, belly side down, on a chopping board and cut it in half. Open it out and remove the tail meat from both halves of the shell. Remove the dark intestinal tract with the point of a knife and discard. Snap off the claws and break them into pieces at the joints, then crack the shells with a heavy knife. Remove the meat and cut it into small pieces. Heat the remaining oil in a pan, add the lobster meat and tomatoes, and cook for 5 minutes. Cook the stracci in plenty of salted, boiling water for 2–3 minutes until al dente, drain, and add to the vegetables. Mix well, add the lobster mixture, and transfer to a warmed serving dish.

STRACCI WITH LOBSTER

STRACCI WITH ZUCCHINI SAUCE

STRACCI ALLA SALSA DI ZUCCHINE

Preparation time: *50 min*
Cooking time: *20 min*
Serves 4

— 2 tablespoons olive oil
— 1 pound 5 ounces (600 g)
  zucchini (courgettes), sliced
— 1 shallot, chopped
— 3 tablespoons vegetable
  broth (stock)
— 1½ quantity Fresh Pasta
  Dough (see page 139)
— all-purpose (plain) flour,
  for dusting
— ½ cup (40 g) grated
  Parmesan cheese
— salt and pepper

Heat the oil in a pan. Add half the zucchini (courgettes) and the shallot and cook over medium–low heat, stirring occasionally, for 10 minutes. Put the remaining zucchini into a food processor, add the broth (stock) and a pinch each of salt and pepper, and process to a puree. Roll out the pasta on a lightly floured counter to a thin sheet and cut into uneven wide pieces. Cook in plenty of salted boiling water for 2–3 minutes until al dente. Drain, transfer to the pan with the zucchini, and stir. Add the zucchini puree and toss the stracci for 2 minutes. Transfer to a warmed serving dish, sprinkle with the Parmesan, and serve immediately.

STRACCI WITH CLAMS

STRACCI ALLE VONGOLE

Preparation time: *30 min*
Cooking time: *30 min*
Serves 4

— 2¼ pounds (1 kg) clams
— 4 garlic cloves
— 2 tablespoons olive oil
— 7 ounces (200 g) canned
  chopped tomatoes
— 14 ounces (400 g) fresh stracci
  (see Stracci with Zucchini
  Sauce, above)
— 1 sprig fresh flat-leaf
  parsley, chopped
— salt and pepper

Scrub the clams under cold running water and discard any with damaged shells or that do not shut immediately when sharply tapped. Put them into a shallow pan, add 3 of the garlic cloves and pour in half the oil. Cover and cook over high heat, shaking the pan occasionally, for 3–5 minutes until the shells open. Lift out the clams with a slotted spoon. Strain the cooking liquid through a strainer lined with cheesecloth (muslin) into a bowl and set aside.

Chop the remaining garlic clove. Heat the remaining oil in a pan. Add the tomatoes and chopped garlic, cover, and simmer, stirring occasionally, for 10 minutes. Add the clams, pour in 1 cup (250ml) of the reserved cooking liquid (add water to make up the amount, if needed), season with salt and pepper and cook over high heat for 5 minutes. Cook the stracci in plenty of salted boiling water for 2–3 minutes until al dente. Drain, tip into the pan with the clam sauce, and toss. Sprinkle with the parsley and serve.

TAGLIATELLE

These long, pale gold ribbons are made with a flour and egg dough, rolled out very thinly and cut into strips ¼–⅜ inch (5–8 mm) wide. The name comes from *tagliare*, "to cut," and tagliatelle is usually homemade but can be found commercially, both fresh and dried. It originated in the city of Bologna in Emilia-Romagna, in northern Italy, where the chamber of commerce displays a gold reproduction of a perfect tagliatella. The classic sauce to accompany tagliatelle is the iconic Bolognese, but it goes equally well with other meat or creamy sauces. Tagliatelle comes in different sizes, such as the smaller version tagliatelline, and can also be colored. The green is usually achieved by adding spinach to the dough, the black by adding squid ink. A dish of green tagliatelle mixed with ordinary tagliatelle is called Paglia e Fieno (see page 184), meaning "straw and hay." Pizzocheri is another type of thick tagliatelle—¾ inch (1.5 cm wide)—originating from Valtellina, a valley in Lombardy in northern Italy, made with a mixture of buckwheat flour and all-purpose wheat flour (see Valtellina Pizzocheri, page 186).

TAGLIATELLE WITH ARTICHOKES

TAGLIATELLE CON CARCIOFI

Preparation time: *1 hour*
Cooking time: *30 min*
Serves 4

— 1 quantity Fresh Pasta
  Dough (see page 139)
— 4 globe artichokes
— juice of 1 lemon
— 4 tablespoons olive oil,
  plus extra for drizzling
— 1 garlic clove
— 6 fresh basil leaves
— 1 sprig fresh flat-leaf parsley
— 5 canned tomatoes, drained
  and chopped
— 4 tablespoons grated
  Parmesan cheese
— salt

Roll out the pasta dough on a lightly floured counter into a thin sheet. Cut into strips ¼–⅜ inch (5–8 mm) wide and let dry on floured dish towels. Break off the artichoke stalks and remove the tough outer leaves and the chokes. Rub all over with lemon juice to prevent discoloration. Cook in lightly salted boiling water for 7 minutes, then drain and slice thinly. Heat the oil in a skillet or frying pan, add the garlic, and cook for a few minutes until browned. Remove and discard the garlic and add the artichokes, basil, parsley, and tomatoes to the pan. Season with salt and cook over low heat for 10 minutes. Cook the tagliatelle in plenty of salted boiling water for 2–3 minutes until al dente, then drain, reserving some of the cooking water, and add to the pan and toss. If necessary, add a few tablespoonfuls of the pasta cooking water to thin the sauce. Drizzle with olive oil and sprinkle with the Parmesan. Remove and discard the parsley, transfer the tagliatelle to a warmed serving dish, and serve.

SPICY TAGLIATELLE WITH CAULIFLOWER

TAGLIATELLE AL CAVOLFIORE PICCANTE

Preparation time: *30 min*
Cooking time: *30 min*
Serves 6

— 1 small cauliflower,
   cut into florets
— 2 tablespoons olive oil
— 2 garlic cloves, lightly crushed
— 1 tablespoon fresh
   bread crumbs
— ½ dried red chile, crumbled
— 1–2 tablespoons chopped
   fresh thyme
— 1 egg yolk
— scant 1 cup (200 ml) heavy
   (double) cream
— 14 ounces (400 g) fresh
   tagliatelle (see Tagliatelle
   with Artichokes, page 171)
— salt

Cook the cauliflower florets in lightly salted boiling water for 10 minutes, then drain, reserving the cooking water. Heat the oil in a shallow pan. Add the garlic cloves and cook over low heat, stirring frequently, for a few minutes until golden brown. Remove with a slotted spoon and discard. Add the bread crumbs, chile, and cauliflower to the pan and stir. Sprinkle with the thyme, pour in 5 tablespoons of the reserved cooking water, and simmer for 10 minutes. Remove the pan from the heat, beat in the egg yolk, and then gently stir in the cream. Cook the tagliatelle in the remaining reserved cooking water, topped up with more boiling water if necessary, for 2–3 minutes until al dente. Drain, tip into a warmed serving dish, and pour the sauce over. Serve immediately.

TAGLIATELLE WITH LEEK BÉCHAMEL

TAGLIATELLE CON BESCIAMELLA AI PORRI

Preparation time: *20 min*
Cooking time: *18 min*
Serves 4

— 2 tablespoons butter
— 2 tablespoons olive oil
— 2 leeks, white parts only,
   finely chopped
— ⅓ cup (50 g) diced speck
   or smoked bacon
— scant ½ cup (100 ml)
   béchamel sauce (see
   Baked Rigatoni, page 124)
— 1 tablespoon chopped
   fresh flat-leaf parsley
— 10 ounces (275 g) fresh
   tagliatelle (see Tagliatelle
   with Artichokes, page 171)
— salt and pepper

Melt the butter with the oil in a pan. Add the leeks and cook over low heat, stirring occasionally, for 5 minutes. Add the speck or bacon and cook, stirring occasionally, for 2 minutes, then stir the mixture into the béchamel sauce. Season with salt and pepper, stir in the parsley, and keep warm. Cook the tagliatelle in plenty of salted boiling water for 2–3 minutes until al dente. Drain, transfer to a warmed serving dish, pour the béchamel mixture over, and serve.

SPICY TAGLIATELLE WITH CAULIFLOWER

TAGLIATELLE BOLOGNESE

TAGLIATELLE ALLA BOLOGNESE

Preparation time: *30 min,*
plus 30 min soaking
Cooking time: *1 hour 20 min*
Serves 6

— 1 cup (50 g) dried mushrooms
— 2 tablespoons olive oil
— 1 garlic clove
— 1 small carrot, finely chopped
— 1 celery stalk, finely chopped
— ½ onion, finely chopped
— ⅓ cup (50 g) finely
   chopped prosciutto
— 7 ounces (200 g) ground
   (minced) pork
— ¾ cup (175 ml) red wine
— 1¾ cup (400 ml) pureed
   canned tomatoes (passata)
— pinch of freshly grated nutmeg
— 4–5 tablespoons hot vegetable
   broth (stock) (optional)
— 14 ounces (400 g) fresh
   tagliatelle (see Tagliatelle
   with Artichokes, page 171)
— ⅓ cup (25 g) grated
   Parmesan cheese
— salt and pepper

Put the mushrooms into a bowl, pour in lukewarm water to cover, and let soak for 30 minutes. Drain and squeeze out the excess liquid. Heat the oil in a flameproof earthenware dish. Add the garlic clove and cook over low heat, stirring frequently, for a few minutes until lightly browned. Remove the garlic with a slotted spoon and discard. Add the carrot, celery, onion, and prosciutto and cook over low heat, stirring occasionally, for 8 minutes until lightly browned. Increase the heat to medium, add the ground (minced) pork and mushrooms, and cook, stirring frequently, for 8–10 minutes, until lightly browned. Pour in the wine and cook until the alcohol has evaporated. Add the pureed canned tomatoes (passata) and nutmeg, season with salt and pepper, lower the heat, cover, and simmer for 1 hour. Add a little hot broth (stock) occasionally if the sauce begins to dry out. Cook the tagliatelle in plenty of salted boiling water for 2–3 minutes until al dente. Drain, tip into a warmed serving dish, pour the sauce over, and sprinkle with the Parmesan. Serve immediately.

This fresh pasta dish, made at home using a board and rolling pin, has brought worldwide fame to the cuisine of Emilia-Romagna in northern Italy. Characteristically, simple ingredients contrast with incredibly rich and robust flavors. The meat sauce from Bologna differs from the recipes of other towns by the addition of prosciutto instead of sausage.

TAGLIATELLE WITH OLIVES

TAGLIATELLE CON OLIVE

Preparation time: *5 min*
Cooking time: *5 min*
Serves 4

— 4 tablespoons (50 g) butter
— 11 ounces (300 g) fresh
   tagliatelle (see Tagliatelle
   with Artichokes, page 171)
— 24 green olives, pitted
— fresh basil leaves, to garnish
— salt

Melt the butter in a heatproof bowl set over a pan of simmering water. Cook the tagliatelle in plenty of salted boiling water for 2–3 minutes, until al dente. Drain and tip onto a warmed serving dish. Toss with the melted butter and olives, sprinkle with a few small basil leaves, and serve immediately.

TAGLIATELLE WITH EGGPLANT

TAGLIATELLE ALLE MELANZANE

Preparation time: *30 min*
Cooking time: *30 min*
Serves 4

— 6 tablespoons olive oil
— 2 eggplants (aubergines), thinly sliced
— 1 garlic clove
— 9 ounces (250 g) tomatoes, peeled, and chopped
— 10 fresh basil leaves
— 10 ounces (275 g) fresh tagliatelle (see Tagliatelle with Artichokes, page 171)
— scant 1 cup (100 g) grated firm ricotta cheese
— salt and pepper

Heat 4 tablespoons of the olive oil in a skillet or frying pan, add the eggplant (aubergine) slices, and cook over low heat for 8–10 minutes until golden brown all over. Heat the remaining oil in a pan, add the garlic and the tomatoes, and cook over low heat for 10 minutes, then remove and discard the garlic. Remove the pan from the heat and season with salt and pepper, then chop one of the basil leaves, and stir in. Cook the tagliatelle in plenty of salted boiling water for 2–3 minutes until al dente, then drain and place in a warmed serving dish. Cover with the ricotta, then spoon the tomato sauce over. Top with the eggplant slices and sprinkle with the remaining basil.

TAGLIATELLE WITH LEMON

TAGLIATELLE AL LIMONE

Preparation time: *25 min*
Cooking time: *9 min*
Serves 4

— 3 unwaxed lemons
— 4 tablespoons (50 g) butter
— ¼ cup (4 tablespoons) light (single) cream
— 10 ounces (275 g) fresh tagliatelle (see Tagliatelle with Artichokes, page 171)
— grated Parmesan cheese, to serve
— salt

Grate the zest of 2 of the lemons. Peel the remaining lemon, removing all traces of pith from the zest and cut it into thin strips. Melt the butter in a skillet or frying pan. When it foams, add the grated lemon zest and cook, stirring occasionally, for a few minutes, then stir in the cream and season with salt. Do not let the mixture boil. Cook the tagliatelle in plenty of salted boiling water for 2–3 minutes until al dente. Drain, tip into the pan, and toss gently. Transfer to a serving dish, sprinkle with plenty of Parmesan, and garnish with the strips of lemon zest.

TAGLIATELLE WITH ASPARAGUS

TAGLIATELLE AI ASPARAGI

Preparation time: *25 min*
Cooking time: *30 min*
Serves 4

— 1½ pounds (700 g) asparagus spears, trimmed
— 4 tablespoons (50 g) butter
— 1 onion, chopped
— 10 ounces (275 g) fresh tagliatelle (see Tagliatelle with Artichokes, page 171)
— ½ cup (40 g) grated Parmesan cheese
— salt

Cook the asparagus in salted boiling water for 10 minutes, then drain. Melt 3 tablespoons of the butter in a shallow pan. Add the onion and cook over low heat, stirring occasionally, for 5 minutes. Do not let it brown. Add the asparagus and cook for another 5 minutes. Cook the tagliatelle in plenty of salted boiling water for 2–3 minutes until al dente. Drain, tip into a warmed serving dish, and pour the asparagus sauce over. Add the remaining butter and the Parmesan and toss lightly. Serve immediately.

TAGLIATELLE WITH LEMON

TAGLIATELLE WITH CREAM, PEAS, AND HAM

TAGLIATELLE PANNA, PISELLI, E PROSCIUTTO

Preparation time: *10 min*
Cooking time: *35 min*
Serves 4

— 2 tablespoons butter
— 2 tablespoons olive oil
— 1 onion, very thinly sliced
— 1¾ cups (200 g) shelled peas
— scant ½ cup (100 ml) heavy (double) cream
— 2 cooked ham slices, diced
— 10 ounces (275 g) fresh tagliatelle (see Tagliatelle with Artichokes, page 171)
— ⅔ cup (50 g) grated Parmesan cheese
— salt

Melt the butter with the oil in a pan, add the onion and cook over low heat, stirring occasionally, for 5 minutes until softened. Add the peas and cook, stirring occasionally, for 20 minutes, then stir in the cream. Cook for 5 minutes, then add the ham. Cook the tagliatelle in plenty of salted boiling water for 2–3 minutes until al dente, then drain and toss with the Parmesan and sauce. Transfer to a warmed serving dish and serve immediately.

TAGLIATELLE WITH MUSHROOMS

TAGLIATELLE AI FUNGHI

Preparation time: *30 min*
Cooking time: *45 min*
Serves 4

— ½ cup dried mushrooms
— 1 small onion
— 2 tablespoons olive oil
— 5 tablespoons dry white wine
— 3 tablespoons concentrated tomato paste (puree)
— 10 ounces (275 g) fresh tagliatelle (see Tagliatelle with Artichokes, page 171)
— ½ cup (40 g) grated Parmesan cheese
— salt

Put the mushrooms in a bowl, add warm water to cover, and let soak for 20 minutes. Drain, squeeze out the liquid, and chop finely with the onion. Heat the oil in a pan, add the mushrooms and onion, and cook over low heat, stirring occasionally, for 5 minutes. Stir in ½ cup (120 ml) water and season lightly with salt. Add the white wine and cook until the alcohol has evaporated, then stir in the tomato paste (puree). Simmer over low heat for 30 minutes. Cook the tagliatelle in plenty of salted boiling water for 2–3 minutes until al dente. Sprinkle with the Parmesan and toss with the mushroom sauce.

TAGLIATELLE WITH RICOTTA

TAGLIATELLE ALLA RICOTTA

Preparation time: *18 min*
Cooking time: *10 min*
Serves 4

— scant 1 cup (200 g) ricotta cheese
— 3 egg yolks
— 10 ounces (275 g) fresh tagliatelle (see Tagliatelle with Artichokes, page 171)
— salt and pepper

Beat the ricotta with a fork in a heatproof bowl, then beat in the egg yolks. Set the bowl over a pan of simmering water and heat through, whisking constantly. Season with salt and pepper and remove from the heat. Cook the tagliatelle in plenty of salted boiling water for 2–3 minutes until al dente. Drain, tip into the bowl with the ricotta mixture and toss well. Transfer to a serving dish and serve immediately.

TAGLIATELLE WITH SAGE AND TARRAGON CHICKEN SAUCE

TAGLIATELLE CON RAGÙ DI GALLINA
AL DRAGONCELLO E SALVIA

Preparation time: *30 min*
Cooking time: *30 min*
Serves 6

— 3 tablespoons butter
— 2 shallots, finely chopped
— 2 carrots, finely chopped
— 2 skinless boneless chicken
   breasts, diced
— scant 1 cup (200 ml)
   dry white wine
— 1¾ cups (400 ml)
   chicken broth (stock)
— 1 teaspoon tomato
   paste (puree)
— 1 sprig fresh tarragon, chopped
— grated zest of 1 lemon
— 14 ounces (400 g) fresh
   tagliatelle (see Tagliatelle
   with Artichokes, page 171)
— ½ cup (40 g) grated
   Parmesan cheese
— 12 large fresh sage leaves,
   fried in butter
— salt

Melt 2 tablespoons of the butter in a shallow pan. Add the shallots and carrots and cook over low heat, stirring occasionally, for 5 minutes. Add the chicken, increase the heat to medium, and cook, stirring occasionally, for about 8 minutes until lightly browned. Pour in the wine and cook until the alcohol has evaporated. Pour in the broth (stock), stir in the tomato paste (puree), lower the heat, cover, and simmer gently for 15 minutes. Stir in the tarragon and lemon zest. Cook the tagliatelle in plenty of salted boiling water for 2–3 minutes until al dente. Drain, tip into the pan with the sauce and toss for 1 minute. Add the remaining butter and the Parmesan, transfer to a warmed serving dish, and garnish with the fried sage leaves.

TAGLIATELLINE WITH CHICKEN LIVERS

TAGLIATELLINE AI FEGATINI DI POLLO

Preparation time: *1 hour*
Cooking time: *30 min*
Serves 6

— 1 quantity Fresh Pasta
   Dough (see page 139)
— 2 tablespoons butter,
   plus extra for serving
— ½ small onion, chopped
— ½ celery stalk, chopped
— 2 ounces (50 g) ground
   (minced) veal
— 3½ ounces (100 g) chicken
   livers, trimmed and
   coarsely chopped
— 1¼ cups (300 ml) pureed
   canned tomatoes (passata)
— salt

Roll out the pasta dough into a thin sheet on a lightly floured counter. Cut into strips about ¼ inch (5 mm) wide and let dry on floured dish towels. Melt the butter in a small skillet or frying pan. Add the onion and celery and cook over low heat, stirring occasionally, for 5 minutes. Add the ground (minced) veal and cook, stirring occasionally, for 10 minutes until lightly browned. Add the chicken livers, mix well, and pour in the pureed canned tomatoes (passata). Simmer gently for another 10 minutes. Cook the pasta in plenty of salted boiling water for 2–3 minutes until al dente. Drain and toss with the sauce, then stir in a pat of butter if you like.

TAGLIATELLE WITH FAVA BEANS AND BABY SQUID

TAGLIATELLE, FAVE E CALAMARETTI

Preparation time: 25 *min*
Cooking time: 35 *min*
Serves 4

— ¾ cup (100 g) shelled fava (broad) beans
— 4 tablespoons (50 g) butter
— 1 shallot, chopped
— 11 ounces (300 g) baby squid, cleaned and cut into strips
— scant 1 cup (200 ml) dry white wine
— 14 ounces (400 g) fresh tagliatelle (see Tagliatelle with Artichokes, page 171)
— salt

Pop the fava (broad) beans out of their skins by pressing gently between your finger and thumb. Melt half the butter in a shallow pan. Add the shallot and cook over very low heat, stirring occasionally, for 5 minutes. Add the squid and cook, stirring occasionally, for 10 minutes. Season lightly with salt, drizzle with the wine, and cook until the alcohol has evaporated. Add the beans and a pinch of salt and simmer for 20 minutes. Cook the tagliatelle in plenty of salted boiling water for 2–3 minutes until al dente. Drain, tip into the pan of sauce, and toss over the heat for 1 minute. Serve immediately.

CUTTLEFISH INK TAGLIATELLE

TAGLIATELLE AL NERO DI SEPPIA

Preparation time: 30 *min*
Cooking time: 5 *min*
Serves 4

— ¾ cups (200 g) all-purpose (plain) flour, preferably Italian type 00, plus extra for dusting
— 2 eggs, lightly beaten
— 1 or 2 cuttlefish ink sacs
— 5 ounces (150 g) canned tuna in oil, drained and flaked
— 1 tablespoon capers, rinsed
— 3 tablespoons olive oil
— salt

Sift the flour with a pinch of salt into a mound on the counter and make a well in the middle. Add the eggs and cuttlefish ink and gradually incorporate the flour into the eggs with your fingers. Knead the dough until soft and smooth, then roll out into a thin sheet on a lightly floured counter, fold over several times, and cut into ¼–⅜-inch (5–8 mm) wide tagliatelle. Combine the tuna, capers, and olive oil in a bowl. Cook the tagliatelle in plenty of salted boiling water for 2–3 minutes until al dente, then drain and toss with the tuna sauce. Transfer to a warmed serving dish and serve immediately.

TAGLIATELLE WITH FAVA BEANS AND BABY SQUID

TAGLIATELLE WITH SALMON

Preparation time: *5 min*
Cooking time: *15 min*
Serves *4*

— 4 tablespoons (50 g) butter
— 3½ ounces (100 g) smoked salmon, chopped
— juice of ½ lemon, strained
— scant ½ cup (100 ml) heavy (double) cream
— 5 tablespoons whiskey
— 10 ounces (275 g) fresh tagliatelle (see Tagliatelle with Artichokes, page 171)
— salt and pepper

Melt the butter in a pan, add the salmon, stir, and sprinkle with the lemon juice. Cook for a few minutes, then add the cream and whiskey and season with salt and pepper. Cook over low heat for 5 minutes. Cook the tagliatelle in plenty of salted boiling water for 2–3 minutes until al dente, drain, add to the sauce, and cook for a few minutes. Toss gently and transfer to a warmed serving dish.

Tip: This recipe also works with dried short pasta like penne.

TAGLIATELLE WITH SPINACH

Preparation time: *20 min*
Cooking time: *20 min*
Serves *4*

— 5 tablespoons (65 g) butter, plus extra for greasing
— 1½ pounds (700 g) spinach
— 1 onion, finely chopped
— 1⅓ cups (120 g) grated Parmesan cheese
— 10 ounces (275 g) fresh tagliatelle (see Tagliatelle with Artichokes, page 171)
— scant 1 cup (200 ml) heavy (double) cream
— salt and pepper

Preheat the oven to 400°F (200°C/Gas Mark 6) and grease an ovenproof dish with butter. Put the spinach into a pan with just the water clinging to the leaves after washing and cook over low heat, turning occasionally, for 5 minutes until wilted. Drain and chop. Heat half the butter in a pan, add the onion, and cook over low heat, stirring occasionally, for 5 minutes until softened. Add the spinach and cook for a few minutes more. Season with salt and pepper and sprinkle with half the Parmesan. Cook the tagliatelle in plenty of salted boiling water for 2–3 minutes until al dente, then drain, return to the pan, and toss with the remaining butter. Make layers of tagliatelle, most of the remaining Parmesan, and the spinach in the prepared dish, ending with a layer of spinach. Pour the cream on top, sprinkle with the rest of the Parmesan, and bake for 10 minutes until golden and bubbling.

TAGLIATELLE WITH MOZZARELLA

TAGLIATELLE ALLA MOZZARELLA

Preparation time: *15 min*
Cooking time: *6 min*
Serves 4

— 12 ounces (350 g) fresh
  tagliatelle (see Tagliatelle
  with Artichokes, page 171)
— 4 ounces (120 g) mozzarella
  cheese, diced
— ½ cup (80 g) diced ham
— 3 tablespoons butter, shaved
  into curls
— ½ cup (40 g) grated
  Parmesan cheese
— salt and pepper

Cook the tagliatelle in plenty of salted boiling water for
2–3 minutes until al dente. Drain and toss with the mozzarella
and ham, then transfer to a serving dish. Sprinkle the curls
of butter over the surface, season lightly with pepper, and
garnish with the Parmesan. Serve immediately.

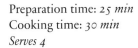

TAGLIATELLE WITH ZUCCHINI SAUCE

TAGLIATELLE CON SALSA SAPORITA ALLE ZUCCHINE

Preparation time: *25 min*
Cooking time: *30 min*
Serves 4

— 3 tablespoons butter
— 1 shallot, chopped
— 3 zucchini (courgettes),
  thinly sliced
— 2 tablespoons heavy
  (double) cream
— 12 ounces (350 g) fresh
  tagliatelle (see Tagliatelle
  with Artichokes, page 171)
— ¼ cup (50 g) mascarpone cheese
— salt and pepper

Melt the butter in a shallow pan. Add the shallot and cook
over low heat, stirring occasionally, for 5 minutes. Add the
zucchini (courgettes) and cook, stirring occasionally, for
10 minutes. Pour in the cream, season with salt and pepper,
and simmer gently for another 10 minutes. Warm a serving
dish and dot the base with the mascarpone. Cook the
tagliatelle in plenty of salted boiling water until al dente.
Drain, tip into the serving dish, and stir. Add the zucchini
sauce and serve.

PAGLIA E FIENO WITH SPECK

PAGLIA E FIENO CON SPECK

Preparation time: *50 min*
Cooking time: *15 min*
Serves 4

— 1 quantity Green Pasta
   Dough (see page 139)
— semolina or all-purpose
   (plain) flour, for dusting
— scant ½ cup (100 ml)
   heavy (double) cream
— ⅔ cup (50 g) grated
   Parmesan cheese
— 3 tablespoons butter
— 1 sprig fresh rosemary
— ½ cup (80 g) diced speck
   or smoked bacon
— 5 ounces (150 g) fresh
   tagliatelle (see Tagliatelle
   with Artichokes, page 171)
— salt and pepper

Roll out the green pasta dough on a lightly floured counter into a thin sheet. Cut into strips about ¼–⅜ inch (5–8 mm) wide and let dry on floured dish towels. Combine the cream and Parmesan in a serving dish. Melt the butter in a pan. Add the rosemary and speck or bacon, season with salt and pepper, and cook over low heat, stirring frequently, for 5 minutes. Remove and discard the rosemary and transfer the speck or bacon to the dish. Cook both types of tagliatelle in plenty of salted boiling water for 2–3 minutes until al dente. Drain, tip into the dish, stir and serve.

Tip: Green tagliatelle is slightly moist because of the spinach used to color it. To prevent the ribbons from sticking together when they are left to rest, sprinkle the cloth they are laid on with semolina flour rather than all-purpose (plain) flour.

BAKED SPICY TAGLIATELLE

SFORMATO DI TAGLIATELLE PICCANTI

Preparation time: *30 min*
Cooking time: *25 min*
Serves 4

— butter, for greasing
— ½ cup (80 g) diced smoked
   pancetta or bacon
— 8¾ cups (2 litres) milk
— 10 ounces (275 g) fresh
   tagliatelle (see Tagliatelle
   with Artichokes, page 171)
— 3 eggs, separated
— ¾ cup (80 g) grated
   Gruyère cheese
— 1 teaspoon paprika
— salt and pepper

Preheat the oven to 350°F (180°C/Gas Mark 4) and grease an ovenproof dish with butter. Dry-fry the pancetta or bacon in a small pan over low heat, stirring occasionally, for 4–5 minutes until lightly browned. Remove the pan from the heat. Pour the milk into a large pan and bring just to a boil. Add the tagliatelle and cook for 2–3 minutes until al dente. Drain, reserving scant 1 cup (200 ml) of the cooking liquid. Beat the egg yolks with the cheese and paprika in a large bowl and season with salt and pepper. Stir in the reserved cooking liquid, then stir in the tagliatelle and pancetta or bacon. Stiffly whisk the egg whites in a grease-free bowl and fold into the mixture. Pour the mixture into the prepared dish and bake for 10–15 minutes until golden brown and slightly risen. Serve immediately.

PAGLIA E FIENO WITH SPECK

TAGLIATELLINE WITH ONIONS

TAGLIATELLINE ALLE CIPOLLE

Preparation time: *10 min*
Cooking time: *15 min*
Serves 4

— 3 tablespoons butter
— 4 tablespoons olive oil
— 14 ounces (400 g) white
  onions, thinly sliced
— 10 ounces (275 g) fresh
  tagliatelline (see Tagliatelline
  with Chicken Livers, page 179)
— ⅔ cup (50 g) grated
  Parmesan cheese
— salt and pepper

Melt the butter with the oil in a flameproof casserole. Add the onions and cook over low heat, stirring occasionally, for 5–10 minutes until translucent, then season with salt. Meanwhile, cook the tagliatelline in plenty of salted boiling water for 2–3 minutes until al dente, then drain and tip into the casserole. Season lightly with pepper and toss. Remove from the heat and sprinkle with the Parmesan.

VALTELLINA PIZZOCCHERI

PIZZOCCHERI DELLA VALTELLINA

Preparation time: *50 min,*
plus 30 min resting
Cooking time: *45 min*
Serves 6

— 1¼ cups (150 g)
  buckwheat flour
— ¾ cup (80 g) all-purpose
  (plain) flour, preferably Italian
  type 00, plus extra for dusting
— 1 egg, lightly beaten
— 2 tablespoons milk
— salt

For the sauce:
— 4⅓ cups (400 g) shredded
  savoy cabbage
— 1 potato, chopped
— scant ½ cup (100 g) butter
— 1 onion, thinly sliced
— 1 garlic clove, thinly sliced
— 4 fresh sage leaves, shredded
— 5 ounces (150 g) sliced
  low-fat cheese
— 1 cup (80 g) grated
  Parmesan cheese
— salt and pepper

Sift together both flours and a pinch of salt into a mound on the counter and make a well in the middle. Add the egg, 1 tablespoon warm water, and the milk and gradually incorporate the flour with your fingers, adding more warm water if necessary. Knead until smooth. Roll in a damp dish towel and let rest for 30 minutes. Meanwhile, put the cabbage and potato into a pan, add water to cover, and season with salt and pepper. Bring to a boil, then lower the heat, and simmer for 20 minutes until the cabbage is tender and the potato is almost disintegrating. Divide the butter between three small pans and cook the onion, garlic, and sage in the separate pans until soft and golden brown. Roll out the pasta dough into a fairly thick sheet on a lightly floured counter and cut into ½-inch (1-cm) wide ribbons about 8 inches (20 cm) long. Add the pizzoccheri to the pan of vegetables, cook for 5 minutes, then drain, and transfer to a large dish. Pour the hot butters over the mixture and toss lightly. Arrange a layer of vegetables and pizzoccheri on the base of a soup tureen, place a layer of cheese slices on top, and sprinkle with the Parmesan. Continue making alternating layers until all the ingredients are used. Serve hot.

Buckwheat flour, originally from Asia, is often replaced by cornstarch (cornflour) in Italian cooking. However, buckwheat is still produced near Carnia in Friuli-Venezia Giulia, northeast Italy, and in Valtellina in Lombardy, in the north, where Pizzoccheri is a traditional dish.

BAKED TAGLIATELLE AND SPINACH

PASTICCIO DI TAGLIATELLE E SPINACI

Preparation time: *1 hour,*
plus 2–2 ½ hours rising
Cooking time: *55 min*
Serves 6

— oil, for brushing
— 4 cups (450 g) strong white
   bread flour, plus extra
   for dusting
— 1 tablespoon salt
— 1 envelope rapid-rise
   (sachet fast-action) yeast
— 1 tablespoon olive oil
— 1¾ cups (400 ml)
   lukewarm water
— butter, for greasing

For the filling:
— 7 ounces (200 g) spinach,
   coarse stalks removed
— 6 tablespoons (80 g) butter
— scant ½ cup (100 ml) milk
— 4 tablespoons heavy
   (double) cream
— 11 ounces (300 g) fresh
   tagliatelle (see Tagliatelle
   with Artichokes, page 171)
— scant 1 cup diced ham
— 3 eggs
— ⅔ cup (50 g) grated
   Parmesan cheese
— salt and pepper

Make the bread dough. Brush a bowl with oil. Sift together the flour and salt onto a counter, mix in the yeast, and shape into a mound. Make a well in the middle and pour the oil and half the lukewarm water into it. Knead thoroughly, gradually incorporating the dry ingredients and adding more water to make a firm dough (you may not need all the water). Shape into a ball, put it into the prepared bowl, cover with a damp dish towel, and let rise in a warm place for 2–2½ hours. Preheat the oven to 350°F (180°C/Gas Mark 4) and grease an ovenproof dish with butter. Punch down (knock back) the dough and roll out on a lightly floured counter into a sheet ⅛–¼ inch (3–5 mm) thick. Put it into the base of the prepared dish, trimming off any excess.

Put the spinach into a pan with just the water clinging to the leaves after washing and cook over low heat, turning occasionally, for 5–10 minutes until wilted. Add the butter, pour in the milk and cream, stir well, and season with salt and pepper. Cook the tagliatelle in plenty of salted boiling water for 2–3 minutes until al dente. Drain, return to the pan, and add the spinach mixture and ham. Spoon the mixture into the dough-lined dish. Beat the eggs with the Parmesan and a pinch of salt in a bowl, then pour the mixture over the tagliatelle. Bake for 30 minutes, remove from the oven, and serve.

TAGLIATELLE WITH WHITE TRUFFLE

TAGLIATELLE AL TARTUFO BIANCO

Preparation time: *10 min*
Cooking time: *20 min*
Serves 4

— 5 tablespoons (65 g) butter,
   plus extra for greasing
— 1 garlic clove
— 1 sprig fresh rosemary
— 14 ounces (400 g) fresh
   tagliatelle (see Tagliatelle with
   Artichokes, page 171)
— 1 egg yolk
— pinch of freshly grated nutmeg
— 1 quantity hot béchamel sauce
   (see Baked Rigatoni, page 124)
— 1 white truffle, thinly shaved
— ⅔ cup (50 g) grated
   Parmesan cheese
— salt and pepper

Preheat the oven to 350°F (180°C/Gas Mark 4) and grease an ovenproof dish with butter. Melt 4 tablespoons of the butter in a skillet or frying pan. Add the garlic clove and rosemary sprig and cook over low heat for a few minutes, but do not let the garlic burn, then remove the garlic and rosemary, and discard. Cook the tagliatelle in plenty of salted boiling water for 2–3 minutes until al dente. Drain, tip into the pan, and toss in the herb butter. Beat the egg yolk and nutmeg into the béchamel sauce and season with salt and pepper. Gently stir the sauce and truffle shavings into the tagliatelle and sprinkle with the grated cheese. Transfer the mixture to the prepared dish, dot with the remaining butter, and bake for 10 minutes. Serve immediately.

TAGLIATELLE WITH MEATBALLS AND TOMATO SAUCE

Preparation time: *1 hour*
Cooking time: *1 hour 15 min*
Serves 4–6

— 4 tablespoons (50 g) butter
— 2 tablespoons olive oil
— 2 onions, finely chopped
— 1 celery stalk, finely chopped
— 4 carrots, finely chopped
— 14 ounces (400 g) ground (minced) beef
— scant 1 cup (200 ml) dry white wine
— 1 cup (120 g) cooked or frozen baby peas (petits pois)
— 11 ounces (300 g) canned chopped tomatoes
— all-purpose (plain) flour, for dusting
— oil, for deep-frying
— 14 ounces (400 g) fresh tagliatelle (see Tagliatelle with Artichokes, page 171)
— 10 ounces (275 g) mozzarella cheese, diced
— scant ½ cup (100 ml) tomato sauce (see Baked Capellini, page 25)
— ⅔ cup (50 g) grated pecorino cheese, plus extra to serve
— salt and pepper

Melt half the butter with the oil in a shallow pan. Add the onions, celery, and carrots and cook over low heat, stirring occasionally, for 5 minutes. Add the ground (minced) meat, increase the heat to medium, and cook, stirring frequently and breaking it up with a wooden spoon, for 8–10 minutes until lightly browned. Pour in the wine and cook until the alcohol has evaporated. Add the peas and tomatoes, season with salt and pepper, lower the heat, cover, and simmer, stirring occasionally, for 30 minutes.

Remove the pan from the heat and transfer the mixture to a food processor. Process in pulses until thoroughly combined, then scrape into a bowl. Shape scoops of the mixture into small balls with your hands and dust with flour. Heat the oil in a deep-fryer to 350–375°F (180–190°C) or until a cube of day-old bread browns in 30 seconds. Add the meatballs, in batches if necessary, and cook until browned all over. Remove with a slotted spoon and drain on paper towels. Preheat the oven to 325°F (160°C/Gas Mark 3). Cook the tagliatelle in plenty of salted boiling water for 2–3 minutes until al dente. Drain and arrange in an ovenproof dish in alternating layers with the mozzarella, tomato sauce, meatballs, and pecorino until all the ingredients are used up. Dot with the remaining butter and bake for about 10 minutes until golden. Remove from the oven, sprinkle with pecorino, and season with pepper. Serve immediately.

TAGLIERINI

A type of fresh pasta also known as tagliolini, taglierini is a very thin version of tagliatelle that originated in northern Italy and is about ⅛ inch (3 mm) wide. Rolled out into a thin sheet and cut with a knife in the old-fashioned way, homemade taglierini is made from rich egg dough, whereas industrially produced taglierini is made from durum wheat semolina flour and water. Taglierini is suitable for serving with a sauce, but can also be cooked in broth (stock). It is ideal with delicate and creamy sauces based on butter, eggs, and cheese, as well as with fish and shellfish.

TAGLIERINI WITH MUSHROOMS AND PANCETTA

TAGLIERINI AI FUNGHI E PANCETTA

Preparation time: *1 hour 10 min*
Cooking time: *22 min*
Serves 6

— 1½ quantity Fresh Pasta Dough (see page 139)
— 4 tablespoons (50 g) butter
— 5 ounces (150 g) smoked pancetta or bacon, cut into strips
— 2¾ cups (200 g) sliced porcini mushrooms
— 2 tablespoons heavy (double) cream
— 1 tablespoon chopped fresh flat-leaf parsley
— salt and pepper

Roll out the pasta dough on a lightly floured counter into a thin sheet. Cut into strips about ⅛ inch (3 mm) wide and let dry on floured dish towels. Melt the butter in a small pan. Add the pancetta or bacon and cook over low heat, stirring occasionally, for 4–5 minutes until lightly browned. Increase the heat to high, add the mushrooms, season with salt, and cook, stirring occasionally, for 10 minutes. Cook the taglierini in plenty of salted boiling water for 2–3 minutes until al dente. Drain and tip into the pan with the mushrooms. Lower the heat, add the cream and heat through, stirring constantly. Transfer to a warmed serving dish, sprinkle with the parsley, and season with pepper. Serve immediately.

TAGLIERINI WITH SMOKED SALMON, TOMATO, AND CREAM SAUCE

TAGLIERINI WITH SMOKED SALMON, TOMATO, AND CREAM SAUCE

TAGLIERINI AL SUGO DI SALMONE, POMODORO, E PANNA

Preparation time: *10 min*
Cooking time: *25 min*
Serves 4

— 2 tablespoons butter
— 2 tablespoons olive oil
— 1 onion, chopped
— 1 garlic clove, chopped
— 3½ ounces (100 g) canned chopped tomatoes
— 3 ounces (80 g) smoked salmon, cut into strips
— scant 1 cup (200 ml) dry white wine
— 2 tablespoons heavy (double) cream
— 1 teaspoon chopped fresh thyme
— 10 ounces (275 g) fresh taglierini (see Taglierini with Mushrooms and Pancetta, page 191)
— 1 tablespoon snipped fresh chives
— salt and pepper

Melt the butter with the oil in a pan. Add the onion and garlic and cook over low heat, stirring occasionally, for 5 minutes. Add the tomatoes and salmon and cook, stirring occasionally, for 10 minutes. Drizzle with the wine and cook until the alcohol has evaporated. Stir in the cream and thyme, season with salt and pepper, and heat through gently. Cook the taglierini in plenty of salted boiling water for 2–3 minutes until al dente. Drain, tip into the pan with the sauce, and toss for a few minutes. Sprinkle with the chives and serve immediately.

TAGLIERINI WITH BUTTER AND WHITE WINE

TAGLIERINI AL BURRO E VINO BIANCO

Preparation time: *15 min*
Cooking time: *15 min*
Serves 4

— 3 tablespoons butter
— grated zest and strained juice of ½ lemon
— scant 1 cup (200 ml) dry white wine
— 1 dried red chile, crumbled
— 3 tablespoons heavy (double) cream
— 14 ounces (400 g) fresh taglierini (see Taglierini with Mushrooms and Pancetta, page 191)
— ½ cup (40 g) grated Parmesan cheese
— 1 tablespoon chopped fresh flat-leaf parsley
— salt

Melt half the butter in a shallow pan. Add the lemon zest, stir, drizzle with the wine, and cook until the alcohol has evaporated. Stir in the chile and cream and simmer gently for 10 minutes. Remove the pan from the heat and keep warm. Cook the taglierini in plenty of salted boiling water for 2–3 minutes until al dente. Drain, tip into the pan with the sauce, set over medium–high heat and toss for a few minutes. Remove from the heat, transfer to a warmed serving dish, drizzle with the lemon juice, and stir. Add the remaining butter, Parmesan and parsley, and serve immediately.

GREEN TAGLIERINI WITH ARTICHOKES, SHRIMP, AND BRANDY

TAGLIERINI VERDI AI GAMBERI SFUMATI AL COGNAC

Preparation time: *40 min*
Cooking time: *30 min*
Serves 4

— 3 young globe artichokes, trimmed and thinly sliced
— juice of ½ lemon
— 20 cooked shrimp (prawns)
— 3 tablespoons butter
— 4 tablespoons heavy (double) cream
— ½ cup (120 ml) brandy
— 10 ounces (275 g) fresh taglierini (see Taglierini with Mushrooms and Pancetta, page 191)
— 8–12 fresh basil leaves
— salt

Put the artichokes into a pan, add the lemon juice and a pinch of salt, and pour in water just to cover. Bring to a boil, lower the heat, cover, and simmer for 10 minutes. Meanwhile, reserve 8 shrimp (prawns) for the garnish and peel, devein, and chop the remainder. Drain the artichokes, transfer to a food processor, and process to a puree. Melt 1 tablespoon of the butter in a small pan. Add the artichoke puree and cook over low heat, stirring frequently, for 5 minutes. Stir in the cream and heat through over low heat, stirring constantly, for a few minutes.

Melt the remaining butter in a skillet or frying pan. Add the shrimp and cook over low heat, stirring frequently, for 5 minutes. Drizzle with the brandy and cook until the alcohol has evaporated. Cook the taglierini in plenty of salted boiling water for 2–3 minutes until al dente. Drain, tip into the pan with the shrimp and toss for 2 minutes. Pour a small ladleful of artichoke puree onto each of 4 individual plates and top with the taglierini twisted into a turban shape. Garnish with the reserved whole shrimp and a few basil leaves.

CREAMY TAGLIERINI WITH PROSCIUTTO

TAGLIERINI ALLA CREMA CON PROSCIUTTO

Preparation time: *15 min*
Cooking time: *8 min*
Serves 4

— 1¾ cups (400 ml) low-fat cream cheese
— 2 egg yolks
— generous ½ cup (100 g) diced prosciutto
— 2 tablespoons heavy (double) cream
— 10 ounces (275 g) fresh taglierini (see Taglierini with Mushrooms and Pancetta, page 191)
— 2 tablespoons butter
— ½ cup (40 g) grated Parmesan cheese
— salt and pepper

Beat the cream cheese in a bowl, then stir in the egg yolks, prosciutto, and cream, and season with salt and pepper. Cook the taglierini in plenty of salted boiling water for 2–3 minutes until al dente. Drain, tip onto a warmed serving dish, pour the sauce over, and add the butter. Serve immediately, handing the Parmesan separately.

TAGLIERINI WITH HAZELNUTS

Preparation time: *10 min*
Cooking time: *15 min*
Serves 4

— 2 tablespoons olive oil
— 1 onion, chopped
— ⅓ cup (50 g) diced
  pancetta or bacon
— scant ½ cup (100 ml) dry
  white wine
— 3 tablespoons butter, softened
— scant 1 cup (100 g)
  chopped hazelnuts
— 9 ounces (250 g) fresh
  taglierini (see Taglierini with
  Mushrooms and Pancetta,
  page 191)
— salt and pepper

Heat the oil in a pan. Add the onion and cook over low heat, stirring occasionally, for 5 minutes. Increase the heat to medium, add the pancetta or bacon, and cook, stirring frequently, for 2 minutes. Pour in the wine and cook until the alcohol has evaporated. Beat the butter in a bowl until creamy, then beat in the chopped hazelnuts. Stir the mixture into the pan, season with salt and pepper, remove from the heat, and keep warm. Cook the taglierini in plenty of salted boiling water for 2–3 minutes until al dente. Drain, tip into a warmed serving dish, and pour the sauce over. Serve immediately.

TAGLIERINI WITH MASCARPONE

Preparation time: *15 min*
Cooking time: *20 min*
Serves 4

— 2 tablespoons milk
— ⅓ cup (80 g) mascarpone cheese
— grated zest and strained
  juice of ½ lemon
— 10 ounces (275 g) fresh
  taglierini (see Taglierini with
  Mushrooms and Pancetta,
  page 191)
— salt and freshly ground
  white pepper

Heat the milk in a small pan. Add the mascarpone and cook over very low heat, stirring constantly, until melted. Remove from the heat, stir in the lemon zest, and season with salt and white pepper. Stir well and keep warm. Pour the strained lemon juice onto a warmed serving dish. Cook the taglierini in plenty of salted boiling water for 2–3 minutes until al dente. Drain, tip onto the serving dish, and pour the mascarpone sauce over. Toss well and serve immediately.

COCOA TAGLIERINI

COCOA TAGLIERINI

Preparation time: *1 hour,
plus 30 min resting*
Cooking time: *15 min*
Serves 4

— 1¼ cups (150 g) all-purpose
  (plain) flour, plus extra
  for dusting
— 3 tablespoons unsweetened
  cocoa powder
— 2 eggs
— salt

For the sauce:
— 3 tablespoons butter
— 1 garlic clove
— 3 bay leaves
— ⅓ cup (80 g) mascarpone cheese
— ½ dried red chile, crumbled
— ½ cup (40 g) grated
  Parmesan cheese

Make the pasta dough. Sift together the flour and unsweetened cocoa powder into a mound on a counter and make a well in the middle. Break the eggs into the well and add a pinch of salt. Using your fingers, gradually incorporate the flour into the eggs. Knead thoroughly, shape into a ball, cover with a clean dish towel and let rest for 30 minutes. Roll out the dough on a lightly floured counter to a thin sheet. Roll it up and cut into ⅛-inch (3-mm) wide strips. Make the sauce. Melt the butter in a pan. Add the garlic and bay leaves and cook over low heat, stirring occasionally, for a few minutes until the garlic is lightly browned. Remove the garlic and bay leaves with a slotted spoon and discard. Stir the mascarpone and chile into the pan. Cook the taglierini in plenty of salted boiling water for 2–3 minutes until al dente. Drain, tip into the pan with the sauce, and toss for 30 seconds. Transfer to a warmed serving dish, sprinkle with the Parmesan, and serve immediately.

CHESTNUT FLOUR TAGLIERINI WITH ONION BUTTER

Preparation time: *1 hour,
plus 1 hour resting*
Cooking time: *20 min*
Serves 4

— 1¼ cups (150 g) chestnut flour
— 2¼ cups (250 g) all-purpose
  (plain) flour, preferably Italian
  type 00, plus extra for dusting
— 2 eggs
— salt

For the sauce:
— 2 tablespoons butter
— 1 small onion, finely chopped
— 2 ounces (50 g) mild fontina
  cheese, diced
— 1½ ounces (40 g) fontina
  Val d'Aosta cheese, finely diced
— salt

Make the pasta dough. Sift both types of flour into a mound on a counter and make a well in the middle. Break the eggs into the well and add a pinch of salt. Using your fingers, gradually incorporate the flour into the eggs. Knead thoroughly, shape into a ball, cover with a clean dish towel and let rest for 1 hour. Meanwhile, make the sauce. Melt half the butter in a small shallow pan. Add the onion, season lightly with salt, and cook over low heat, stirring occasionally, for 10 minutes. Remove the pan from the heat and set aside. Roll out the dough into a fairly thick sheet on a lightly floured counter, then roll it up, and slice into ⅛-inch (3-mm) strips. Dice the remaining butter and put it into a serving dish with the onions and both types of cheese. Cook the taglierini in plenty of salted boiling water for 2–3 minutes until al dente. Drain, leaving it slightly wet, tip into the serving dish, and toss well. Serve immediately.

Preparation time: *10 min*
Cooking time: *20 min*
Serves 4

— 4 tablespoons (50 g) butter
— 2 shallots, thinly sliced
— 10 ounces (275 g) fresh
  taglierini (see Taglierini with
  Mushrooms and Pancetta,
  page 191)
— ½ cup (50 g) grated
  Gruyère cheese
— generous ⅓ cup (30 g)
  grated Parmesan cheese
— salt

Preparation time: *14 min*
Cooking time: *8 min*
Serves 4

— 4 tablespoons (50 g) butter
— 1 tablespoon heavy
  (double) cream
— 1-ounce (25-g) tube
  truffle paste
— 10 ounces (275 g) fresh
  taglierini (see Taglierini with
  Mushrooms and Pancetta,
  page 191)
— ½ cup (40 g) grated Parmesan
  cheese, to serve
— salt and freshly ground
  white pepper

TAGLIERINI WITH SHALLOTS

TAGLIERINI ALLO SCALOGNO

Melt the butter in a skillet or frying pan. Add the shallots and
cook over very low heat, stirring occasionally, for 25–30 minutes
until golden brown and caramelized. Cook the taglierini in
plenty of salted boiling water for 2–3 minutes until al dente.
Drain and immediately tip the pasta into the hot pan.
Toss well, transfer to a warmed serving dish, sprinkle with
the Gruyère and Parmesan, and serve immediately.

TAGLIERINI WITH TRUFFLES

TAGLIERINI TARTUFATI

Melt the butter in a heatproof bowl set over a pan of
simmering water. Add the cream and mix well. Add about
4 inches (10 cm) of the truffle paste and mix well again.
Taste and, if necessary, add more truffle paste. Cook the
taglierini in plenty of salted boiling water for 2–3 minutes
until al dente. Drain, transfer to a warmed serving dish,
and toss with the truffle butter. Season with white pepper,
sprinkle with Parmesan, and serve immediately.

TAGLIERINI WITH RICOTTA

TAGLIERINI ALLA RICOTTA

Preparation time: *30 min*
Cooking time: *25 min*
Serves 4

— 2 small eggplants
   (aubergines), diced
— 6 tablespoons olive oil
— scant 1 cup (200 g)
   ricotta cheese
— 10 ounces (275 g) fresh
   taglierini (see Taglierini with
   Mushrooms and Pancetta,
   page 191)
— 1 sprig fresh flat-leaf parsley,
   chopped
— salt and pepper

Spread out the eggplants (aubergines) on a plate, sprinkle with salt, and let sit for 30 minutes. Rinse under cold running water and pat dry with paper towels. Heat 5 tablespoons of the oil in a large skillet or frying pan. Add the eggplants and cook over low heat, stirring frequently, for 8–10 minutes until golden brown. Remove with a slotted spoon and drain on paper towels. Keep warm. Combine the ricotta and remaining oil in a bowl and season with salt and pepper. Cook the taglierini in plenty of salted boiling water for 2–3 minutes until al dente. Drain, return to the pan, and add the ricotta mixture and eggplants. Sprinkle with the parsley, stir, and serve immediately.

TAGLIERINI WITH ROSEMARY

TAGLIERINI AL ROSMARINO

Preparation time: *10 min*
Cooking time: *25 min*
Serves 4

— 3 tablespoons butter
— 1 tablespoon olive oil
— 1 garlic clove, finely chopped
— 1 onion, finely chopped
— 1 sprig fresh rosemary,
   finely chopped
— ⅓ cup (40 g) finely chopped
   pine nuts
— scant 1 cup (200 ml) dry
   white wine
— 10 ounces (275 g) fresh
   taglierini (see Taglierini with
   Mushrooms and Pancetta,
   page 191)
— ½ cup (40 g) grated
   pecorino cheese
— 1 dried red chile, crumbled
— salt and pepper

Melt half the butter with the oil in a shallow pan. Add the garlic and onion and cook over low heat, stirring occasionally, for 5 minutes. Add the rosemary and pine nuts and cook, stirring constantly, for a few minutes. Drizzle with the wine and cook until the alcohol has evaporated, then stir, season with salt and pepper, lower the heat, and simmer for 10 minutes. Cook the taglierini in plenty of salted boiling water for 2–3 minutes until al dente. Drain, tip into a warmed serving dish, and pour the sauce over. Sprinkle with pecorino and chile, and serve immediately.

TAGLIERINI WITH TUNA

TAGLIERINI AL TONNO

Preparation time: *15 min*
Cooking time: *28 min*
Serves *4*

— 2 tablespoons olive oil
— 1 small onion, chopped
— 1 garlic clove
— 3 ounces (80 g) canned tuna in oil, drained and flaked
— 1 canned anchovy fillet, drained and chopped
— 7 ounces (200 g) canned chopped tomatoes
— 10 ounces (275 g) fresh taglierini (see Taglierini with Mushrooms and Pancetta, page 191)
— salt and pepper

Heat the oil in a shallow pan. Add the onion and garlic clove and cook over low heat, stirring occasionally, for 5 minutes. Remove the garlic with a slotted spoon when it becomes golden brown and discard. Add the tuna and anchovy, stir, and cook for 3 minutes, then stir in the chopped tomatoes, and season with salt and pepper. Cover and simmer, stirring occasionally, for 15 minutes. Cook the taglierini in plenty of salted boiling water for 2–3 minutes until al dente. Drain, tip into a warmed serving dish, pour the tuna sauce over, and serve.

TAGLIERINI AND PEA TIMBALE

TIMBALLO DI TAGLIERINI AI PISELLI

Preparation time: *50 min*
Cooking time: *1 hour*
Serves *6*

— 4 tablespoons (50 g) butter, plus extra for greasing
— 2 tablespoons olive oil
— ½ onion, chopped
— 1¾ cups (200 g) shelled peas
— scant ½ cup (100 ml) lukewarm water
— 5–6 tablespoons fresh bread crumbs
— 3½ ounces (100 g) sliced ham
— 15 ounces (425 g) fresh taglierini (see Taglierini with Mushrooms and Pancetta, page 191)
— 2 eggs
— ½ cup (40 g) grated Parmesan cheesed
— salt and pepper

Melt half the butter with the oil in a shallow pan. Add the onion and cook over low heat, stirring occasionally, for 5 minutes. Add the peas and lukewarm water, cover, and simmer for 30 minutes. Preheat the oven to 350°F (180°C/Gas Mark 4). Grease an ovenproof dish with butter and sprinkle with bread crumbs. Line the dish with the slices of ham. Cook the taglierini in plenty of salted boiling water for 2–3 minutes until al dente. Drain, tip into the pan with the peas and stir, then remove the pan from the heat. Beat the eggs with the grated cheese and a pinch of pepper in a bowl, then stir into the pasta mixture. Spoon the mixture over the ham, dot with the remaining butter, and bake for about 20 minutes. Remove from the oven and let stand for 5 minutes, then serve.

Preparation time: *15 min*
Cooking time: *30 min*
Serves 4

— 2 red bell peppers
— 2 tablespoons olive oil
— 1 tablespoon chopped onion
— ⅓ cup (80 g) mascarpone cheese
— 10 ounces (275 g) fresh
    taglierini (see Taglierini with
    Mushrooms and Pancetta,
    page 191)
— salt and pepper

TAGLIERINI WITH MASCARPONE AND BELL PEPPERS

TAGLIERINI CON MASCARPONE E PEPERONI

Peel the bell peppers with a vegetable peeler or paring knife, then halve, seed, and cut the flesh into thin strips. Heat the oil in a pan with the chopped onion and cook until it becomes translucent. Add the bell pepper strips and cook over low heat, stirring occasionally, for 15 minutes. Season with salt and pepper, add the mascarpone, and stir until melted. Cook the taglierini in plenty of salted boiling water for 2–3 minutes until al dente. Drain, tip into the pan with the sauce, and toss gently for a few seconds. Transfer to a warmed serving dish and serve immediately.

Preparation time: *14 min*
Cooking time: *8 min*
Serves 4

— 6 tablespoons (80 g) butter
— pinch of freshly grated nutmeg
— 1 quantity Fresh Pasta Dough
    (see page 139)
— 1 cup (80 g) grated
    Parmesan cheese
— 1 small white truffle
— salt and pepper

TAGLIERINI WITH BUTTER AND TRUFFLE

TAGLIERINI AL BURRO E TARTUFO

Roll out the pasta dough on a lightly floured counter into a thin sheet. Cut into strips about ⅛ inch (3 mm) wide and let dry on floured dish towels. Melt the butter in a small pan and season with the nutmeg and a pinch each of salt and pepper. Cook the taglierini in plenty of salted boiling water for 2–3 minutes until al dente, then drain and tip into a warmed serving dish. Pour the melted butter over the pasta, sprinkle with the Parmesan and then shave the truffle over the top.

Preparation time: *20 min*
Cooking time: *20 min*
Serves 4

— 3 tablespoons butter,
    plus extra for greasing
— 2 egg yolks
— 3 tablespoons heavy
    (double) cream
— 3½ ounces (100 g) ham in
    a single slice, cut into strips
— 12 ounces (350 g) fresh
    taglierini (see Taglierini with
    Mushrooms and Pancetta,
    page 191)
— ½ cup (40 g) grated
    Parmesan cheese
— salt and pepper

BAKED TAGLIERINI WITH HAM

TAGLIERINI AL FORNO CON PROSCIUTTO

Preheat the oven to 350°F (180°C/Gas Mark 4) and grease an ovenproof dish with butter. Beat the egg yolks with the cream in a bowl, season with salt and pepper, and stir in the ham. Cook the taglierini in plenty of salted boiling water for 2–3 minutes until al dente. Drain, return to the pan, and add the butter and grated cheese. Transfer to the prepared dish, pour the ham and cream mixture over it, and stir. Bake for 10 minutes, then remove from the oven, and let stand for 5 minutes before serving.

TAGLIERINI WITH LANGOUSTINES

TAGLIERINI AGLI SCAMPI

Preparation time: *35 min*
Cooking time: *25 min*
Serves *4*

— 14 ounces (400 g) langoustines
or lobsterettes
— 1 onion, roughly chopped
— 1 carrot, roughly chopped
— 1 celery stalk, roughly chopped
— 3 tablespoons olive oil
— 1 tablespoon chopped fresh
flat-leaf parsley
— 1 teaspoon concentrated
tomato paste (puree)
— 10 ounces (275 g) fresh
taglierini (see Taglierini with
Mushrooms and Pancetta,
page 191)
— salt

Peel the langoustines or lobsterettes, reserving the shells. Put the shells in a pan with the onion, carrot, and celery, add water to cover and a pinch of salt. Bring to a boil, lower the heat, and simmer for 15 minutes, then strain into a bowl. Reserve some of the broth (stock). Heat the oil in a skillet or frying pan, add the langoustines or lobsterettes and cook for 3 minutes, then sprinkle with the parsley. Stir the tomato paste with a little of the shellfish broth in a bowl and add to the pan. Cook the taglierini in plenty of salted boiling water for 2–3 minutes until al dente, then drain, toss with the sauce, and transfer to a warmed serving dish.

TAGLIERINI WITH MASCARPONE AND LEMON

TAGLIERINI AL MASCARPONE E LIMONE

Preparation time: *10 min*
Cooking time: *10 min*
Serves *4*

— 2 tablespoons milk
— ⅓ cup (80 g) mascarpone cheese
— grated zest and strained juice
of ½ lemon
— 1 tablespoon green
peppercorns
— 12 ounces (350 g) fresh
taglierini (see Taglierini with
Mushrooms and Pancetta,
page 191)
— salt and freshly ground
white pepper

Heat the milk in a small pan. Add the mascarpone and stir over very low heat until melted. Remove the pan from the heat, add the lemon zest and peppercorns, and season to taste with salt and a little white pepper. Stir well, set aside, and keep warm. Pour the lemon juice into a warmed serving dish. Cook the taglierini in plenty of salted boiling water for 2–3 minutes until al dente. Drain and tip into the prepared serving dish. Add the mascarpone sauce and toss to coat. Serve immediately.

TRENETTE

Ribbons of fresh, narrow, and flat pasta, trenette are very similar to linguine but slightly thinner, with a width of ½ inch (1 cm). It originates from Liguria in the northwest of Italy and is commonly served with pesto, as in the most traditional recipe Trenette con il Pesto (Trenette with Pesto, see page 206). Trenette also goes well with delicate fish and shellfish sauces.

  ◷

Preparation time: *10 min*
Cooking time: *10 min*
Serves 4

— 3 tablespoons olive oil
— 1 garlic clove
— 1 chile
— 12 ounces (350 g) langoustines or lobsterettes, thawed if frozen, peeled
— 12 ounces (350 g) fresh trenette (see Trenette with Pesto, page 206)
— chopped fresh flat-leaf parsley, to garnish
— salt

TRENETTE WITH LANGOUSTINES

TRENETTE AGLI SCAMPI

Heat the oil in a skillet or frying pan. Add the garlic clove and chile and cook, stirring frequently, for a few minutes until lightly browned. Remove the garlic and chile with a slotted spoon and discard. Add the langoustines or lobsterettes to the pan, season with salt, and cook for 3–5 minutes. Meanwhile, cook the trenette in plenty of salted boiling water for 2–3 minutes until al dente. Drain, tip into the pan, and toss to mix. Serve immediately, garnished with chopped parsley.

TRENETTE WITH ANCHOVIES

TRENETTE CON LE ALICI

Preparation time: *25 min*
Cooking time: *20 min*
Serves 4

— 3 tablespoons olive oil
— 1 garlic clove
— 1 fresh red chile,
  seeded and chopped
— 2 ounces (50 g) canned
  anchovy fillets, drained
  and chopped
— 1 sprig fresh flat-leaf
  parsley, chopped
— 14 oz (400 g) canned tomatoes,
  drained and chopped
— 12 ounces (350 g) fresh
  trenette (see Trenette with
  Pesto, below)
— salt

Heat the oil in a shallow pan. Add the garlic clove and chile and cook over low heat, stirring frequently, for a few minutes until the garlic is lightly browned. Remove the garlic with a slotted spoon and discard. Add the anchovy fillets and parsley to the pan and cook, stirring constantly, for 4 minutes. Add the tomatoes, season with salt, cover, and simmer gently, stirring occasionally, for about 10 minutes until thickened. Cook the trenette for 2–3 minutes in plenty of salted boiling water until al dente. Drain, tip into a warmed serving dish, pour the sauce over, and serve.

TRENETTE WITH PESTO

TRENETTE CON IL PESTO

Preparation time: *1 hour 10 min*
Cooking time: *25 min*
Serves 4

— 1 quantity Fresh Pasta Dough
  (see page 139)
— 2 potatoes
— scant 1 cup (150 g) green
  beans, trimmed

For the pesto:
— 10 fresh basil leaves
— ½ cup (50 g) pine nuts
— ½ cup (40 g) grated
  Parmesan cheese
— ½ cup (40 g) grated
  pecorino cheese
— ½ cup (120 ml) olive oil
— salt

Roll out the pasta dough into a thin sheet on a lightly floured counter. Cut into strips about ½ inch (1 cm) wide and let dry on floured dish towels. Peel and cut the potatoes into thin batons and put them into a bowl of cold water. To make the pesto, put the basil, pine nuts, both cheeses, a pinch of salt, and the oil in a food processor and process at medium speed until blended. Alternatively, pound the ingredients with a mortar and pestle until a smooth paste is obtained. Cook the potatoes and green beans in plenty of salted boiling water for 10–15 minutes until tender. Remove them from the pan with a slotted spoon and in the same water, cook the pasta for 2–3 minutes until al dente. Drain, leaving it quite moist, and tip into a warmed serving dish. Add the green beans and potatoes, spoon the sauce over the top, and serve immediately.

TROFIE

These tiny dumplings are a specialty of the coastal area in Liguria (northwest Italy) from Camogli to Bogliasco and, along with trenette, trofie is the most typical pasta from Liguria. The name derives from the dialect word *strufuggià*, meaning "to rub," referring to the way in which it is made—by rolling pieces of pasta into thin twists. Trofie is typically served with pesto sauce (see overleaf). The classic version is to boil potatoes and green beans in the same pan and add the trofie at the end of cooking. In some areas, trofie is often mixed with boiled fresh white beans. A small amount of chestnut flour can sometimes be added to the white flour, which sweetens the trofie and complements the pesto.

TROFIE WITH ARUGULA

TROFIE ALLA RUCOLA

Preparation time: *20 min*
Cooking time: *35 min*
Serves 4

— 1 green bell pepper
— ¾ cup (100 g) arugula (rocket)
— ¼ cup (25 g) pine nuts
— 1 garlic clove
— 3 tablespoons olive oil
— ½ cup (40 g) grated sharp pecorino cheese
— 11 ounces (300 g) fresh trofie (see Trofie with Pesto, page 208)
— salt and pepper

Preheat the oven to 400°F (200°C/Gas Mark 6). Put the bell pepper onto a baking sheet and roast, turning occasionally, for 30 minutes until charred. Remove from the oven and when cool enough to handle, peel, seed, and coarsely chop the flesh. Put the bell pepper, arugula (rocket), pine nuts, garlic, oil, and a pinch of salt into a food processor and process until smooth. Pour the mixture into a large bowl and mix with the grated pecorino. Cook the trofie in plenty of salted boiling water until al dente. Drain, tip into the bowl with the sauce, season with pepper, and serve.

TROFIE WITH PESTO

Preparation time: *30 min,*
plus 1 hour resting
Cooking time: *4–5 min*
Serves 4

— 3 cups (350 g) all-purpose
  (plain) flour, plus extra
  for dusting
— salt
— pesto, to serve (see Trenette
  with Pesto, page 206)

TROFIE AL PESTO

Sift the flour into a mound on a counter and make a well
in the middle. Add a pinch of salt and enough water to make
a fairly firm dough. Using your fingers, gradually incorporate
the flour into the water. Knead well, then break off very
small pieces of dough, and roll them on the counter to make
1¼–1½-inch (3–4 cm) long rolls that are thicker in the middle
and thinner at the ends. Let dry on floured dish towels for
up to 1 hour. Cook the trofie in plenty of salted boiling water
for 2–3 minutes until al dente. Drain, toss with pesto, and
serve immediately.

TROFIE WITH POTATOES
AND TURNIP GREENS

Preparation time: *50 min*
Cooking time: *50 min*
Serves 4

— 9 ounces (250 g) turnip
  greens (tops)
— 2 potatoes
— 2 tablespoons olive oil
— 1 onion, chopped
— 1 garlic clove
— 12 ounces (350 g) fresh trofie
  (see Trofie with Pesto, above)
— 3 ounces (80 g) crescenza
  cheese, diced
— ½ cup (40 g) grated
  pecorino cheese
— salt and pepper

TROFIE CON PATATE E BROCCOLETTI

Blanch the turnip greens (tops) in boiling salted water for
5 minutes, then remove with a slotted spoon, squeeze out the
excess liquid, and chop. Cook the potatoes in boiling salted
water for 20–30 minutes until tender but not falling apart.
Drain, peel, and dice. Heat the oil in a shallow pan. Add the
onion and garlic clove and cook over low heat, stirring
occasionally, for 5 minutes. Remove the garlic clove when it
becomes golden brown. Stir the potatoes into the pan, then
add the turnip greens. Season with salt and pepper and cook,
stirring occasionally, for 10–15 minutes. Cook the trofie in
plenty of salted boiling water for 2–3 minutes until al dente.
Drain, tip into a warmed serving dish, sprinkle with the
crescenza, and stir. Add the turnip greens and potatoes,
sprinkle with grated pecorino, season with pepper, and serve.

The Italian word broccoletti *refers both to broccoli and turnip*
greens (cime di rapa). *They are very similar, but broccoli requires*
a longer cooking time (8 minutes).

TROFIE WITH PESTO

FILLED PASTA

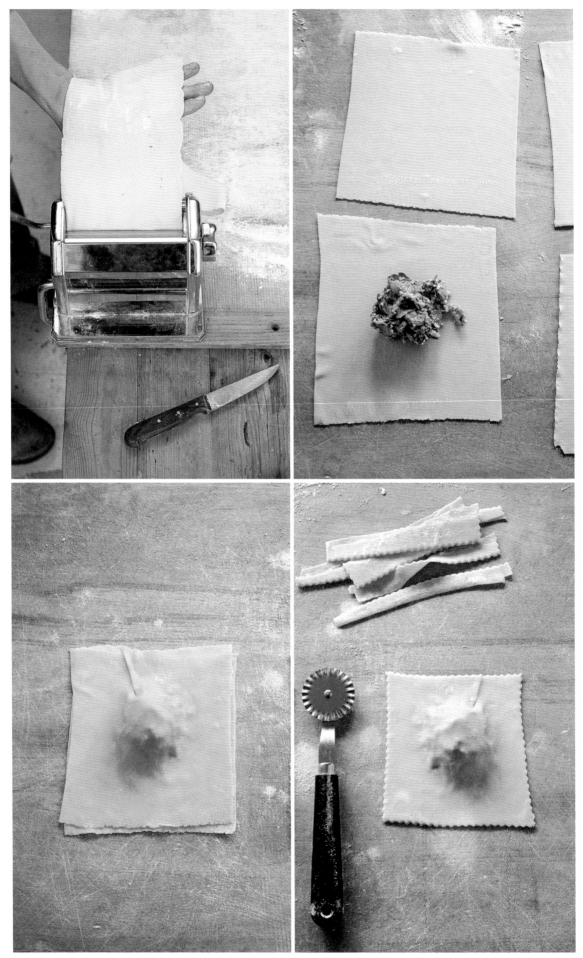

AGNOLOTTI

Agnolotti, a specialty of the Piedmont region in northwest Italy, is a square or round type of filled pasta. The alleged story behind its name is that the Marquis of Monferrato asked his chef, Angelot, to prepare a feast to celebrate a long-awaited victory. Using the few ingredients that were available to him, Angelot created the diminutive pieces for his piat d'Angelot (Angelot's dish), which eventually became agnolotti. The filling generally consists of cooked meat, and agnolotti is typically served with a simple dressing of either the meat juices saved from the filling or melted butter. For Agnolotti alla Piemontese (Agnolotti Piedmontese, see below), the most traditional recipe, the filling calls for a mixture of veal and pork, or braised beef.

⊛

Preparation time: *1 hour 15 min, plus 1 hour resting*
Cooking time: *25 min*
Serves *6*

— 2⅔ cups (300 g) all-purpose (plain) flour, preferably Italian type 00, plus extra for dusting
— 3 eggs, lightly beaten
— salt

For the filling:
— 9 ounces (250 g) spinach
— 14 ounces (400 g) braised beef, ground (minced), with its gravy
— 2 egg yolks, lightly beaten
— 1 egg, lightly beaten
— ⅔ cup (50 g) grated Parmesan cheese, plus more to serve
— scant 1 cup chopped cooked ham
— salt and pepper

AGNOLOTTI PIEDMONTESE

AGNOLOTTI ALLA PIEMONTESE

Make the pasta dough with the quantities specified (see Fresh Pasta Dough, page 139) and let rest for 1 hour. Blanch the spinach in boiling water, drain, chop, and combine with the beef in a bowl. Stir in the egg yolks, whole egg, Parmesan, and ham and season with salt and pepper. If the mixture is a little dry, soften with a few tablespoons of gravy from the braised beef. Roll out the pasta dough into strips on a lightly floured counter. Put mounds – about 1 teaspoon – of filling at regular intervals along one strip, place another strip on top, and press down well around the filling. Cut square agnolotti with a pasta or pastry wheel. Cook in salted boiling water for about 10 minutes. Drain and dress with gravy from the braised beef or with melted butter and Parmesan.

PUMPKIN AGNOLOTTI

AGNOLOTTI DI ZUCCA

Preparation time: *45 min,*
plus 30 min resting
Cooking time: *45 min*
Serves 4

— 3½ cups (400 g) all-purpose
   (plain) flour, preferably
   Italian type 00
— 4 eggs
— salt

For the filling:
— olive oil, for brushing
— 1 pound 2 ounces (500 g)
   pumpkin, seeded and cut
   into chunks
— ½ onion, chopped
— ⅓ cup (40 g) chopped walnuts
— 1 tablespoon chopped
   fresh sage
— salt and pepper

For the sauce:
— generous ⅓ cup (50 g)
   golden raisins (sultanas)
— 2 tablespoons butter
— 1 shallot, chopped
— 4 tablespoons medium sherry
— salt and pepper

Preheat the oven to 400°F (200°C/Gas Mark 6) and brush an ovenproof dish with oil. Meanwhile, make the pasta dough with the quantities specified (see Fresh Pasta Dough, page 139), cover with a damp cloth and rest for 30 minutes. Put the pieces of pumpkin in the prepared dish and bake in the oven for 30 minutes until softened. Remove the pumpkin from the oven and when it is cool enough to handle, scoop the pulp from the skin and mash well. Discard the skin. Add the onion, walnuts, and sage and season with salt and pepper.

Roll out the pasta dough on a lightly floured counter or with a pasta machine into thin strips. Put small mounds—about 1 teaspoon—of the filling at regular intervals along one strip, place another strip on top and press down well around the filling. Cut square agnolotti with a pasta or pastry wheel. To make the sauce, put the golden raisins (sultanas) into a heatproof bowl, pour in warm water to cover, and let soak and plump up. Melt the butter in a skillet or frying pan. Add the shallot and cook over low heat, stirring occasionally, for 5 minutes. Add the sherry and cook for a few minutes until the alcohol has evaporated. Drain the golden raisins and add to the pan, then season with salt and pepper. Cook the agnolotti in plenty of salted boiling water until it floats to the surface and is al dente. Drain, toss with the sauce, and serve immediately.

ANOLINI

Anolini is a type of fresh, filled pasta of ancient origin, from the city of Parma in the northern Italian region of Emilia-Romagna. It is made by placing small portions of the filling on a sheet of pasta, about 1¾ inches (45 mm) apart. A second sheet is placed over this, and the pieces are cut out using a stamp about 1¼ inches (30 mm) in diameter. Anolini is also common in Piacenza, in the same region, where the pieces are smaller and the meat for the filling is stewed in wine. Anolini can also be served in brodo, or beef broth.

⊗

Preparation time: *1 hour 30 min, plus 1 hour resting*
Cooking time: *25 min*
Serves 6

— generous 2¾ cups (320 g) all-purpose (plain) flour, plus extra for dusting
— 3 eggs
— 4 cups (1 litre) beef broth (stock)
— salt

For the filling:
— 1¾ cups (100 g) fresh bread crumbs
— 2–3 tablespoons boiling vegetable broth (stock)
— 2 eggs
— 3 cups (250 g) grated Parmesan cheese
— salt and pepper

ANOLINI WITH PARMESAN

ANOLINI AL PARMIGIANO

Make the pasta dough. Sift the flour into a mound on a counter and make a well in the middle. Break the eggs into the well and add a pinch of salt. Using your fingers, gradually incorporate the flour into the eggs. Knead thoroughly, shape into a ball, cover with a clean dish towel, and let rest in a cool place for 1 hour. Meanwhile, make the filling. Put the bread crumbs into a heatproof bowl, add a pinch each of salt and pepper, pour in 2 tablespoons of the boiling broth (stock), and stir well. Add the eggs and then stir in the Parmesan. The mixture must be fairly firm but if it is too dry, add the remaining tablespoon of broth. Roll out the dough on a lightly floured counter into a thin sheet. Cut out 1¼-inch (3-cm) circles with a pasta wheel or stamp out with a cookie cutter. Put a small mound of filling in the middle of each, fold the dough over, and shape into a half moon. Alternatively, put a mound of filling in the middle of half the circles and cover with the remaining circles, pressing the edges to seal. Bring the beef broth to a boil in a large pan. Add the anolini, bring back to a boil, and cook until al dente. Serve immediately in the hot broth.

CANNELLONI

Cannelloni, meaning "large tubes," is a type of fresh pasta related to lasagna. These 4-inch (10-cm) squares of pasta are covered with a thin layer of filling and rolled up to enclose it. For this reason, cannelloni is sometimes confused with manicotti, which is a pre-fabricated tube. The composer Gioacchino Rossini from Pesaro, in the central Italian region of Marche, allegedly invented the shape in the nineteenth century, and cannelloni is common in both the Marche and in Abruzzo, further south. Cannelloni lends itself to a wide variety of fillings and is frequently served with thick sauces.

Preparation time: *35 min,
plus 1 hour resting*
Cooking time: *5 min*
Makes about 12 cannelloni

— 3½ cups (400 g) all-purpose
(plain) flour, preferably
Italian type 00
— 4 eggs
— salt

CANNELLONI (BASIC RECIPE)

CANNELLONI (RICETTA BASE)

Sift the flour into a mound on a counter and make a well in the middle. Break the eggs into the well and add a pinch of salt. Using your fingers, gradually incorporate the flour into the eggs. Knead thoroughly, shape into a ball, cover with a clean cloth and leave to rest in a cool place for 1 hour. Roll out into a thin sheet on a lightly floured counter. Cut into 4-inch (10-cm) squares. Cook the pasta squares, a few at a time, in plenty of salted boiling water for a few minutes. Remove with a slotted spoon, rinse under cold running water, and spread out on clean dish towels to dry. They are then ready for your chosen filling.

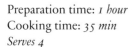

Preparation time: *1 hour*
Cooking time: *35 min*
Serves 4

— 1 quantity Cannelloni
(see page 216)

For the filling:
— 2 tablespoons butter,
plus extra for greasing
— 11 ounces (300 g) spinach
— 7 ounces (200 g) roast veal,
chopped
— 1 slice cooked ham, chopped
— 2 tablespoons grated
Parmesan cheese
— 1 egg, lightly beaten
— 1 quantity béchamel sauce (see
Baked Pumpkin Pasta, page 236)
— salt and pepper

CANNELLONI WITH BÉCHAMEL SAUCE

CANNELLONI ALLA BESCIAMELLA

Preheat the oven to 400°F (200°C/Gas Mark 6). Grease an ovenproof dish with butter. Put the spinach into a pan with just the water clinging to the leaves after washing and cook over low heat, turning occasionally, for 5 minutes until wilted. Drain well and pulse until finely chopped in a food processor, then combine with the veal, ham, Parmesan, and egg, and season to taste. Put some of the spinach mixture and a little béchamel sauce on each cannelloni square and roll up from one side. Arrange the cannelloni in a single layer in the prepared dish, pour the remaining béchamel sauce over, and dot with the butter. Bake for 20 minutes, then let rest for 5 minutes before serving.

CANNELLONI FROM PIACENZA

CANNELLONI ALLA PIACENTINA

Preparation time: *50 min*
Cooking time: *1 hour*
Serves 4

— 3 tablespoons butter
— 1¾ cups (200 g) all-purpose
(plain) flour
— 2 eggs
— 2 egg yolks
— 2¼ cups (500 ml) milk
— salt

For the filling:
— 1¾ pounds (800 g) spinach,
coarse stalks removed
— 2⅔ cups (600 g) ricotta cheese
— 1 small garlic clove,
coarsely chopped
— scant ½ cup (100 g)
mascarpone cheese
— 1 egg
— 1 egg yolk
— pinch of freshly grated nutmeg
— salt

For the sauce:
— ⅓ cup (25 g) grated
Parmesan cheese
— 5 tablespoons (65 g)
butter, melted

Melt 1 tablespoon of the butter in a heatproof bowl set over a pan of simmering water, then remove from the heat. Sift the flour with a pinch of salt into a bowl and make a well in the middle. Break the eggs into the well, add the egg yolks and melted butter, and mix well. Gradually stir in the milk, a little at a time, and continue stirring for 10 minutes to make a fairly thick batter. Melt the remaining butter in a small skillet. or frying pan. Pour in a ladleful of the batter and cook until the underside is set. Flip over and cook the second side, then remove from the pan. Continue making fritters in this way until all the batter has been used.

Preheat the oven to 350°F (180°C/Gas Mark 4). To make the filling, put the spinach into a pan with just the water clinging to its leaves after rinsing and cook over low heat, turning occasionally, for 5–10 minutes until wilted. Drain and squeeze out the excess liquid. Put the spinach into a food processor or blender, add the ricotta, and garlic and process until thoroughly combined. Transfer to a bowl and stir in the mascarpone, egg, egg yolk, and nutmeg, and season with salt. Divide the filling among the fritters, roll them up, and put them into an ovenproof dish. Sprinkle with Parmesan and drizzle with the melted butter. Bake for about 30 minutes until golden brown. Serve immediately.

ARTICHOKE CANNELLONI

ARTICHOKE CANNELLONI

CANNELLONI AI CARCIOFI

Preparation time: *30 min*
Cooking time: *55 min*
Serves 4

— 1 quantity Cannelloni
  (see page 216)

For the filling:
— 4 tablespoons (50 g) butter,
  plus extra for greasing
— juice of ½ lemon
— 6 globe artichokes
— 1 small onion, finely chopped
— 1 garlic clove, finely chopped
— 1 tablespoon finely chopped
  fresh flat-leaf parsley
— 2 tablespoons all-purpose
  (plain) flour
— pinch of freshly grated nutmeg
— scant 1 cup (200 ml) beef
  broth stock)
— 1 egg, lightly beaten
— 1 cup (80 g) grated
  Parmesan cheese
— 1 quantity béchamel sauce
  (see Baked Rigatoni, page 124)
— salt and pepper

Preheat the oven to 400°F (200°C/Gas Mark 6) and grease an ovenproof dish with butter. Half-fill a large bowl with water and stir in the lemon juice. Break off the artichoke stalks and remove and discard the coarse outer leaves. Thinly slice, discarding the chokes, then add to the acidulated water to avoid discoloration.

Melt the butter in a pan. Add the onion, garlic, and parsley and cook over low heat, stirring occasionally, for 5 minutes. Drain the artichokes, add to the pan, and cook over medium–low heat, stirring occasionally. Sprinkle in the flour and nutmeg and stir well to mix. Gradually pour in the broth (stock), stirring until smooth and thoroughly combined, and bring to a boil, stirring constantly. Remove the pan from the heat, season the mixture with salt and pepper and leave it to cool slightly. Transfer the mixture to a food processor and process until smooth. Alternatively, push the mixture through a meat grinder (mincer). Transfer the mixture to a bowl, if necessary. Stir in the egg, a little Parmesan, and some of the béchamel sauce.

Spread a little artichoke mixture on each cannelloni square and roll up. Put them into the prepared dish in a single layer, pour the remaining béchamel sauce over, and sprinkle with the remaining Parmesan. Bake for 20–25 minutes, remove from the oven, let stand for 5 minutes, then serve.

CANNELLONI NAPOLETANA

Preparation time: *40 min*
Cooking time: *1 hour 5 min*
Serves 4

— 1 quantity Cannelloni
  (see page 216)
— butter, for greasing
— ⅓ cup (25 g) grated
  pecorino cheese
— olive oil, for drizzling

For the filling:
— 12 ounces (350 g) lean beef
  or pork, or a mixture
— 3 ounces (80 g)
  Neapolitan salami
— 2 tablespoons olive oil
— 3½ ounces (100 g) Italian
  sausage, skinned and cut
  into pieces
— 2 hard-boiled eggs, chopped
— salt and pepper

CANNELLONI NAPOLETANA

CANNELLONI ALLA NAPOLETANA

To make the filling, finely chop the meat with the salami.
Heat the oil in a flameproof shallow earthenware dish.
Add the meat mixture and pieces of sausage, season lightly
with salt and pepper, and cook over low heat, stirring
occasionally, for 30 minutes until thickened. Remove the dish
from the heat and let cool. Preheat the oven to 350°F (180°C/
Gas Mark 4) and grease an ovenproof dish with butter.
Stir the hard-boiled eggs into the cooled meat mixture.
Reserve a quarter of this mixture and divide the rest among
the cannelloni squares, then roll them up. Put the cannelloni
into the prepared dish, spoon the reserved filling over them,
sprinkle with the pecorino, and drizzle with a little olive oil.
Bake for about 20 minutes until golden brown. Remove from
the oven, let stand for 5 minutes, then serve.

The aroma of freshly cooked ragù *(or "meat sauce") is a permanent
feature in Naples, where Neapolitans dedicate a great deal of time
and patience to its preparation, using an earthenware pan to
perfectly blend the various ingredients.*

Preparation time: *40 min*
Cooking time: *1 hour*
Serves 4

— 1 quantity Cannelloni
  (see page 216)

For the filling:
— 14 ounces (400 g) radicchio,
  trimmed and coarse
  leaves removed
— 3 tablespoons butter,
  plus extra for greasing
— 2 tablespoons olive oil
— 1 shallot, finely chopped
— 5 ounces (150 g) ground
  (minced) chicken breast
— 2 tablespoons hot water
— ½ quantity béchamel sauce
  (see Baked Rigatoni, page 124)
— 5 ounces (150 g) fontina
  cheese, thinly sliced
— 2 tablespoons grated
  Parmesan cheese
— salt and pepper

CANNELLONI WITH RADICCHIO CREAM

CANNELLONI ALLA CREMA DI RADICCHIO

Blanch the radicchio leaves in lightly salted boiling water for
2 minutes, then drain, squeeze out the excess liquid, and chop.
Melt the butter with the oil in a shallow pan. Add the shallot
and cook over low heat, stirring occasionally, for 5 minutes.
Stir in the chicken, season with salt and pepper, drizzle with
the hot water, cover, and simmer, stirring occasionally, for
20 minutes. Add the chopped radicchio and cook for another
5 minutes. Preheat the oven to 400°F (200°C/Gas Mark 6) and
grease an ovenproof dish with butter. Spread 1 tablespoon
of the béchamel sauce on each cannelloni square, put a slice
of fontina on top, add a little of the radicchio mixture, and
roll them up. Put the rolls into the prepared dish, pour the
remaining béchamel sauce over, and sprinkle with the Parmesan.
Bake for about 20 minutes until golden brown. Remove from
the oven, let stand for 5 minutes, then serve.

CANNELLONI WITH STRACCHINO AND VEGETABLES

Preparation time: *1 hour*
Cooking time: *1 hour 25 min*
Serves 6

— butter, for greasing
— 1½ quantity Cannelloni
  (see page 216)
— ½ cup (40 g) grated
  Parmesan cheese

For the filling:
— 3 young globe artichokes,
  trimmed
— 2 carrots, sliced
— scant 1 cup (150 g) green
  beans, trimmed
— 2 zucchini (courgettes), sliced
— 4 tablespoons (50 g) butter
— 1 leek, chopped
— 1 firm tomato, cut into strips
— 7 ounces (200 g) stracchino
  cheese
— 1 cup (80 g) grated
  Parmesan cheese
— salt and pepper

For the béchamel sauce:
— scant 1 cup (100 g)
  shelled peas
— 4 tablespoons (50 g) butter
— 4 tablespoons all-purpose
  (plain) flour
— 2½ cups (600 ml)
  lukewarm milk
— salt

To make the filling, blanch the artichokes, carrots, beans, and zucchini (courgettes) in boiling water for a few minutes, then drain. Melt the butter in a pan. Add the leek and cook over low heat, stirring occasionally, for 5 minutes. Season with salt and pepper, add the blanched vegetables, and cook over low heat, stirring occasionally, for 30 minutes. Stir in the tomato, remove the pan from the heat, and let cool. Meanwhile, briefly blanch the peas in boiling water, then drain and stir in half the butter.

Make the béchamel sauce. Melt the butter in a pan. Stir in the flour and cook over medium heat, stirring constantly, for 2–3 minutes until golden brown. Gradually stir in the milk, a little at a time. Bring to a boil, stirring constantly, lower the heat, and simmer gently, stirring constantly, for 20 minutes until thickened and smooth. Remove the pan from the heat and season with salt.

Stir the peas into the béchamel. Stir the stracchino and Parmesan into the cooled vegetable filling.

Preheat the oven to 350°F (180°C/Gas Mark 4) and grease an ovenproof dish with butter. Divide the filling among the cannelloni squares and roll up. Spoon a little of the béchamel sauce over the base of the prepared dish, put the cannelloni on top, and cover with the remaining béchamel sauce. Sprinkle with the grated cheese and bake for about 20 minutes until golden brown. Remove from the oven and let stand for 5 minutes, then serve.

CAPPELLACCI

Cappellacci is a type of fresh egg pasta from the Ferrara area in the northern Italian region of Emilia-Romagna. Known locally as *caplaz*, the name refers to a type of informal cap. Cappellacci is bigger than cappelletti and looks like round ravioli. It is made by placing a small amount of filling in the middle of a square of pasta dough; the pasta dough is then folded in half, and the two opposing corners are joined and pressed closed. The most traditional filling for cappellacci consists of a mixture of pumpkin and Parmesan cheese, served with melted butter and more Parmesan. Cappellacci is also often combined with tomato, meat, or sausage sauces.

Ⓐ

Preparation time: *1 hour 10 min, plus 1 hour resting*
Cooking time: *30 min*
Serves 6

— 4½ cups (500 g) all-purpose (plain) flour, plus extra for dusting
— 5 eggs
— salt

For the filling:
— 1¾ pounds (800 g) pumpkin or butternut squash
— 1 egg
— ½ cup (40 g) grated Parmesan cheese
— pinch of freshly grated nutmeg
— 1–2 tablespoons fresh bread crumbs
— salt and pepper

For the sauce:
— 6 tablespoons (80 g) butter, melted
— ⅔ cup (50 g) grated Parmesan cheese

PUMPKIN CAPPELLACCI

CAPPELLACCI DI ZUCCA

Make the pasta dough. Sift the flour into a mound on a counter and make a well in the middle. Break the eggs into the well and add a pinch of salt. Using your fingers, gradually incorporate the flour into the eggs. Knead thoroughly, shape into a ball, cover with a clean dish towel, and let rest for 1 hour. Meanwhile, make the filling. Preheat the oven to 350°F (180°C/Gas Mark 4). Put the pumpkin or squash on a baking sheet and bake for 20 minutes until softened. Remove from the oven, halve, and scoop out and discard the seeds. Scoop out the flesh and pass it through a strainer into a bowl. Beat in the egg, Parmesan, and nutmeg and season with salt and pepper. Stir well and add bread crumbs if the mixture is too runny. Roll out the dough on a lightly floured counter into a thin sheet and cut out 2½-inch (6-cm) squares. Put a mound of filling in the middle of each and fold the dough in half diagonally to make a triangle, pressing the edges firmly together. Bring the tips of the longest side together, one on top of the other, pressing firmly to seal but without flattening the cappellacci. Cook in plenty of salted boiling water until they rise to the surface and are all dente. Drain, transfer to a warmed serving dish, pour the melted butter over, and sprinkle with Parmesan. Serve immediately.

CAPPELLETTI

Cappelletti is a type of filled pasta originating from the northern Italian region of Emilia-Romagna. It resembles small peaked hats, hence its name, which means "small caps." In the Middle Ages, cappelletti was known as *galoza* and was mentioned as early as the thirteenth century. Cappelletti is made by cutting sheets of dough into 1¼-inch (3-cm) squares and placing a small amount of filling in the middle. The squares are folded into triangles and the two corners are joined at the base and pressed together.

Preparation time: *45 min,*
plus 1 hour resting
Cooking time: *5 min*
Serves *4*

— 1¾ cups (200 g) all-purpose
  (plain) flour, plus extra
  for dusting
— 2 eggs
— 1 tablespoon grated
  Parmesan cheese
— salt

For the sauce:
— 1 quantity tomato sauce
  (see Baked Capellini, page 25)
— butter, for tossing
— grated Parmesan cheese,
  for sprinkling

CAPPELLETTI WITH TOMATO SAUCE

CAPPELLETTI CON SUGO DI POMODORO

Sift the flour into a mound on a counter. Make a well in the middle and break the eggs into it. Add the Parmesan and a pinch of salt. Using your fingers, gradually incorporate the flour into the eggs. Knead quickly to make a smooth, pliable dough. Shape the dough into a ball, cover, and let rest for 1 hour. Roll out into a thin sheet on a lightly floured counter or use a pasta machine. Cut the dough into 1¼-inch (3-cm) squares. Fold the dough in half diagonally to make a triangle, pressing the edges firmly together. Bring the tips of the longest side together, one on top of the other, pressing firmly to seal but without flattening the cappelletti. Cook in plenty of boiling salted water until al dente. Drain, toss with the tomato sauce and butter, and serve immediately sprinkled with the Parmesan.

CAPPELLETTI WITH TOMATO SAUCE

CARAMELLE

Caramelle, so called because of its resemblance to wrapped candies, is a type of filled egg-based pasta. It is made by cutting out 2-inch (5-cm) squares from a sheet of pasta dough, placing a small amount of filling in the middle and rolling up into a tube, then twisting the two sides of the square in opposite directions. Caramelle is typically filled with cheese.

CARAMELLE WITH CREAMY CHEESE FILLING

CARAMELLE ALLA CREMA DI FORMAGGIO

Ⓐ

Preparation time: *1 hour 25 min, plus 1 hour resting*
Cooking time: *10 min*
Serves 4

— 2¼ cups (250 g) all-purpose (plain) flour, plus extra for dusting
— 2 eggs
— melted butter, for brushing

For the filling:
— scant 1 cup (200 g) ricotta cheese
— 3½ ounces (100 g) stracchino cheese, diced
— scant ½ cup (100 g) low-fat cream cheese
— 1 cup (80 g) grated Parmesan cheese
— pinch of freshly grated nutmeg
— salt and pepper

For the sauce:
— 4 tablespoons (50 g) butter, melted
— black truffle, thinly sliced

First make the pasta dough. Sift the flour into a mound on a counter and make a well in the middle. Break the eggs into the well and add a pinch of salt. Using your fingers, gradually incorporate the flour into the eggs. Knead thoroughly, shape into a ball, cover with a clean dish towel, and let rest for 1 hour. Meanwhile, make the filling. Pass the ricotta through a strainer into a bowl, beat in the stracchino, cream cheese, Parmesan, and nutmeg, and season with salt and pepper. Cover and chill in the refrigerator. Roll out the dough into a thin sheet on a lightly floured counter and cut out 2-inch (5-cm) squares with a pasta wheel. Lightly brush the surface of each square with melted butter and put a teaspoon of the cheese mixture on top. Roll up into a tube and twist the ends in opposite directions to resemble a paper-wrapped taffy. Cook the caramelle in plenty of salted boiling water until they rise to the surface and are al dente. Drain and transfer to a warmed serving dish. Pour the melted butter over, garnish with slices of truffle, and serve immediately.

CARAMELLE WITH CREAMY CHEESE FILLING

CASÔNSÈI

Casônsèi dates back to the fourteenth century and is a specialty of Brescia in the Lombardy region of northern Italy. It is also known as *casunzièi* in Belluno, in the northeastern region of Veneto. The name casônsèi comes from the ancient term *cassoncelle*, which probably meant "small caskets." Similar to ravioli, these half-moon-shaped parcels are made of an egg-based dough and can have a variety of fillings. The Renaissance version was bittersweet in taste, combining cinnamon and almonds. In the traditional cuisine of Brescia, casônsèi is typically filled with a mixture of sausage, bread dipped in milk, and grated Parmesan.

Preparation time: *1 hour,*
plus 30 min resting
Cooking time: *20 min*
Serves 4

— 2¾ cups (300 g) all-purpose
  (plain) flour, plus extra
  for dusting
— 3 eggs
— 1 tablespoon olive oil
— salt

For the filling:
— 1 pound 2 ounces (500 g)
  potatoes, diced
— 14 ounces (400 g) Swiss chard,
  stalks removed
— 3 tablespoons butter
— 1 garlic clove, finely chopped
— 1 sprig fresh flat-leaf
  parsley, chopped
— 1 leek, chopped
— 7 ounces (200 g) Italian
  sausage, skinned and chopped
— ¾ cups (100 g) bread crumbs
— generous 1 cup (100 g) grated
  Parmesan cheese
— 1 egg, lightly beaten
— salt and pepper

For the sauce:
— 4 tablespoons (50 g)
  butter, melted
— ⅔ cup (50 g) grated
  Parmesan cheese

CASÔNSÈI FROM VAL CAMONICA

CASÔNSÈI DELLA VAL CAMONICA

Make the pasta dough. Sift the flour into a mound on a counter and make a well in the middle. Break the eggs into the well and add the oil and a pinch of salt. Using your fingers, gradually incorporate the flour into the eggs. Knead to a soft dough, shape into a ball, cover with a clean dish towel, and let rest for 30 minutes.

Meanwhile, make the filling. Cook the potatoes in lightly salted boiling water for 15–20 minutes until tender. Drain and mash. Cook the chard leaves in just enough boiling water to cover for 5–10 minutes until tender. Drain, squeeze out the excess liquid, and chop. Melt the butter in a pan. Add the garlic and parsley and cook over low heat, stirring frequently for a few minutes. Add the leek and sausage and cook, stirring occasionally, for 10 minutes. Remove the pan from the heat and let cool. Combine the sausage mixture, mashed potatoes, chard, bread crumbs, Parmesan, and egg in a bowl and season to taste with salt and pepper.

Roll out the dough into a thin sheet on a lightly floured counter. Cut out rectangles about 3¼ × 6¼ inches (8 x 16 cm). Put a mound of filling on each one, roll the dough up, and press the edges well to seal, then gently bend into a horseshoe shape. Cook the casônsèi in plenty of salted boiling water for 5 minutes until al dente. Drain, transfer to a warmed serving dish, pour the melted butter over them, and sprinkle with Parmesan. Serve immediately.

FAGOTTINI

Fagottini is a type of filled pasta similar to ravioli, whose name means "small bundles" in Italian. It is made by cutting 4½-inch (12-cm) squares out of a sheet of pasta and drawing all four corners up together to create small parcels. This shape is ideally suited to vegetable fillings.

Ⓞ Ⓧ

Preparation time: *25 min*
Cooking time: *25 min*
Serves 4

— 1½ quantity Fresh Pasta
 Dough (see page 139)

For the filling:
— 2 tablespoons butter,
 plus extra for greasing
— 1 onion, chopped
— 1 pound 5 ounces (600 g)
 asparagus spears, trimmed
 and chopped
— 6 ounces (175 g) Gorgonzola
 cheese, crumbled
— 3 ounces (80 g) fontina
 cheese, diced
— salt

For the sauce:
— ½ quantity béchamel sauce
 (see Baked Rigatoni, page 124)
— butter

ASPARAGUS AND CHEESE FAGOTTINI

FAGOTTINI DI PUNTE D'ASPARAGI E FORMAGGI

Preheat the oven to 350°F (180°C/Gas Mark 4) and grease an ovenproof dish with butter. To make the filling, melt the butter in a pan. Add the onion and asparagus and cook over low heat, stirring occasionally, for 15 minutes. Season with salt, remove the pan from the heat, and stir in the Gorgonzola and fontina until thoroughly combined. Cut the pasta dough into long thin strips and then into squares. Briefly blanch in boiling salted water and drain. Put a small mound of the filling on each one and bring the four corners together to make parcels or bundles. Put them into the prepared dish, pour the béchamel over, and dot with the butter. Bake for 20 minutes until golden brown. Serve immediately.

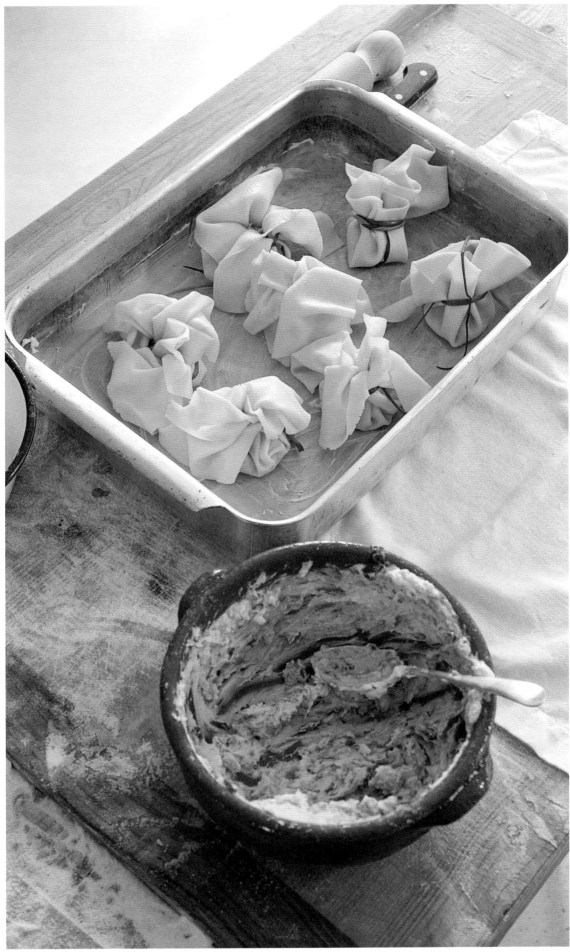

FAGOTTINI WITH PUMPKIN, ONION, AND RAISIN FILLING (PAGE 233)

FAGOTTINI WITH PUMPKIN, ONION, AND RAISIN FILLING

FAGOTTINI WITH PUMPKIN, ONION, AND RAISIN FILLING

FAGOTTINI RIPIENI DI ZUCCA, CIPOLLA, E UVETTA

Preparation time: *1 hour 30 min,*
plus 1 hour resting
Cooking time: *1 hour*
Serves *4*

— 2¼ cups (250 g) all-purpose
(plain) flour, plus extra
for dusting
— 2 eggs
— 16 blanched fresh chives
— butter, for greasing
— salt

For the filling:
— 2 tablespoons raisins
— 1 tablespoon olive oil
— 1½ cups (200 g) peeled,
seeded and diced pumpkin
or butternut squash
— 2 small white onions,
finely chopped
— generous 1 cup (250 g)
ricotta cheese
— 2 teaspoons roughly
chopped chives
— salt

For the béchamel sauce:
— 4 tablespoons (50 g) butter
— ½ cup (50 g) all-purpose
(plain) flour
— 2¼ cups (500 ml) hot milk
— salt and pepper

Make the pasta dough. Sift the flour into a mound on a counter and make a well in the middle. Break the eggs into the well and add a pinch of salt. Using your fingers, gradually incorporate the flour into the eggs. Knead thoroughly, shape into a ball, cover with a clean dish towel, and let rest for 1 hour. Meanwhile, make the filling. Put the raisins into a bowl, pour in hot water to cover, and let soak. Heat the oil in a pan. Add the pumpkin, season with salt and pepper, and cook over low heat, stirring occasionally, for 15 minutes. Add the onions and cook, stirring occasionally, for another 5 minutes. Taste and adjust the seasoning if necessary. Beat the ricotta in a bowl, then stir in the pumpkin and onion mixture. Drain the raisins, squeeze out the excess liquid, and stir into the bowl, along with the chopped chives.

Roll out the dough into a thin sheet on a lightly floured counter and cut into 8 fairly large squares. Cook in plenty of salted boiling water until al dente. Drain and spread out on clean dish towels. Put a generous tablespoon of the filling in the middle of each square, bring the 4 corners together holding them fairly high, and tie at the base with 2 blanched chives.

Preheat the oven to 350°F (180°C/Gas Mark 4) and grease an ovenproof dish with butter. To make the sauce, melt the butter in a pan. Stir in the flour and cook over medium heat, stirring constantly, for 2–3 minutes until golden brown. Gradually stir in the milk, a little at a time. Bring to a boil, stirring constantly, lower the heat, and simmer gently, stirring constantly, for 20 minutes until thickened and smooth. Season with salt and pepper. Put the fagottini in the prepared dish, pour the sauce over, and bake for 10–15 minutes. Remove from the oven and let stand for 5 minutes, then serve.

LASAGNA

The starting point for a huge range of dishes, this large, flat sheet of egg dough cut into strips is considered the basis for all fresh pasta. It was already popular with the Greeks as early as the first millennium BC. The name itself is of Greek origin, from the word *laganon*, referring to a flat sheet of pasta cut into strips. The dough is cut into rectangular sheets measuring 4×8 inches (10 x 20 cm), arranged in layers alternating with sauce, and then baked in the oven. Lasagnette, popular in the northern region of Emilia-Romagna and in central and southern Italy, is a narrower version and is also known as pappardelle in Tuscany. Lasagna itself is popular throughout Italy, but the classic lasagna recipe remains Lasagne alla Bolognese (Lasagna Bolognese, see page 237), which layers pasta, meat sauce, béchamel sauce, and grated Parmesan.

Preparation time: *40 min, plus 15 min resting*
Cooking time: *5 min*
Serves 6
Makes about 12 lasagna sheets

— 2¾ cups (300 g) all-purpose (plain) flour, plus extra for dusting
— 3 eggs
— 1 tablespoon olive oil
— salt

LASAGNA (BASIC RECIPE)

LASAGNE (RICETTA BASE)

Sift the flour into a mound on a counter and make a well in the middle. Break the eggs into the well and add a pinch of salt. Using your fingers, gradually incorporate the flour into the eggs. Knead for about 10 minutes, adding a little flour if it is too soft or a little water if it is too firm. Shape into a ball, cover with a clean dish towel, and let rest for 15 minutes. Roll out into a fairly thick sheet on a lightly floured counter, then cut into 4×8-inch (10 x 20 cm) rectangles. Cook, a few at a time, in plenty of salted boiling water to which the oil has been added, until al dente, then remove, and spread out to dry on clean dish towels.

LASAGNA VERDI (BASIC RECIPE)

LASAGNE VERDI (RICETTA BASE)

Preparation time: *40 min,*
plus 15 min resting
Cooking time: *5 min*
Serves 6
Makes about 12 lasagna sheets

— 2¾ cups (300 g) all-purpose
  (plain) flour, plus extra
  for dusting
— 3 eggs
— 1⅔ cups (150 g) spinach,
  chopped, cooked, and
  squeezed dry
— 1 tablespoon olive oil
— salt

Sift the flour into a mound on a counter and make a well in the center. Break the eggs into the well and add the chopped spinach and a pinch of salt. Using your fingers, gradually incorporate the flour into the eggs. Knead for a few minutes, adding more flour, a little at a time, if the spinach has made the dough too wet. Shape into a ball, cover with a clean dish towel, and let rest for 15 minutes. Roll out into a fairly thick sheet on a lightly floured counter, then cut into 4×8-inch (10 x 20 cm) wide rectangles. Cook, a few at a time, in plenty of salted boiling water to which the oil has been added, until al dente, then remove, and spread out to dry on clean dish towels.

EGGPLANT AND RICOTTA LASAGNA

LASAGNE CON MELANZANE E RICOTTA

Preparation time: *1 hour 15 min*
Cooking time: *50 min*
Serves 4

— 1 quantity Lasagna
  (see opposite)
— 1 large eggplant
  (aubergine), sliced
— butter, for greasing
— ½ cup (50 g) pine nuts,
  chopped
— ⅔ cup (150 g) crumbled
  ricotta cheese
— ½ cup (120 ml) concentrated
  tomato paste (puree)
— 12 fresh basil leaves
— olive oil, for drizzling
— 4 tablespoons grated
  Parmesan cheese
— salt

Put the eggplant (aubergine) slices in a colander, sprinkle with salt, and let drain for 1 hour. Rinse, pat dry, and cook under a preheated broiler until tender. Preheat the oven to 350°F (180°C/Gas Mark 4). Grease an ovenproof dish with butter. Arrange a layer of lasagna sheets on the base of the prepared dish, place half the eggplant slices on top, and sprinkle with half the pine nuts, half the ricotta, 4 tablespoons of the tomato paste (puree) and 6 of the basil leaves. Drizzle with olive oil and repeat the layers. Sprinkle with the Parmesan, bake for about 40 minutes, and serve.

BAKED PUMPKIN PASTA

Preparation time: *1 hour,
plus 30 min soaking,
plus 15 min resting*
Cooking time: *1 hour*
Serves 4

— butter, for greasing
— 7 ounces (200 g) cooked
   pumpkin or canned
   unsweetened pumpkin puree
— 2¾ cups (300 g) all-purpose
   (plain) flour, plus extra
   for dusting
— 1 egg
— salt

For the filling:
— 1 cup (50 g) dried mushrooms
— 2 tablespoons butter
— ½ shallot, chopped
— ½ carrot, chopped
— salt and pepper

For the béchamel sauce:
— 4 tablespoons (50 g) butter
— ½ cup (50 g) all-purpose
   (plain) flour
— 2¼ cups (500 ml)
   lukewarm milk
— salt and pepper

Make the filling. Put the mushrooms into a bowl and pour in hot water to cover. Let soak for 30 minutes, then drain, squeeze out the excess liquid, and chop. Melt the butter in a shallow pan. Add the shallot and carrot and cook over low heat, stirring occasionally, for 5 minutes. Add the mushrooms and cook, stirring occasionally, for 30 minutes. Meanwhile, make the béchamel sauce. Melt the butter in a pan. Stir in the flour and cook over medium heat, stirring constantly, for 2–3 minutes until golden brown. Gradually stir in the milk, a little at a time. Bring to a boil, stirring constantly, lower the heat, and simmer gently, stirring constantly, for 20 minutes until thickened and smooth. Remove the pan from the heat, season with salt and pepper, and stir in the mushroom mixture. Preheat the oven to 400°F (200°C/Gas Mark 6) and grease an ovenproof dish with butter.

Make the pasta dough. Put the cooked pumpkin into a food processor or blender, add a pinch of salt, and process to a puree. Combine the pumpkin puree with the flour and egg and knead well. Shape into a ball, cover with a clean cloth and leave to rest for 15 minutes. Roll out into a thin sheet on a lightly floured counter and cut into 10 rectangles. Cook in plenty of salted boiling water until al dente. Drain and arrange them alternately with the béchamel mixture in the prepared dish. Bake for 10 minutes, then serve.

ARTICHOKE LASAGNETTE

Preparation time: *1 hour 20 min*
Cooking time: *30 min*
Serves 4

— 1 quantity Fresh Pasta Dough
  (see page 139)
— juice of ½ lemon
— 4 globe artichokes
— 4 tablespoons olive oil
— ½ onion, chopped
— 5 ounces (150 g) ham,
  cut into strips
— ⅔ cup (50 g) grated
  Parmesan cheese
— salt

Roll out the dough into a fairly thick sheet on a lightly floured counter, then cut into strips about 2½ inches (6 cm) long and ½ inch (1 cm) wide. Partly fill a bowl with water and stir in the lemon juice. Break off the stems of the artichokes and remove and discard the coarse outer leaves, then slice. As you prepare each artichoke, put it into the acidulated water to prevent discoloration. Heat the oil in a pan. Add the onion and cook over low heat, stirring occasionally, for 5 minutes, until softened. Drain the artichokes, add them to the pan, cover, and cook, stirring occasionally, for 10–15 minutes until tender. Add the strips of ham to the artichoke mixture and sauté, stirring occasionally, for 2 minutes, then remove the pan from the heat. Cook the lasagnette in plenty of salted boiling water until al dente, then drain and toss with the artichoke mixture. Sprinkle with the Parmesan and serve immediately.

LASAGNA BOLOGNESE

Preparation time: *30 min*
Cooking time: *1 hour 20 min*
Serves 4

— 1 quantity Fresh Pasta Dough
  (see page 139)

For the filling:
— 3 tablespoons olive oil
— 1 carrot, chopped
— 1 onion, chopped
— 11 ounces (300 g) ground
  (minced) beef
— scant ½ cup (100 ml)
  dry white wine
— 1 cup (250 ml) pureed
  canned tomatoes (passata)
— 2 tablespoons butter,
  plus extra for greasing
— 1 quantity béchamel sauce
  (see Baked Pumpkin Pasta,
  page 236)
— scant 1 cup (65 g) grated
  Parmesan cheese
— salt and pepper

Heat the olive oil in a pan, add the carrot and onion, and cook over low heat, stirring occasionally, for 5 minutes. Add the meat and cook until browned, then pour in the wine, and cook until the alcohol has evaporated. Season with salt, add the pureed canned tomatoes (passata), and simmer for 30 minutes, then season with pepper. Preheat the oven to 400°F (200°C/Gas Mark 6). Grease an ovenproof dish with butter. Roll out the pasta dough into a thin sheet on a lightly floured counter. Cut into 4 × 8-inch (10 x 20-cm) rectangles and cook, a few at a time, in plenty of lightly salted boiling water for a few minutes. Drain and place on a damp dish towel. Arrange a layer of lasagna on the base of the prepared dish, spoon some of the meat sauce, then some of the béchamel sauce on top, sprinkle with some of the Parmesan, and dot with some of the butter. Repeat the layers until all the ingredients have been used, ending with a layer of béchamel sauce. Bake for 30 minutes.

LASAGNA VERDI WITH PORCINI MUSHROOMS

LASAGNE VERDI AI FUNGHI PORCINI

Preparation time: *25 min*
Cooking time: *50 min*
Serves 6

— 1 quantity Lasagna Verdi
   (see page 235)
— 2 tablespoons butter,
   plus extra for greasing

For the filling:
— 2 tablespoons olive oil
— 2 garlic cloves, lightly crushed
— 2¾ cups (200 g) sliced
   porcini mushrooms
— 1 tablespoon chopped
   fresh thyme
— scant 1 cup (200 ml)
   dry white wine
— pinch of freshly grated nutmeg
— 1 quantity béchamel sauce
   (see Baked Rigatoni, page 124)
— ⅔ cup (50 g) grated Parmesan
   cheese, plus extra for serving
— salt and pepper

To make the filling, heat the oil in a shallow pan. Add the garlic cloves and cook over low heat, stirring frequently, for a few minutes until lightly browned. Remove the garlic with a slotted spoon and discard. Add the mushrooms, sprinkle with the thyme, drizzle with the wine, and cook until the alcohol has evaporated. Season with salt and pepper and simmer, stirring occasionally, for 10 minutes, then remove from the heat. Stir the nutmeg into the béchamel sauce. Preheat the oven to 350°F (180°C/Gas Mark 4) and grease an ovenproof dish with butter. Place a layer of lasagna in the base of the prepared dish, cover with a layer of mushrooms, top with béchamel sauce, and sprinkle with Parmesan. Continue making layers in this way until all the ingredients have been used, ending with a layer of béchamel sauce. Dot with the butter and bake for about 20 minutes until golden brown. Sprinkle Parmesan over and serve immediately.

LASAGNA WITH MUSHROOMS AND PARMESAN CREAM

LASAGNE CON CREMA DI PARMIGIANO E FUNGHI

Preparation time: *40 min*
Cooking time: *1 hour*
Serves 6

— 1 quantity Lasagna
   (see page 234)
— 1 tablespoon butter,
   plus extra for greasing

For the filling:
— 6 tablespoons (80 g) butter
— 4–5 fresh sage leaves
— 4 tablespoons heavy
   (double) cream
— generous 1 cup (100 g) grated
   Parmesan cheese
— 2 tablespoons olive oil
— 1 garlic clove
— 7¼ cups (500 g) chopped
   chanterelle mushrooms
— salt

To make the filling, melt the butter in a pan. Add the sage leaves and cook over low heat until lightly browned, then remove and discard. Pour in the cream and bring just to a boil. Stir in the Parmesan, remove from the heat, and set aside. Heat the oil in another shallow pan. Add the garlic clove and cook over low heat, stirring frequently, until lightly browned. Remove the garlic with a slotted spoon and discard. Add the mushrooms to the pan, season with salt, and cook over low heat, stirring occasionally, for 30 minutes. Meanwhile, preheat the oven to 350°F (180°C/Gas Mark 4) and grease an oven-proof dish with butter. Make a layer of lasagna in the base of the prepared dish, cover with the Parmesan and cream mixture, and top with mushrooms. Continue making layers until all the ingredients have been used, ending with a layer of pasta. Dot with the butter and bake for 20 minutes until golden brown. Remove from the oven and let stand for 5 minutes, then serve.

LASAGNA NAPOLETANA

Preparation time: *1 hour,*
plus 15 min resting
Cooking time: *2 hours 30 min*
Serves 6

— 2¾ cups (300 g) all-purpose
  (plain) flour, preferably Italian
  type 00, plus extra for dusting
— 3 eggs, lightly beaten
— salt

For the filling:
— 5 tablespoons olive oil
— 1 onion, chopped
— 1 carrot, chopped
— 1 celery stalk, chopped
— ½ garlic clove, chopped
— 4 cups (900 g) pureed canned
  tomatoes (passata)
— 5 eggs
— 11 ounces (300 g) ground
  (minced) beef
— ⅔ cup (50 g) grated
  Parmesan cheese
— 3 tablespoons butter,
  plus extra for greasing
— 5 ounces (150 g) mozzarella
  cheese, sliced
— salt and pepper

LASAGNE ALLA NAPOLETANA

For the filling, heat 3 tablespoons of the oil in a pan, add the onion, carrot, celery, and garlic, and cook over low heat, stirring occasionally, for 5 minutes, then add the pureed canned tomatoes (passata). Season with salt and pepper and simmer for about 1 hour. Meanwhile, boil 4 of the eggs for 12 minutes, then plunge into cold water, peel, and slice. Combine the ground (minced) beef, Parmesan, and remaining egg in a bowl and season with salt. Shape the mixture into small balls. Heat 2 tablespoons of the butter and the remaining oil in a skillet or frying pan, add the meatballs, and cook until browned all over, then add them to the tomato sauce.

Make the pasta (see Fresh Pasta Dough, page 139) with the quantities specified and roll out into 2 thin sheets on a lightly floured counter. Cut into 4-inch (10-cm) squares and cook, a few at a time, in plenty of salted boiling water for a few minutes. Drain and place on a damp dish towel. Preheat the oven to 325°F (160°C/Gas Mark 3). Grease a large ovenproof dish with butter, arrange a layer of lasagna on the base, and cover with some of the tomato sauce and meatballs, then the mozzarella, and a few slices of hard-boiled eggs. Repeat the layers until all the ingredients have been used, ending with a layer of tomato sauce. Dot the top with the remaining butter, cover the dish with aluminum foil or baking paper, and bake for about 1 hour. Let stand for 10 minutes before serving.

FRESH PASTA • FILLED

Preparation time: *30 min*
Cooking time: *55 min*
Serves 6

— 1 quantity Lasagna
  (see page 234)
— 2 tablespoons butter,
  plus extra for greasing

For the filling:
— 2 tablespoons butter
— 2 tablespoons olive oil
— 2 garlic cloves
— 3–4 fresh sage leaves
— 1 pound 2 ounces (500 g)
  pumpkin, peeled, seeded,
  and sliced
— 4–5 tablespoons hot water
— ½ quantity béchamel sauce
  (see Baked Rigatoni, page 124)
— pinch of freshly grated nutmeg
— 1 cup (120 g) grated
  Gruyère cheese
— salt and pepper

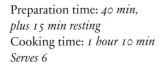

Preparation time: *40 min,
plus 15 min resting*
Cooking time: *1 hour 10 min*
Serves 6

— 2¾ cups (300 g) all-purpose
  (plain) flour, preferably Italian
  type 00, plus extra for dusting
— 3 eggs, lightly beaten
— salt

For the sauce:
— 3 tablespoons heavy
  (double) cream
— 11 ounces (300 g) radicchio,
  cut into strips
— 2 tablespoons butter,
  plus extra for greasing
— 1 quantity béchamel sauce
  (see Baked Pumpkin Pasta,
  page 236)
— salt and pepper

PUMPKIN LASAGNA

LASAGNE ALLA ZUCCA GIALLA

To make the filling, melt the butter with the olive oil in a shallow pan. Add the garlic cloves and sage leaves and cook over low heat, stirring occasionally, for a few minutes until the garlic is lightly browned. Add the pumpkin, cover, and cook, stirring occasionally and adding a little hot water as required, for 30 minutes. Remove and discard the garlic and sage. Remove the pan from the heat and mash the pumpkin with a fork, then mix with the béchamel sauce. Stir in the nutmeg and season to taste with salt and pepper. Preheat the oven to 350°F (180°C/Gas Mark 4) and grease an ovenproof dish with butter. Make a layer of lasagna in the base of the prepared dish, spoon a layer of the pumpkin mixture on top, and sprinkle with Gruyère. Continue making layers in this way until all the ingredients have been used, ending with a layer of lasagna. Dot with butter and bake for 20 minutes until light golden brown. Remove from the oven and let stand for 5 minutes, then serve.

RADICCHIO LASAGNA

LASAGNE DI RADICCHIO

Make the pasta (see Fresh Pasta Dough, page 139) with the quantities specified. Heat the cream in a pan over low heat, stir in the radicchio, add the butter, and cook until the radicchio is soft. Stir in the béchamel sauce and season with salt and pepper to taste. Preheat the oven to 300°F (150°C/Gas Mark 2). Grease an ovenproof dish with butter. Cook the lasagna sheets, a few at a time, in a large pan of salted boiling water until al dente, drain, and place on a damp dish towel to cool. Place a layer of lasagna on the base of the prepared dish and top with a layer of radicchio sauce. Continue making alternate layers until all the ingredients have been used, ending with a layer of radicchio sauce. Bake for 30 minutes, then serve.

THREE-COLOR RICOTTA LASAGNA

SEAFOOD LASAGNA

Preparation time: *40 min*
Cooking time: *30 min*
Serves 6

— 1 quantity Lasagna
   (see page 234)

For the filling:
— 2 canned tomatoes,
   drained and chopped
— 3 ounces (80 g) pesto
   (see Trenette with Pesto,
   page 206)
— 2 tablespoons olive oil
— 7 ounces (200 g) shelled
   scallops
— 2½ cups (600 ml) dry
   white wine
— ½ bunch snipped fresh chives
— 1 cup (250 ml) heavy
   (double) cream
— ½ cup (40 g) grated mild
   pecorino cheese
— 7 ounces (200 g) crab meat,
   drained if canned
— salt and pepper

For the filling, combine the tomatoes and pesto in a bowl. Heat the oil in a shallow pan over low heat. Add the scallops and cook for 2 minutes on each side. Remove from the pan and keep warm. Pour the wine into the pan, increase the heat to medium–high, and cook until reduced by half. Stir in the chives and cream and cook until reduced by half again. Meanwhile, preheat the oven to 350°F (180°C/Gas Mark 4). Remove the pan from the heat, stir in the pecorino and crab meat, and season with salt and pepper. Make a layer of lasagna sheets in the base of an ovenproof dish, spoon some of the crab filling on top, and cover with a layer of seared scallops. Continue making layers in this way until all the ingredients have been used, ending with a layer of pasta. Cover with the pesto and tomato mixture. Turn off the oven and let the lasagna heat through in the oven for 10 minutes, then serve.

THREE-COLOR RICOTTA LASAGNA

Ⓦ

Preparation time: *30 min*
Cooking time: *20 min*
Serves 6

— 1 quantity Lasagna
   (see page 234)
— 5 tablespoons (65 g) butter,
   plus extra for greasing

For the filling:
— 2 cups (450 g) ricotta cheese
— 3 ounces (80 g) cooked
   spinach, drained and pureed
— 1 cup (250 ml) pureed canned
   tomatoes (passata)
— 1 cup (80 g) grated
   pecorino cheese
— salt and pepper

To make the filling, press the ricotta through a strainer into a bowl and beat well with a pinch of salt and pepper. Put one-third of the ricotta into another bowl and beat in the spinach puree. Put half the remaining ricotta into another bowl and beat in the pureed canned tomatoes (passata). Leave the remaining ricotta plain. Preheat the oven to 350°F (180°C/Gas Mark 4) and grease an ovenproof dish with butter. Make a layer of lasagna in the base of the prepared dish, spread the spinach and ricotta mixture on top, and sprinkle with grated pecorino. Make another layer of lasagna, spread the white ricotta on top and sprinkle with grated pecorino. Make a final layer of lasagna, spread the ricotta and tomato mixture on top, and sprinkle with the remaining pecorino. Dot with butter and bake for 20 minutes. Serve immediately.

VINCISGRASSI

VINCISGRASSI

Preparation time: *1 hour,
plus 15 min resting*
Cooking time: *1 hour 30 min*
Serves 6–8

— butter, for greasing
— 3 cups (350 g) all-purpose
(plain) flour, preferably Italian
type 00, plus extra for dusting
— generous 1 cup (200 g)
semolina flour
— 3 tablespoons Vin Santo
or Marsala
— 3 eggs, lightly beaten
— salt

For the filling:
— ½ cup (25 g) dried mushrooms
— 3½ ounces (100 g) sweetbreads,
soaked in several changes of
water for 5 hours or overnight
— 4 tablespoons (50 g) butter
— 2 tablespoons olive oil
— ½ onion, chopped
— 1 black truffle, diced
— 2 tablespoons chicken
broth (stock)
— 1 skinless chicken breast fillet,
cut into strips
— 7 ounces (200 g) chicken
giblets, trimmed and chopped
— 5 tablespoons dry Marsala
— 1 cup (80 g) grated
Parmesan cheese
— 1 quantity béchamel sauce
(see Baked Pumpkin Pasta,
page 236)
— salt and pepper

Preheat the oven to 350°F (180°C/Gas Mark 4). Grease an oven-proof dish with butter. For the filling, put the mushrooms in a bowl, add hot water to cover, and let soak for 20 minutes, then drain, squeeze dry, and chop. Blanch the sweetbreads in boiling water for a few minutes, drain, let cool, then dice.

Melt half the butter in a skillet or frying pan, add the sweetbreads, and cook, stirring occasionally, for a few minutes. Heat the remaining butter with the oil in another pan, add the onion, and cook over low heat, stirring occasionally, for 5 minutes, then stir in the mushrooms, truffle, and broth (stock). Add the chicken strips and cook over high heat until browned, then add the giblets and cook for a few minutes more. Pour in the Marsala, lower the heat, and cook until half the wine has evaporated. Pour in just enough hot water to cover, season with salt and pepper, cover, and cook over low heat for about 30 minutes, then add the sweetbreads.

Make the pasta dough (see Fresh Pasta Dough, page 139) with the ingredients specified, then roll out into a thin sheet on a lightly floured counter, and cut into strips about 4 inches (10 cm) wide and 20 inches (50 cm) long. Bring a large pan of salted water to a boil, add the pasta strips, and boil for a few minutes until half-cooked, then remove, and plunge into a bowl of cold water. Drain the pasta and spread out on a damp dish towel. Overlap pasta strips in the base of the prepared dish to cover the base, allowing the excess to overhang the sides. Cut the remaining strips into rectangles.

Fill the dish with alternate layers of filling and pasta, sprinkled with Parmesan and tablespoonfuls of béchamel sauce, ending with a layer of béchamel sauce. Fold over the overhanging ends of the pasta strips to make a pie. Place the dish in a roasting pan, add hot water to the pan to come about halfway up the sides of the dish, and bake for 30 minutes.

VINCISGRASSI

PANSOTTI

Pansotti, a specialty of the city of Genoa in Liguria in northwest Italy, is a type of filled pasta that looks like large triangular ravioli. The word *pansotti* means "pot-bellied" in Italian. Pansotti is made from 2-inch (5-cm) squares of pasta, which are folded over to make a triangle. The edges may be either straight or serrated, and pansotti is typically served with a walnut sauce.

GENOESE PANSOTTI

Preparation time: *1 hour 15 min, plus 30 min resting*
Cooking time: *20 min*
Serves 6

— 3½ cups (400 g) all-purpose (plain) flour, preferably Italian type 00, plus extra for dusting
— 1 tablespoon dry white wine
— 2 tablespoons butter, diced
— ⅔ cup (50 g) grated Parmesan cheese
— salt

For the filling:
— 2¼ pounds (1 kg) borage, escarole, Swiss chard, or turnip tops (greens)
— ½ garlic clove
— scant 1 cup (200 g) ricotta cheese
— 2 eggs, lightly beaten
— 4–6 tablespoons grated Parmesan cheese

For the sauce:
— 1 slice bread, crusts removed
— 2 tablespoons milk
— 1¾ cups (200 g) shelled walnuts
— ½ garlic clove
— ⅔ cup (150 ml) olive oil

PANSOTTI ALLA GENOVESE

Make the pasta dough (see Fresh Pasta Dough, page 139) with the flour, 5 tablespoons water, the wine, and a pinch of salt. To make the filling, cook the greens in salted boiling water for 5 minutes or until tender. Drain, reserve some of the water, squeeze the greens dry, and chop the greens with the garlic, then mix with the ricotta, eggs, and enough Parmesan to thicken the mixture. Roll out the pasta dough into a thin sheet on a lightly floured counter and place mounds of the filling at regular intervals on top. Cut the dough into squares around each mound, then fold them in half. To make the sauce, tear the bread into pieces, place in a bowl, add the milk, and let soak. Blanch the walnuts in boiling water and peel off the skins. Squeeze out the bread. Pound the walnuts, garlic, and bread in a mortar and gradually whisk in the oil to make a runny sauce. If necessary, add 1–2 tablespoons of the cooking water from the greens. Cook the pansotti in a large pan of salted boiling water until al dente, then drain and transfer to a warmed serving dish. Add the walnut sauce, the butter, and Parmesan, mix well, and serve.

In Liguria in northwest Italy, there are numerous variations on this traditional dish. Pansotti can vary in shape and are found as squares, triangles, half-moons, or tortelloni (see page 273), but they are always served with a walnut sauce.

RAVIOLI

Square, rectangular, or half-moon-shaped, ravioli is a popular type of filled pasta. Ravioli is also the generic name for all bite-size pasta shapes with fillings. Ravioli ranges in size from the small raviolini to the large raviolone, but commonly consists of 1¼-inch (3-cm) squares. It is made by placing portions of filling on a sheet of dough, laying another sheet over it, and then cutting the pieces out using a serrated pasta wheel. The filling has changed over the centuries—wild herbs have been replaced by escarole, borage, chard, or spinach, and pecorino cheese has often been replaced by Parmesan. Ravioli is usually served with melted butter or simple sauces with aromatic herbs, and with grated cheese on top. It can also be served in broth (stock).

RAVIOLI WITH WHITE TRUFFLE

RAVIOLI AL TARTUFO BIANCO

Preparation time: *1 hour,*
plus 30 min resting
Cooking time: *8 min*
Serves *4*

— 2¾ cups (300 g) all-purpose (plain) flour, plus extra for dusting
— 3 eggs
— salt

For the filling:
— 1½ cups (350 g) ricotta cheese
— ⅔ cup (50 g) grated Parmesan cheese
— 1 egg
— 2 pinches of freshly grated nutmeg
— salt and pepper

For the sauce:
— 6 tablespoons (80 g) butter, melted
— 1 white truffle, shaved

Sift the flour into a mound on a counter and make a well in the middle. Break the eggs into the well and add a pinch of salt. Using your fingers, gradually incorporate the flour into the eggs. Knead thoroughly and form the dough into a ball. Cover with a clean dish towel and let rest for 30 minutes. Meanwhile, make the filling. Push the ricotta through a strainer into a large bowl, beat in the Parmesan, egg, and nutmeg, and season with salt and pepper.

Roll out the dough into a thin sheet on a lightly floured counter. Put small mounds of the filling in an even row over the bottom half of the pasta sheet. Fold the top half of the dough sheet over and press around the filling with your fingers to seal. Cut out the ravioli and press the edges firmly together. Cook in plenty of salted boiling water until the ravioli rise to the surface and are al dente. Using a slotted spoon, transfer to a warmed serving dish, pour the melted butter over, and sprinkle with the truffle shavings. Serve immediately.

FISH RAVIOLI

Preparation time: *1 hour 15 min, plus 30 min resting*
Cooking time: *25 min*
Serves 4

— 3½ cups (400 g) all-purpose (plain) flour, preferably Italian type 00, plus extra for dusting
— 4 eggs
— 2 tablespoons olive oil
— beaten egg, for brushing
— salt

For the filling:
— 1¾ pounds (800 g) mixed small oily fish such as anchovies and sardines
— 7 ounces (200 g) bread, crusts removed
— 2 tablespoons olive oil
— ½ onion, chopped
— scant ½ cup (100 ml) white wine
— salt and pepper

To serve:
— 6 tablespoons (80 g) butter
— chopped fresh flat-leaf parsley, to garnish

Make a fairly firm pasta dough (see Fresh Pasta Dough, page 139) with the quantities specified. Cover with a damp dish towel and let rest for 30 minutes. Meanwhile, make the filling. Rub off the scales of the fish with your fingers or the back of a knife and rinse under cold running water. Cut the head off each fish. Gently squeeze the belly until the guts protrude, trap them with a knife, and pull them out. Rinse well, then slit open the belly of each fish and place, skin side up, on a cutting (chopping) board. Press firmly along the backbone with your fingers until the fish is flat. Turn it over and gently pull out the bones, snipping the backbone at the tail end with kitchen scissors. Chop the flesh.

Tear the bread into pieces, put into a bowl and pour in water to cover. Let soak. Heat the oil in a skillet or frying pan. Add the onion and cook over low heat, stirring occasionally, for 8–10 minutes until lightly browned. Add the fish and cook, stirring occasionally, for 2–3 minutes. Pour in the wine and cook for a few minutes until the alcohol has evaporated. Squeeze out the bread and stir into the pan. Season with salt and pepper, remove the pan from the heat, and let cool.

Roll out the pasta dough into a thin sheet on a lightly floured counter or use a pasta machine. Put small mounds—about 1 teaspoon—of the filling in an even row spaced about 1½ inches (4 cm) apart on the bottom half of the sheet. Brush the spaces between the filling with beaten egg and fold over the top half of the sheet. Press down around the filling, pushing out any air. Using a ravioli cutter or sharp knife, cut into squares. Cook the ravioli in plenty of salted boiling water until they rise to the surface and are al dente, remove from the pan, and drain. Melt the butter in a pan, add the ravioli, and toss gently over low heat for a few minutes. Tip into a warmed serving dish, sprinkle with the parsley, and serve immediately.

BUTTERED EGGPLANT RAVIOLI

Preparation time: *1 hour,*
plus 30 min resting
Cooking time: *1 hour 15 min*
Serves 4

— 2¾ cups (300 g) all-purpose
    (plain) flour, plus extra
    for dusting
— 3 eggs
— salt

For the filling:
— 1 pound 2 ounces (500 g)
    eggplants (aubergines), sliced
— 2 tablespoons butter
— 2 tablespoons olive oil
— 1 onion, chopped
— 2 garlic cloves, chopped
— 7 ounces (200 g) tomatoes,
    blanched, peeled, and diced
— 6 fresh basil leaves, torn
— ½ cup (40 g) grated
    Parmesan cheese
— salt

For the sauce:
— 3 tablespoons butter
— ½ cup (40 g) grated
    Parmesan cheese

Preheat the oven to 200°F (100°C/Gas Low). Put the eggplants (aubergines) into an ovenproof dish, sprinkling salt between each layer, and dry out in the oven for 30 minutes. Meanwhile, make the pasta dough. Sift the flour into a mound on a counter and make a well in the middle. Break the eggs into the well and add a pinch of salt. Using your fingers, gradually incorporate the flour into the eggs. Knead thoroughly, shape into a ball, cover with a clean dish towel, and let rest for 30 minutes.

Remove the eggplant from the oven and leave until cool enough to handle, then peel and finely chop the flesh. Melt the butter with the oil in a shallow pan. Add the onion and garlic and cook over low heat, stirring occasionally, for 5 minutes. Add the tomatoes and simmer, stirring occasionally, for 15 minutes. Add the eggplant flesh and cook for about 10 minutes until thickened. Remove the pan from the heat and stir in the basil and Parmesan.

Roll out the pasta dough into a thin sheet on a lightly floured counter. Put small mounds of the filling in an even row over the bottom half of the pasta sheet. Fold over the top half and press around the filling with your fingers to seal. Cut out the ravioli and press the edges together firmly. Cook in plenty of salted boiling water until the ravioli rise to the surface and are al dente. Drain and transfer to a pan with the butter and Parmesan, heat gently, and serve.

ZUCCHINI AND ALMOND RAVIOLI

Preparation time: *1 hour 20 min, plus 1 hour resting*
Cooking time: *1 hour 10 min*
Serves 6

— 2¾ cups (300 g) all-purpose (plain) flour, plus extra for dusting
— 3 eggs
— a pinch of dried marjoram
— salt

For the filling:
— 2 tablespoons olive oil
— 3 shallots, chopped
— 4⅔ cups (800 g) grated zucchini (courgettes)
— 2 sprigs fresh marjoram, chopped
— 1 cup (80 g) grated Parmesan cheese
— ½ cup (50 g) ground almonds
— 2 eggs, lightly beaten
— 3 tablespoons fresh bread crumbs
— pinch of freshly grated nutmeg
— salt and pepper

For the sauce:
— 5 zucchini (courgettes)
— 6 tablespoons (80 g) chilled butter
— 2 tablespoons olive oil
— 1 shallot, chopped
— 2 tablespoons heavy (double) cream
— 2 sprigs fresh marjoram, chopped
— ¼ cup (25 g) lightly toasted slivered almonds
— 4 torn fresh basil leaves
— ⅔ cup (50 g) grated Parmesan cheese
— salt and pepper

Make the pasta dough. Sift the flour into a mound on a counter and make a well in the middle. Break the eggs into the well and add the marjoram and a pinch of salt. Using your fingers, gradually incorporate the flour into the eggs. Knead thoroughly, shape into a ball, cover with a clean dish towel, and let rest for 1 hour.

Meanwhile, make the filling. Heat the oil with 4 tablespoons water in a shallow pan. Add the shallots and cook over low heat, stirring occasionally, for 5 minutes. Add the grated zucchini (courgettes) and cook, stirring occasionally, for 15 minutes until tender and dry. Season with salt and pepper and stir in the marjoram. Transfer to a bowl and stir in the Parmesan, ground almonds, eggs, bread crumbs, and nutmeg.

Make the sauce. Using a citrus zester, cut long, thin strips of peel from 3 of the zucchini. Melt 2 tablespoons of the butter in a pan. Add the zucchini peel strips, season with salt and pepper, and cook over low heat, shaking the pan occasionally and taking care not to break them, for a few minutes until softened. Remove the pan from the heat. Dice all the zucchini. Heat the oil in a shallow pan. Add the shallot and cook over low heat, stirring occasionally, for 5 minutes. Add the diced zucchini, pour in water to cover, season with salt and pepper, and bring to a boil over medium heat. Lower the heat and simmer for 15 minutes. Stir in the cream and simmer for another 5 minutes. Remove the pan from the heat and add the marjoram. Transfer the mixture to a food processor and process to a puree. Return the sauce to the rinsed-out pan and reheat gently.

Roll out the pasta dough on a lightly floured counter into a thin sheet or use a pasta machine. Put small mounds of the filling in an even row over the bottom half of the pasta sheet. Fold over the top half of the sheet and press around the filling with your fingers to seal. Cut out the ravioli and press the edges together firmly. Cook the ravioli in plenty of salted boiling water until they rise to the surface and are al dente. Drain, add to the pan with the sauce, and mix gently over the heat. Transfer the mixture to a warmed serving dish and garnish with the strips of zucchini peel, toasted almonds, pieces of cold butter, basil leaves, and Parmesan. Serve immediately.

CHANTERELLE AND THYME RAVIOLI

CHANTERELLE AND THYME RAVIOLI

RAVIOLI DI GALLINACCI AL TIMO

Preparation time: *1 hour 15 min,*
plus 1 hour resting
Cooking time: *35 min*
Serves 4

— 2¾ cups (300 g) all-purpose
  (plain) flour, plus extra
  for dusting
— 2 eggs
— 2 egg yolks
— 1 tablespoon olive oil
— salt

For the filling:
— 2 tablespoons olive oil
— 1 onion, chopped
— 1 garlic clove, finely chopped
— pinch of fresh thyme
— 7¼ cups (500 g) chopped
  chanterelle mushrooms
— ⅔ cup (50 g) grated
  Parmesan cheese
— salt and pepper

For the sauce:
— 4 tablespoons (50 g) butter
— 1 tablespoon chopped
  fresh thyme
— ½ cup (40 g) grated
  Parmesan cheese

Make the pasta dough. Sift the flour into a mound on a counter and make a well in the middle. Break 1 egg into the well and add the egg yolks, oil, and a pinch of salt. Using your fingers, gradually incorporate the flour into the eggs. Knead thoroughly, shape into a ball, cover with a clean dish towel, and let rest for 1 hour.

Meanwhile, make the filling. Heat the oil in a shallow pan. Add the onion and garlic and cook over low heat, stirring occasionally, for 5 minutes. Add the thyme and mushrooms, season with salt, and cook, stirring occasionally, for 20 minutes. Remove from the heat and let cool. Break up the cooled mixture, stir in the cheese, and season with salt and pepper.

Lightly beat the remaining egg in a bowl. Roll out the dough into a thin sheet on a lightly floured counter and cut out 3¼-inch (8-cm) circles. Brush the surface of each with beaten egg, place a little filling on top, and fold the circles in half, pressing the edges to seal. Cook the ravioli in plenty of salted boiling water until they rise to the surface and are al dente. Meanwhile, make the sauce. Melt the butter in a shallow pan and stir in the thyme. Drain the ravioli, tip into the sauce, and toss lightly. Transfer to a warmed serving dish and serve immediately, handing the Parmesan separately.

ONION RAVIOLI

RAVIOLI ALLA CIPOLLA

Preparation time: *1 hour 10 min,*
plus 30 min resting
Cooking time: *20 min*
Serves 4–6

— 3½ cups (400 g) all-purpose
  (plain) flour, plus extra
  for dusting
— 4 eggs
— salt

For the filling:
— 4 tablespoons (50 g) butter
— 1 pound 2 ounces (500 g)
  onions, chopped
— 1 tablespoon chopped fresh
  pennyroyal or mint
— generous 1 cup (100 g)
  grated pecorino cheese

To serve:
— 1 cup (250 ml) pureed
  canned tomatoes (passata)
— grated pecorino cheese
— pepper

Sift the flour into a mound on a counter and make a well in the middle. Break the eggs into the well and add a pinch of salt. Using your fingers, gradually incorporate the flour into the eggs. Knead thoroughly, shape into a ball, cover with a clean dish towel, and let rest for 30 minutes. Meanwhile, make the filling. Melt the butter in a pan. Add the onions and cook over low heat, stirring occasionally, for 10 minutes until softened. Remove from the heat, sprinkle with the pennyroyal or mint and the pecorino, and mix well. Divide the pasta dough in half and roll out each piece into a thin sheet on a lightly floured counter. Put small mounds of the filling in an even row on one sheet. Lay the second sheet on top and press around the filling with your fingers to seal. Using a ravioli cutter, stamp out square ravioli. Dust them lightly with flour and let rest for 15 minutes. Put the pureed canned tomatoes (passata) into a heatproof bowl set over a pan of simmering water to heat through. Cook the ravioli in plenty of salted boiling water until they rise to the surface and are al dente. Remove with a slotted spoon and transfer to a warmed serving dish. Pour the tomatoes over, sprinkle with the pecorino, season with pepper, and serve.

RICOTTA RAVIOLI WITH ZUCCHINI AND THYME

RAVIOLI DI RICOTTA CON ZUCCHINE E TIMO

Preparation time: *15 min*
Cooking time: *20 min*
Serves 4

— 14 ounces (400 g) ready-made
  ricotta ravioli

For the sauce:
— 3 tablespoons butter
— 2 zucchini (courgettes), diced
— 1 tablespoon chopped
  fresh thyme
— 3 tablespoons heavy (double)
  cream
— salt

To make the sauce, melt the butter in a shallow pan. Add the zucchini (courgettes) and cook over low heat, stirring occasionally, for a few minutes. Sprinkle with the thyme and drizzle with the cream, season with salt, and simmer, stirring occasionally, for 15 minutes. Cook the ravioli in plenty of salted boiling water until they rise to the surface and are al dente. Remove with a slotted spoon, add to the pan with the zucchini, and stir. Transfer to a warmed serving dish and serve immediately.

POTATO AND PORCINI
MUSHROOM RAVIOLI

Preparation time: *1 hour 10 min,
plus 1 hour resting*
Cooking time: *30 min*
Serves 6

— 3½ cups (400 g) all-purpose
(plain) flour, plus extra
for dusting
— 4 eggs
— salt

For the filling:
— 12 ounces (350 g)
potatoes, diced
— 3 tablespoons butter
— 3 tablespoons olive oil
— 2¾ cups (200 g) chopped
porcini mushrooms
— 1 garlic clove
— 1 sprig fresh rosemary
— 1 egg, lightly beaten
— ½ cup (40 g) grated
Parmesan cheese
— ⅓ cup (50 g) smoked pancetta
or bacon, finely diced
— salt and pepper

For the sauce:
— 3½ ounces (100 g) spinach,
coarse stalks removed
— 1 cup (250 ml) vegetable
broth (stock)
— 1 tablespoon mascarpone cheese
— 1 sprig fresh thyme, chopped
— salt and pepper

To serve:
— ½ cup (50 g) chilled
butter, diced
— ⅔ cup (50 g) grated
Parmesan cheese

Make the pasta dough. Sift the flour into a mound on a counter and make a well in the middle. Break the eggs into the well and add a pinch of salt. Using your fingers, gradually incorporate the flour into the eggs. Knead thoroughly, shape into a ball, cover with a clean dish towel, and let rest for 1 hour.

Meanwhile, make the filling. Cook the potatoes in lightly salted boiling water for about 15 minutes until just tender, then drain. Meanwhile, melt 1 tablespoon of the butter with 1 tablespoon of the oil in a skillet or frying pan. Add the mushrooms and cook over medium–high heat, stirring frequently, for 10 minutes. Remove from the pan with a slotted spoon and set aside. Melt the remaining butter with the remaining oil in a pan. Add the drained potatoes, the garlic, and rosemary and cook over low heat, stirring occasionally, for 5 minutes. Remove from the heat and remove and discard the garlic and rosemary. Put the potatoes and mushrooms into a food processor and process until thoroughly combined. Transfer to a bowl and stir in the egg, Parmesan, and pancetta or bacon, and season with salt and pepper.

Roll out the dough into a thin sheet on a lightly floured counter. Put small mounds of the filling in an even row over the bottom half of the pasta sheet. Fold over the top half of the sheet and press around the filling with your fingers to seal. Cut out the ravioli and press the edges together firmly. Make the sauce. Put the spinach into a pan with just the water clinging to the leaves after washing and cook, turning occasionally, for 5–10 minutes until wilted. Drain and squeeze out the excess liquid, then put into the food processor with the broth (stock) and mascarpone, season with salt and pepper, and process. Cook the ravioli in plenty of salted boiling water until they rise to the surface and are al dente, then drain. Pour a scant ½ cup (100 ml) water into a pan, add the thyme and ravioli, season with salt, and cook for 30 seconds. Pour in the spinach puree, stir, and serve garnished with pieces of chilled butter and sprinkled with Parmesan.

RAVIOLI WITH CASTELMAGNO

Preparation time: *1 hour 10 min,
plus 1 hour resting*
Cooking time: *25 min*
Serves 6

— 2¾ cups (300 g) all-purpose
    (plain) flour, plus extra
    for dusting
— 3 eggs
— salt

For the filling:
— 7 ounces (200 g) diced
    Castelmagno cheese
— ¼ cup (50 ml) milk
— scant ½ cup (100 g)
    ricotta cheese
— ½ cup (40 g) grated
    Parmesan cheese
— 3 egg yolks
— salt

For the sauce:
— 4 tablespoons (50 g) butter
— scant ½ cup (100 ml)
    vegetable broth (stock)
— ½-ounce (15 g) truffle paste

To serve:
— ½ white truffle
— grated Parmesan cheese

Make the pasta dough. Sift the flour into a mound on a counter and make a well in the middle. Break the eggs into the well and add a pinch of salt. Using your fingers, gradually incorporate the flour into the eggs. Knead thoroughly, shape into a ball, cover with a clean dish towel, and let rest for 1 hour. Meanwhile, make the filling. Put the Castelmagno into a heatproof bowl, pour in the milk, and set over a pan of simmering water until softened. Remove from the heat and stir in the ricotta, Parmesan, and egg yolks, then season with salt and let cool.

Roll out the dough into a thin sheet on a lightly floured counter. Put small mounds of the filling in an even row over the bottom half of the pasta sheet. Fold over the top half of the sheet and press around the filling with your fingers to seal. Cut out the ravioli and press the edges together firmly. Make the sauce. Melt the butter in a pan. Add the broth (stock) and truffle paste and simmer, stirring occasionally, until thickened. Cook the ravioli in plenty of salted boiling water until they rise to the surface and are al dente. Drain, transfer to the pan with the sauce, and toss for 1 minute. Transfer to a warmed serving dish and serve sprinkled with truffle shavings. Hand the Parmesan separately.

This recipe is from the Piedmont region in northwest Italy and uses the very best of fall (autumn) produce, particularly truffles. This precious ingredient can be used in a multitude of dishes, from salads and risotto to filled pasta and fondues.

RAVIOLI WITH CASTELMAGNO

RAVIOLI NAPOLETANA

RAVIOLI ALLA NAPOLETANA

Preparation time: *45 min,*
plus 30 min resting
Cooking time: *20 min*
Serves 6

— 2¾ cups (300 g) all-purpose
  (plain) flour, preferably Italian
  type 00, plus extra for dusting
— 3 eggs, lightly beaten
— salt

For the filling:
— scant ½ cup (100 g) ricotta
  cheese
— 1 egg, lightly beaten
— 1 tablespoon chopped
  fresh flat-leaf parsley
— generous 1 cup (100 g)
  grated Parmesan cheese
— generous ½ cup (100 g)
  cooked ham, finely chopped
— 3½ ounces (100 g) mozzarella
  cheese, diced
— 1 quantity tomato sauce
  (see Baked Capellini, page 25)

To serve
— ½ cup (40 g) grated
  Parmesan cheese

Make the pasta dough (see Fresh Pasta Dough, page 139) with the quantities specified, cover with a damp dish towel, and let rest for 30 minutes. Meanwhile, beat the ricotta in a bowl with a wooden spoon, then stir in the egg, parsley, Parmesan, ham and mozzarella. Roll out the pasta dough into a thin sheet on a lightly floured counter and place mounds of the filling at regular intervals on the bottom half of the sheet. Fold over the top half of the dough and press around the filling with your fingers to seal. Cook the ravioli in a large pan of salted boiling water until they rise to the surface and are al dente. Drain, toss with the tomato sauce, transfer to a warmed serving dish, and serve with Parmesan.

RAVIOLI WITH DUCK FILLING

RAVIOLI CON RIPIENO D'ANATRA

Preparation time: *1 hour 50 min,*
plus 1 hour resting
Cooking time: *2 hours 10 min*
Serves 6

— 4½ cups (500 g) all-purpose
  (plain) flour, plus extra
  for dusting
— 5 eggs
— salt

For the filling:
— 6-pound duckling,
  thawed if frozen
— 1 sprig fresh rosemary
— 2 fresh sage leaves
— 2 bay leaves
— 2 tablespoons butter
— 2 tablespoons olive oil
— scant ½ cup (100 ml) brandy
— 2 ounces bread, crusts removed
— scant ½ cup (100 ml) milk

Preheat the oven to 400°F (200°C/Gas Mark 6). To make the filling, season the duckling with salt and pepper and put into a casserole with the rosemary, sage leaves, bay leaves, butter, and oil. Roast, drizzling occasionally with the brandy, for about 2 hours.

Meanwhile, make the pasta dough. Sift the flour into a mound on a counter and make a well in the middle. Break the eggs into the well and add a pinch of salt. Using your fingers, gradually incorporate the flour into the eggs. Knead thoroughly, shape into a ball, cover with a clean dish towel, and let rest for 1 hour.

To finish the filling, tear the bread into pieces, put it into a bowl, pour in the milk, and let soak. When the duckling is cooked, remove it from the oven. Reserve the cooking juices. Remove and discard the skin. Chop the meat from the breast, wings, and legs, and put it into a bowl. Squeeze out the bread

— generous ½ cup
  chopped prosciutto
— 1 egg, lightly beaten
— ⅔ cup (50 g) grated
  Parmesan cheese
— pinch of freshly grated nutmeg
— salt and pepper

For the sauce:
— ⅔ cup chicken broth (stock)
— grated zest of 1 orange
— 2 tablespoons butter
— ⅔ cup (50 g) grated
  Parmesan cheese

and add it to the bowl with the prosciutto, egg, Parmesan, and nutmeg. Mix together well.

Roll out the dough into a thin sheet on a lightly floured counter. Put small mounds of the filling in an even row over the bottom half of the pasta sheet. Fold over the top half of the sheet and press around the filling with your fingers to seal. Cut out the ravioli with a ravioli cutter and press the edges together firmly. To make the sauce, strain the reserved cooking juices into a pan, stir in the broth (stock) and orange zest, and heat, stirring frequently. Cook the ravioli in plenty of salted boiling water until they rise to the surface and are al dente. Drain, return to the pan, pour the sauce over, add the butter and plenty of Parmesan and toss lightly. Transfer to a warmed serving dish and serve immediately.

RAVIOLI WITH MARJORAM

RAVIOLI ALLA MAGGIORANA

Preparation time: *1 hour,
plus 1 hour resting*
Cooking time: *10 min*
Serves 6

— 3 cups (350 g) all-purpose
  (plain) flour, plus extra
  for dusting
— 3 egg yolks
— scant ½ cup (100 ml) dry
  white wine
— salt

For the filling:
— scant 1 cup (200 g)
  ricotta cheese
— 1 egg
— ⅔ cup (50 g) grated
  Parmesan cheese
— 1 cup (50 g) finely chopped
  fresh marjoram
— pinch of ground cinnamon
— salt and pepper

For the sauce:
— scant ½ cup (50 g) butter
— ¼ cup (50 g) superfine
  (caster) sugar
— small pinch of ground
  cinnamon
— ⅓ cup (20 g) finely chopped
  fresh marjoram

Make the pasta dough. Sift the flour into a mound on a counter and make a well in the middle. Add the egg yolks, wine, and a pinch of salt to the well. Using your fingers, gradually incorporate the flour into the eggs. Knead thoroughly, shape into a ball, cover with a clean dish towel, and let rest for 1 hour. Meanwhile, combine the ingredients for the filling, cover with plastic wrap (clingfilm), and store in the refrigerator until required. Roll out the dough into a thin sheet on a lightly floured counter. Put small mounds of the filling in an even row over the bottom half of the pasta sheet. Fold over the top half of the sheet and press around the filling with your fingers to seal. Cut out the ravioli and press the edges together firmly. Make the sauce. Melt the butter in a shallow pan. Stir in the sugar and cinnamon. Cook the ravioli in plenty of salted boiling water until they rise to the surface and are al dente. Drain, tip into the pan, and toss gently. Transfer to a warmed serving dish, sprinkle with the marjoram, and serve.

SALT COD AND RAISIN RAVIOLI

RAVIOLI DI BACCALA E UVETTA

Preparation time: *1 hour 20 min,*
plus 1 hour resting and 24 hours soaking
Cooking time: *1 hour 15 min*
Serves 6

— 4½ cups (500 g) all-purpose
(plain) flour, plus extra
for dusting
— 5 eggs
— salt

For the filling:
— 1 pound 2 ounces (500 g) salt
cod, soaked in several changes
of water for 24 hours
— 2 tablespoons olive oil
— 2 onions, sliced
— 3 tablespoons fresh bread
crumbs
— 3 tablespoons milk
— 1 egg, lightly beaten
— scant ½ cup (100 g) ricotta
cheese
— 2 tablespoons raisins
— salt and pepper

For the sauce:
— scant ½ cup (100 g) butter
— 1 bunch fresh chives, snipped
— 1 garlic clove, finely chopped
— fresh flat-leaf parsley, to
garnish

Make the pasta dough. Sift the flour into a mound on a counter and make a well in the middle. Break the eggs into the well and add a pinch of salt. Using your fingers, gradually incorporate the flour into the eggs. Knead thoroughly, shape into a ball, cover with a clean dish towel, and let rest in a cool place for 1 hour.

Make the filling. Drain the cod, remove and discard the skin and bones, and chop the flesh. Heat the oil in a pan. Add the onions and cook over low heat, stirring occasionally, for 5 minutes. Add the cod and simmer, stirring occasionally, for 1 hour. Meanwhile, soak the bread crumbs in the milk for 10 minutes, then drain, and squeeze out. Remove the pan of fish from the heat, transfer the mixture to a food processor, and process to a puree. Transfer to a bowl, stir in the egg, ricotta, soaked bread crumbs, and 1½ tablespoons of the raisins, and season with salt and pepper.

Roll out the dough into a thin sheet on a lightly floured counter. Put small mounds of the filling in an even row over the bottom half of the pasta sheet. Fold over the top half of the sheet and press around the filling with your fingers to seal. Cut out the ravioli and press the edges together firmly. To make the sauce, melt the butter in a pan. Pour in 4 tablespoons water, add the remaining raisins, the chives and garlic, and simmer gently. Cook the ravioli in plenty of salted boiling water until they rise to the surface and are al dente. Drain, add to the sauce, toss over the heat for 2 minutes, and serve immediately, garnished with parsley sprigs.

RAVIOLI WITH SHEEP MILK CHEESE

RAVIOLI AI FORMAGGI DI PECORA

Preparation time: *1 hour 20 min,*
plus 30 min resting
Cooking time: *23 min*
Serves 6

— 2¾ cups (300 g) all-purpose
 (plain) flour, plus extra
 for dusting
— 3 eggs
— salt

For the filling:
— 3½ ounces (100 g) sheep milk
 ricotta or soft goat cheese
— 1 cup (80 g) grated fresh
 pecorino sardo
— 1 cup (80 g) grated sharp
 pecorino sardo
— 1 egg
— grated zest of 1 orange
— grated zest of 1 lemon
— salt and pepper

For the sauce:
— 1 tablespoon olive oil
— 1 shallot, chopped
— 6 tomatoes, blanched,
 peeled, and diced
— 4 fresh basil leaves, torn
— salt and pepper

To serve:
— 6 tablespoons (80 g) chilled
 butter, cut into pieces
— ½ cup (40 g) grated
 Gruyère cheese
— ⅓ cup (25 g) grated mature
 pecorino cheese
— 4 fresh basil leaves, torn

Sift the flour into a mound on a counter and make a well in the middle. Break the eggs into the well and add a pinch of salt. Using your fingers, gradually incorporate the flour into the eggs. Knead thoroughly, then shape into a ball, cover with a clean dish towel, and let rest for 30 minutes. Meanwhile, make the filling. Combine the ricotta or goat cheese, grated cheeses, egg, orange zest, and lemon zest in a bowl and season with salt and pepper.

Roll out the dough into a thin sheet on a lightly floured counter. Put small mounds of the filling in an even row over the bottom half of the pasta sheet. Fold over the top half of the sheet and press around the filling with your fingers to seal. Cut out the ravioli and press the edges together firmly. To make the sauce, heat the oil in a pan. Add the shallot and cook over low heat, stirring occasionally, for 5 minutes. Add the tomatoes and basil, season with salt and pepper, and cook for 10 minutes. Remove from the heat and process in a food processor or blender, then return to a clean pan, and reheat gently.

Cook the ravioli in plenty of salted boiling water until they rise to the surface and are al dente. Drain, add to the pan with the sauce, and add the pieces of butter. Remove the pan from the heat and sprinkle with the Gruyère, pecorino, and basil. Serve immediately.

SEAFOOD RAVIOLI

RAVIOLI MARINARI

Preparation time: *1 hour 10 min, plus 1 hour resting*
Cooking time: *30 min*
Serves 4

— 3½ cups (400 g) all-purpose (plain) flour, plus extra for dusting
— 4 eggs
— salt

For the filling:
— 2 tablespoons olive oil
— 1 onion, chopped
— 1 celery stalk, chopped
— 1 carrot, chopped
— 2 bay leaves
— 1 garlic clove
— 5 ounces (150 g) cod fillet, skinned and cut into pieces
— 3½ ounces (100 g) shelled langoustines, chopped
— 3½ ounces (100 g) shelled shellfish, such as clams or mussels
— ⅔ cup (150 ml) brandy
— 7 ounces (200 g) canned chopped tomatoes
— 1 tablespoon grated bottarga (salted pressed striped [grey] mullet or tuna roe)
— 1 tablespoon fresh bread crumbs
— salt and pepper

For the sauce:
— 3 tablespoons butter, melted
— 6 fresh basil leaves, torn
— 1½ ounces (40 g) bottarga, grated

First, make the pasta dough. Sift the flour into a mound on a counter and make a well in the middle. Break the eggs into the well and add a pinch of salt. Using your fingers, gradually incorporate the flour into the eggs. Knead thoroughly, shape into a ball, cover with a clean dish towel, and let rest for 1 hour.

Meanwhile, make the filling. Heat the oil in a shallow pan. Add the onion, celery, carrot, bay leaves, and garlic clove and cook over low heat, stirring occasionally, for 5 minutes. Add the cod, langoustines, and shellfish, stir, and cook for about 10 minutes. Pour in the brandy and cook until the alcohol has evaporated, then add the tomatoes. Season with salt and pepper and simmer for 5 minutes. Remove the pan from the heat, transfer the mixture to a food processor, and process to a puree. Transfer to a bowl and stir in the bottarga and bread crumbs.

Roll out the dough into a thin sheet on a lightly floured counter. Put small mounds of the filling in an even row over the bottom half of the pasta sheet. Fold over the top half of the sheet and press around the filling with your fingers to seal. Cut out the ravioli and press the edges together firmly. Cook the ravioli in plenty of salted boiling water until they rise to the surface and are al dente. Drain and tip into a warmed serving dish. Pour the melted butter over and sprinkle with the basil and bottarga. Serve immediately.

ARUGULA, ROBIOLA, RICOTTA, AND MASCARPONE RAVIOLI

Preparation time: *1 hour 10 min, plus 2 hours resting*
Cooking time: *30 min*
Serves 6

— 1½ cups (175 g) all-purpose (plain) flour, plus extra for dusting
— ½ cup (80 g) semolina flour
— 2 eggs
— salt

For the filling:
— 3 ounces (80 g) arugula (rocket)
— 1½ tablespoons butter
— 2 tablespoons chopped shallot
— ½ garlic clove
— 3 ounces (80 g) ricotta cheese
— 3 ounces (80 g) robiola cheese
— 2½ tablespoons mascarpone cheese
— pinch of fresh bread crumbs
— 1–2 tablespoons vegetable broth (stock) (optional)
— salt and pepper

For the cream:
— 5 tablespoons milk
— 1½ tablespoons butter
— pinch of nutmeg, freshly grated
— 5 tablespoons all-purpose (plain) flour, sifted
— 4 tablespoons grated Parmesan cheese
— salt and pepper

For the sauce:
— 2 tablespoons olive oil
— ¾ cup (100 g) shredded arugula (rocket)
— 1 garlic clove, very finely chopped
— 2 tablespoons butter
— 5 ounces (150 g) tomatoes, seeded and diced
— salt and pepper

To make the pasta dough, combine the flour and semolina flour, shape into a mound on a counter and make a well in the middle. Break the eggs into the well and add a pinch of salt. Using your fingers, gradually incorporate the flour into the eggs. Knead thoroughly, then shape into a ball, cover, and let rest for 2 hours.

Meanwhile, make the filling. Put the arugula (rocket) into a small pan with just the water clinging to its leaves after washing and cook over low heat, turning occasionally, for 5 minutes. Drain, squeeze out the excess liquid, and chop. Melt the butter in a shallow pan. Add the shallot and garlic and cook over low heat, stirring occasionally, for 5 minutes, removing and discarding the garlic when it has turned golden brown. Stir in the arugula and ricotta, remove the pan from the heat, and let cool. Stir in the robiola, mascarpone, and bread crumbs, and add the broth (stock) if the mixture is too stiff. Season with salt and pepper and mix well.

To make the cream, pour the milk into a pan, add the butter and nutmeg, season with salt and pepper, and bring just to a boil. Immediately tip in all the sifted flour and stir vigorously. Cook, stirring constantly, for a few minutes until thickened, then season with salt and pepper. Stir in the cooled filling and the Parmesan. Remove the pan from the heat and let cool. Add another pinch of bread crumbs if the mixture is too runny.

Roll out the pasta dough into a thin sheet on a lightly floured counter. Put small mounds of the filling in an even row over the bottom half of the pasta sheet. Fold over the top half of the sheet and press around the filling with your fingers to seal. Cut out the ravioli and press the edges together firmly. Cook the ravioli in plenty of salted boiling water until they rise to the surface and are al dente, then drain. Make the sauce. Heat the oil in a shallow pan. Add the arugula and garlic and cook, stirring constantly, for 1 minute. Add the butter and the ravioli and toss gently. Add the tomatoes and heat through for a few seconds. Transfer the ravioli to a warmed serving dish and serve immediately.

SEA BASS RAVIOLI

RAVIOLI DI BRANZINO

Preparation time: *1 hour 25 min,
plus 1 hour resting*
Cooking time: *20 min*
Serves 6

— 3 cups (350 g) all-purpose
  (plain) flour, preferably Italian
  type 00, plus extra for dusting
— 1¼ cups (150 g) durum wheat
  semolina flour
— 3 eggs
— 4 egg yolks
— salt

For the filling:
— 3 tablespoons olive oil
— 1½ pounds (700 g) sea bass
  fillets, skinned and chopped
— 3 tablespoons
  mascarpone cheese
— grated zest of 1 lemon
— 1 teaspoon snipped fresh chives
— salt and pepper

For the sauce:
— 6 tablespoons (80 g) butter
— 1 tablespoon snipped
  fresh chives

Sift both kinds of flour into a mound on a counter and make
a well in the middle. Break the eggs into the well and add the
egg yolks and a pinch of salt. Using your fingers, gradually
incorporate the flour into the eggs. Knead well, shape into
a ball, cover with a clean dish towel, and let rest for 1 hour.
Meanwhile, make the filling. Heat the oil in a shallow pan.
Add the fish, season with salt and pepper, and cook over low
heat, stirring occasionally, for 10 minutes. Remove from the
pan and let cool, then combine with the mascarpone, lemon
zest, and chives in a bowl. Roll out the dough into a thin
sheet on a lightly floured counter. Put small mounds of the
filling in an even row over the bottom half of the pasta sheet.
Fold over the top half of the sheet and press around the filling
with your fingers to seal. Cut out the ravioli and press the
edges together firmly. Cook the ravioli in plenty of salted
boiling water until they rise to the surface and are al dente.
Drain and toss in a pan over low heat with the butter and
chives, then serve.

SPINACH AND RICOTTA RAVIOLI

RAVIOLI DI SPINACCI E RICOTTA

Preparation time: *50 min*
Cooking time: *20 min*
Serves 6

— 2¾ cups (300 g) all-purpose
  (plain) flour, preferably Italian
  type 00, plus extra for dusting
— 3 eggs
— 4 tablespoons (50 g) butter
— 8 fresh sage leaves
— ½ cup (120 g) crumbled
  ricotta cheese
— ⅔ cup (50 g) grated
  Parmesan cheese
— salt

For the filling:
— 3¼ pounds (1.5 kg) spinach
— 2¼ cups (500 g) ricotta cheese
— 2 eggs, lightly beaten
— 2 tablespoons grated
  Parmesan cheese
— salt and pepper

For the filling, put the spinach into a pan with just the water
clinging to the leaves after washing and cook over low heat,
turning occasionally, for 5 minutes until wilted. Then drain
well and chop. Beat the ricotta in a bowl with a wooden
spoon and stir in the spinach. Stir in the eggs and Parmesan
and season with salt and pepper to taste, stirring until very
smooth. Make the pasta dough with the quantities specified
(see Fresh Pasta Dough, page 139) with the flour, eggs, and
a pinch of salt. Roll out into a thin sheet on a lightly floured
counter. Place mounds of the filling at regular intervals on
the bottom half of the sheet, fold over, and cut out ravioli
(a little larger than normal). Press the edges to seal. Cook in
a large pan of salted boiling water for about 10 minutes, then
drain, and place in a warmed serving dish. Meanwhile, melt
the butter in a small pan and cook the sage leaves until
golden. Sprinkle the ravioli with the ricotta and Parmesan,
pour the sage butter over them, and serve.

RAVIOLINI VOL-AU-VENT

VOL-AU-VENT CON RAVIOLINI

Preparation time: *25 min*
Cooking time: *30 min*
Serves 6

— 4 tablespoons (50 g) butter
— scant 1 cup (100 g) shelled peas
— 2 tablespoons warm water
— 1 pound 2 ounces (500 g) small ravioli
— ½ cup (40 g) grated Parmesan cheese
— 1 large, ready-made vol-au-vent case, about 6–8 inches (15–20 cm) in diameter
— 1 quantity béchamel sauce (see Baked Pumpkin Pasta, page 236)
— salt

Preheat the oven to 300°F (150°C/Gas Mark 2). Line a baking sheet with baking paper. Melt 2 tablespoons of the butter in a pan, add the peas and 2 tablespoons warm water, and cook for about 10 minutes until tender. Season with salt, drain, and set aside. Cook the ravioli in a large pan of salted boiling water until al dente, then drain, tip into a bowl, and gently toss with the remaining butter, 5 tablespoons of the Parmesan, and the peas. Fill the vol-au-vent case with the ravioli and spoon in the béchamel sauce. Sprinkle with the remaining Parmesan, place on the cookie sheet, and heat through in the oven.

WHOLE WHEAT RAVIOLI WITH PEA FILLING

RAVIOLI INTEGRALI FARCITI CON PISELLI

Preparation time: *1 hour 10 min, plus 1 hour resting*
Cooking time: *50 min*
Serves 6

— 1¼ cups (150 g) whole wheat (wholemeal) flour
— 1¼ cups (150 g) all-purpose (plain) flour, preferably Italian type 00, plus extra for dusting
— 3 eggs
— salt

For the filling:
— 5¼ cups (600 g) shelled peas
— 2 tablespoons olive oil
— ¼ cup (50 g) chopped onion
— salt and pepper

For the sauce:
— scant ½ cup (100 g) chilled butter
— 1 cup (80 g) grated Parmesan cheese
— ½ cup (50 g) hazelnuts, chopped
— juice of ½ lemon, strained
— 1 tablespoon chopped fresh flat-leaf parsley

Combine the two types of flour, shape into a mound on a counter and make a well in the middle. Break the eggs into the well and add a pinch of salt. Using your fingers, gradually incorporate the flour into the eggs. Knead thoroughly, shape into a ball, cover with a clean dish towel, and let rest for 1 hour. Meanwhile, make the filling. Cook the peas in salted boiling water for 10–15 minutes until tender. Drain well, transfer to a food processor or blender, and process to a puree. Heat the oil in a pan. Add the onion and cook over low heat, stirring occasionally, for 5 minutes. Add the pea puree, season lightly with salt and pepper, and cook, stirring frequently, for 10–15 minutes until the mixture is fairly dry. Remove the pan from the heat. Roll out the dough into a thin sheet on a lightly floured counter. Put small mounds of the pea filling in even rows over the bottom half of the pasta sheet. Fold over the top half of the sheet and press around the filling with your fingers to seal. Cut out the ravioli and press the edges together firmly. Cook the ravioli in plenty of salted boiling water until they rise to the surface and are al dente. Transfer to a pan and toss with the butter, Parmesan, hazelnuts, lemon juice, and parsley over low heat. Serve immediately.

TORDELLI

Tordelli is a type of filled pasta typical of the city of Lucca in Tuscany. Tordelli is circular, similar to tortelli, and made with 3¼-inch (8-cm) dough circles. Small mounds of filling are then put on each round, the dough is folded over, and the edges pressed together firmly to seal. Tordelli is traditionally accompanied by a sauce made from melted butter and sage.

Ⓐ

Preparation time: *1 hour 20 min, plus 30 min resting*
Cooking time: *20 min*
Serves *4–6*

— 3½ cups (400 g) all-purpose (plain) flour, plus extra for dusting
— 4 eggs
— salt

For the filling:
— 1 thick slice of bread, crusts removed
— 2 tablespoons olive oil
— sprig of fresh thyme
— 5 ounces (150 g) ground (minced) steak
— 5 ounces (150 g) ground (minced) pork
— 2 ounces (50 g) mortadella
— 2 eggs
— ½ cup (40 g) grated Parmesan cheese
— ½ cup (40 g) grated pecorino cheese
— 1 tablespoon chopped fresh flat-leaf parsley
— pinch of freshly grated nutmeg
— salt and pepper

For the sauce:
— 4 tablespoons (50 g) butter, melted
— 4–6 fresh sage leaves, chopped

TORDELLI FROM LUCCA

TORDELLI ALLA LUCCHESE

Make the pasta dough. Sift the flour into a mound on a counter and make a well in the middle. Break the eggs into the well and add a pinch of salt. Using your fingers, gradually incorporate the flour into the eggs. Knead thoroughly, shape into a ball, cover with a clean dish towel, and let rest for 30 minutes.

Meanwhile, make the filling. Put the bread into a bowl, pour in water to cover, and let soak for 10 minutes, then drain, and squeeze out the excess liquid. Meanwhile, heat the oil in a shallow pan with the thyme sprig. Add the ground (minced) meats and cook over medium–low heat, stirring frequently, for about 10 minutes until lightly browned. Remove from the heat and let cool. Using a slotted spoon, transfer the ground meat to a cutting (chopping) board, add the mortadella, and chop together. Transfer to a bowl and mix in the eggs, 2 tablespoons of the Parmesan, 1 tablespoon of the pecorino, the soaked bread, parsley, and nutmeg. Mix well and season with salt and pepper.

Roll out the pasta dough into a thin sheet on a lightly floured counter. Cut out 3¼-inch (8-cm) circles with a pasta wheel. Put small mounds of filling on each round, fold over the dough, and press the edges firmly together to seal. Cook the tordelli in plenty of salted boiling water until they rise to the surface and are al dente. Drain, transfer to a warmed serving dish, pour the melted butter over, and sprinkle with the sage. Sprinkle with the remaining Parmesan and pecorino and serve immediately.

TORDELLI FROM LUCCA

TORTELLI

A type of filled pasta similar to ravioli, tortelli takes its name from *torta*, meaning "tart," and can be square or half-moon-shaped. Originating in the Po Valley in northern Italy, tortelli is mentioned in recipes dating back to the twelfth century and was celebrated by poets in the Middle Ages. The most traditional filling comes from the Emilia-Romagna region and is made from ricotta and spinach. Fillings with potatoes or cured meats are also common.

ARTICHOKE AND CHEESE TORTELLI

TORTELLI DI CARCIOFI E FORMAGGIO

Preparation time: *1 hour 20 min, plus 30 min resting*
Cooking time: *1 hour*
Serves 6

— 3½ cups (400 g) all-purpose (plain) flour, plus extra for dusting
— 4 eggs
— salt

For the filling:
— 4 tablespoons (50 g) butter
— 6 young globe artichokes, trimmed
— 1 onion, thinly sliced
— ¼ cup (25 g) all-purpose (plain) flour
— 2¼ cups (500 ml) lukewarm milk
— 3 eggs, lightly beaten
— ⅓ cup (25 g) grated Parmesan cheese
— salt

For the sauce:
— 3 tablespoons butter, melted
— ½ cup (50 g) grated Parmesan cheese

Make the pasta dough. Sift the flour into a mound on a counter and make a well in the middle. Break the eggs into the well and add a pinch of salt. Using your fingers, gradually incorporate the flour into the eggs. Knead thoroughly, shape into a ball, cover with a clean dish towel, and let rest for 30 minutes.

Meanwhile, make the filling. Melt half the butter in a shallow pan. Add the artichokes, onion, and 2 tablespoons water and cook over low heat, stirring occasionally, for 20 minutes. Remove the artichokes from the pan and chop. Transfer the artichokes and onion to a bowl. Melt the remaining butter in a small pan. Stir in the flour and cook over medium heat, stirring constantly, for 2–3 minutes until golden brown. Gradually stir in the milk, a little at a time. Bring to a boil, stirring constantly, lower the heat, and simmer gently, stirring constantly, for 20 minutes until thickened and smooth. Remove the pan from the heat and add to the artichokes with the eggs and the grated cheese. Mix well and season with salt.

Roll out the pasta into a thin sheet on a lightly floured counter. Put small mounds of the filling in even rows over the bottom half of the pasta sheet. Fold over the top half of the sheet and press around the filling with your fingers to seal. Cut out the tortelli and press the edges together firmly. Cook in plenty of salted boiling water until it rises to the surface and is al dente. Drain, pour the melted butter over, and sprinkle with Parmesan. Serve immediately.

PUMPKIN TORTELLI (PAGE 272)

PUMPKIN TORTELLI

TORTELLI DI ZUCCA

Preparation time: *50 min*
Cooking time: *1 hour 15 min*
Serves *4*

— 4 cups (500 g) peeled, seeded, and chopped pumpkin
— 2 tablespoons olive oil
— ⅔ cups (50 g) grated Parmesan cheese, plus extra to serve
— 2 eggs, lightly beaten
— 1½–2 cups (80–120 g) fresh bread crumbs
— 1 quantity Fresh Pasta Dough (see page 139)
— 4 tablespoons (50 g) butter
— 8 fresh sage leaves
— salt and pepper

Preheat the oven to 350°F (180°c/Gas Mark 4). Put the pumpkin in a roasting pan, drizzle with the oil, cover with aluminum foil, and bake for about 1 hour. Pass the pumpkin through a food mill into a bowl, or process to a puree. Add the Parmesan and eggs, and season with salt and pepper. Stir in enough bread crumbs to make a fairly firm mixture. Roll out the pasta dough into a thin sheet and stamp out 3-inch (7.5-cm) circles with a cookie cutter. Spoon a little of the pumpkin filling into the middle of each round, fold in half, and crimp the edges. Cook the tortelli in a large pan of salted boiling water for 10 minutes. Meanwhile, melt the butter in a skillet or frying pan, add the sage, and cook for a few minutes. Drain the tortelli, place in a warmed serving dish, and sprinkle with the sage butter and extra Parmesan. Serve immediately.

RADICCHIO AND ROBIOLA TORTELLI

TORTELLI AL RADICCHIO E ROBIOLA

Preparation time: *1 hour 15 min,
plus 1 hour resting*
Cooking time: *18 min*
Serves *4*

— 2 tablespoons olive oil
— 9 ounces (250 g) radicchio, cut into strips
— 2¾ cups (300 g) all-purpose (plain) flour, plus extra for dusting
— 2 eggs
— 2 tablespoons dry white wine
— salt

For the filling:
— 7 ounces (200 g) robiola cheese
— ¼ cup (20 g) grated Parmesan cheese
— salt and pepper

For the sauce:
— 1½ tablespoons butter
— 1 tablespoon chopped fresh thyme

First make the pasta dough. Heat the oil in a shallow pan. Add the radicchio, season lightly with salt, and cook over low heat, stirring occasionally, for a few minutes until wilted. Remove from the heat and set aside to cool slightly. Sift the flour into a mound on a counter and make a well in the middle. Break the eggs into the well and add the radicchio, wine, and a pinch of salt. Using your fingers, gradually incorporate the flour into the eggs. Knead thoroughly, shape into a ball, cover with a clean dish towel, and let rest for 1 hour. Meanwhile, make the filling. Beat the robiola in a bowl, then beat in the Parmesan, and season with salt and pepper.

Roll out the pasta dough into a thin sheet on a lightly floured counter. Cut out 3-inch (7.5-cm) squares with a pasta wheel. Put a small mound of filling in the middle of each one and fold over, pressing the edges together firmly. To make the sauce, put the butter and thyme into a heatproof bowl, set over a pan of simmering water and melt, stirring occasionally. Meanwhile, cook the tortelli in plenty of salted boiling water until they rise to the surface and are al dente. Drain, transfer to a warmed serving dish, and pour the melted herb butter over. Serve immediately.

TORTELLINI

Tortellini is a type of small ring-shaped filled pasta, originally from the Emilia-Romagna region of northern Italy. The inspiration for tortellini is supposed to be the navel of Venus. Homemade tortellini is made mainly for festive occasions, as it takes a long time to prepare. Tortellini is made by filling square sheets of dough, folding them into triangles, then wrapping each triangle around the index finger. The points are then pressed together and the rest of the dough gently pushed backward to make the classic tortellini shape. Tortellini can have various fillings and are typically filled with ground (minced) meat and served in broth (stock). The bigger version of tortellini is called tortelloni, which can also sometimes refer to large tortelli.

Preparation time: *1 hour 20 min*
Cooking time: *20 min*
Serves 4

— 2 tablespoons butter
— 2 ounces (50 g) ground (minced) veal
— 2 tablespoons grated Parmesan cheese
— ½ cup (80 g) diced prosciutto
— ¼ cup (40 g) diced mortadella
— 1 egg, lightly beaten
— 1 quantity Fresh Pasta Dough (see page 139)
— 1 quantity tomato sauce (see Baked Capellini, page 25)

TORTELLINI BOLOGNESE

TORTELLINI ALLA BOLOGNESE

Melt the butter in a small pan, add the veal and cook over high heat, stirring frequently, until browned. Transfer to a bowl, let cool, then stir in the Parmesan, prosciutto, mortadella, and egg. Roll out the pasta dough into a thin sheet, put small mounds of the filling at regular intervals on the sheet, and cut into squares. Fold the squares corner to corner into triangles, then wrap each triangle around your index finger, press the points together, and gently push the rest of the dough backward to make the classic tortellini shape. Make 20 tortellini per person. Cook the tortellini in plenty of salted boiling water until they rise to the surface and are al dente. Drain and serve with hot tomato sauce.

PESTO TORTELLONI WITH SQUID

PESTO TORTELLONI WITH SQUID

Preparation time: *50 min*
Cooking time: *30 min*
Serves 4

— 2¾ cups (300 g) all-purpose
  (plain) flour, preferably Italian
  type 00, plus extra for dusting
— 3 eggs, lightly beaten
— salt

For the pesto:
— scant 2 cups (100 g)
  fresh basil leaves
— ¾ cup (40 g) fresh flat-leaf
  parsley
— 3 tablespoons pine nuts
— 1 tablespoon shelled walnuts
— ½ cup (120 ml) olive oil
— scant 1 cup (200 g)
  ricotta cheese
— salt

For the sauce:
— 4 tablespoons olive oil
— 7 ounces (200 g) small
  squid, cleaned
— 1 garlic clove
— 5 tablespoons dry white wine
— 2 tomatoes, blanched, peeled
  and diced
— 1 tablespoon chopped fresh
  flat-leaf parsley
— 6 fresh basil leaves, torn
— salt and pepper

TORTELLONI DI PESTO CON CALAMARETTI

Make the pasta dough (see Fresh Pasta Dough, page 139) with
the quantities specified. For the pesto, put the basil, parsley,
pine nuts, walnuts, and oil into a food processor and process
until combined, then scrape into a bowl. Season with salt
and stir in the ricotta. Roll out the pasta dough on a lightly
floured counter to make a thin sheet and cut out 2-inch
(5-cm) squares. Put a little pesto mixture into the middle of
each square. Fold the squares corner to corner into triangles.
If you like, wrap each triangle around your index finger, press
the points together, and gently push the rest of the dough
backward to make the classic tortelloni shape.

For the sauce, heat 3 tablespoons of the oil in a skillet or frying
pan, add the squid and garlic, and cook, stirring frequently,
for a few minutes until the squid are light golden brown.
Season with salt and pepper to taste, sprinkle with the wine,
and cook until the alcohol has evaporated. Remove the squid
from the pan, leaving the cooking juices in the pan, and slice
into fairly thin circles. Remove and discard the garlic. Cook
the pasta in plenty of salted boiling water until al dente,
drain, and tip into the pan. Add the remaining oil, the tomatoes, and squid circles, and mix well. Sprinkle with the parsley
and basil and mix again. Transfer to a warmed serving dish and
serve immediately.

PESTO TORTELLONI WITH SQUID (PAGE 275)

MUSHROOM TORTELLONI

TORTELLONI DI FUNGHI

Preparation time: *50 min,*
plus 30 min resting
Cooking time: *30 min*
Serves 4

— 4 tablespoons olive oil
— 1 small onion, chopped
— scant 4½ cups (300 g) thinly
  sliced porcini mushrooms
— generous 1 cup (250 g)
  crumbled ricotta cheese
— ⅔ cup (50 g) grated Parmesan
  cheese, plus extra to serve
— 1 sprig fresh flat-leaf parsley,
  chopped
— 1 quantity Fresh Pasta Dough
  (see page 139)
— all-purpose (plain) flour,
  for dusting
— 3 tablespoons butter
— 10 fresh sage leaves
— salt and pepper

Heat the oil in a pan, add the onion and porcini, and cook over low heat, stirring occasionally, for 5 minutes. Season with salt and cook for another 15 minutes. Transfer the mixture to a food processor, add the ricotta, Parmesan, and parsley, and process to a puree. Season with salt and pepper to taste.

Roll out the pasta dough into a thin sheet on a lightly floured counter and cut out 2-inch (5-cm) squares. Put a little ricotta mixture into the middle of each square. Fold the squares corner to corner into triangles, then wrap each triangle around your index finger, press the points together, and gently push the rest of the dough backward to make the classic tortelloni shape. Melt the butter in a large skillet or frying pan, add the sage leaves, and cook for a few minutes. Cook the tortelloni in plenty of salted boiling water until al dente. Drain, add to the pan, and stir over high heat. Transfer to a warmed serving dish, sprinkle with Parmesan, and serve.

INDEX

RECIPE NOTES

— Butter should always be unsalted, unless otherwise specified.

— Pepper is always freshly ground black pepper, unless otherwise specified.

— Eggs, vegetables, and fruits are medium size, unless otherwise specified.

— Milk is whole, unless otherwise specified.

— Garlic cloves are assumed to be large; use two if yours are small.

— Ham refers to cooked ham, unless otherwise specified.

— Prosciutto refers exclusively to raw, dry-cured ham, usually from Parma or San Daniele in northern Italy.

— Cooking and preparation times are for guidance only, as individual ovens vary. If using a fan oven, follow the manufacturer's instructions concerning oven temperatures.

— To test whether your deep-frying oil is hot enough, add a cube of day-old bread. If it browns in 30 seconds, the temperature is 350–375°F (180–190°C), about right for most frying. Exercise caution when deep frying: add the food carefully to avoid splashing, wear long sleeves, and never leave the pan unattended.

— Some recipes include raw or very lightly cooked eggs. These should be avoided particularly by the elderly, infants, pregnant women, convalescents, and anyone with an impaired immune system.

— All spoon measurements are level. 1 teaspoon = 5 ml; 1 tablespoon = 15 ml. Australian standard tablespoons are 20 ml, so Australian readers are advised to use 3 teaspoons in place of 1 tablespoon when measuring small quantities.

— All herbs, shoots, flowers, and leaves should be picked from a clean source. Exercise caution when foraging for ingredients, which should only be eaten if an expert has deemed them safe. In particular, do not gather wild mushrooms yourself before seeking the advice of an expert who has confirmed their suitability for human consumption. As some species of mushrooms have been known to cause allergic reaction and illness, do take extra care when cooking and eating mushrooms, and do seek immediate medical help if you experience a reaction.

Phaidon Press Limited
2 Cooperage Yard
London E15 2QR

Phaidon Press Limited
111 Broadway
New York, NY 10006

www.phaidon.com

© 2009, 2013, 2023 Phaidon Press Limited

ISBN 978 07148 6598 0

The recipes in this book are adapted from various books in *The Silver Spoon* family. The first English edition of *The Silver Spoon* was published by Phaidon in 2005. First published in Italian by Editoriale Domus as *Il cucchiaio d'argento*, 1950. Tenth edition (revised, expanded and redesigned) 2016. © Editoriale Domus

A CIP catalogue record for this book is available from the British Library.

Commissioning Editor: Emilia Terragni
Project Editor: Rachel Malig
Production Controller: Zuzana Cimalova
Photography: Edward Park
Typesetting: Cantina

Interior Design: Phaidon, based on the design of *Vegetables from an Italian Garden* by Astrid Stavro
Cover design: Julia Hasting

Printed in China

The publisher would also like to thank Attilio Bergamaschi, Vanessa Bird, Danielle Centoni, Mary Consonni, Linda Doeser, Carmen Figini, Julia Hasting, Meaghan Kombol, Margot Levy, João Mota, Clelia d'Onofrio, Jane Rollason, Ellie Smith, and Tracey Smith for their contributions to the book.